TURBOCHARGING & SUPERCH...

A practical guide to sup
charging car, motor cycle ε
for road and com...

C000293069

TURBOCHARGING & SUPERCHARGING

ALAN ALLARD

Patrick Stephens, Wellingborough

© Alan Allard, 1982, 1986

All rights reserved. No part of this publication
may be reproduced, stored in a retrieval system or
transmitted, in any form or by any means,
electronic, mechanical, photocopying, recording
or otherwise, without prior permission in writing
from Patrick Stephens Limited.

First published July 1982
Reprinted December 1982
Reprinted December 1983
Reprinted April 1984
Reprinted July 1985
Reprinted July 1986
This edition first published November 1986

British Library Cataloguing in Publication Data

Allard, Alan
    Turbocharging and supercharging.—2nd ed.
    1. Superchargers
    I. Title
    621.43   TJ787

    ISBN 0-85059-744-7

Patrick Stephens Limited is part of the
Thorsons Publishing Group.

Printed and bound in Great Britain.

Contents

Acknowledgements

Arkay; Audi; *Autocar;* BAE; Gale Banks; Beaulieu Museum; Blake Enterprises; Bill Blydenstein; BMW; British Brown-Boveri; Nick Butler; Calaway Cars; Cosworth Engineering; Les Dalton; Detroit Diesel Allison; Roger Gorringe; Bob Hatton, Hatton Enterprises; Lotus; Mathwall Engineering; Peter McDowell, Holset Engineering; Mercedes Benz; Micro Dynamics; *Motor; Motor Sport;* Jan Oder, Janspeed Engineering; PAO Preparations; Ken Parker, Garrett AiResearch; Tim Pitt-Lewis, for the drawings, graphs and diagrams; Porsche; Rajay UK; Renault; Rotomaster; Saab; Shelby Spearco; Schwitzer; David Vizard; Volvo; McLaren Cars; Citroen; Peugeot; Lancia; Ford; Ferrari; Mitsubishi; Nissan; Daihatsu; Pontiac; Bentley; Maserati.

Introduction

It is no exaggeration to say that in the automobile world there are few subjects which conjure up so much interest as supercharging or turbocharging. Yet, despite this, there are very few books available on the subject, although magazine articles and technical papers abound. I have, therefore, with this book, set out to cover an outline of the history and development of the art of forced induction from the beginnings of blowing in the early 1900s to the sophisticated turbocharged vehicles of the 1980s.

However, as it was my intention to make this book of practical value and interest to as wide a range of readers as possible, I have attempted to include a large percentage of practical information, laced with sufficient technical detail to give adequate technical back-up. There are chapters covering almost all aspects of forced induction, from carburation to exhaust systems, together with sections on diesel turbocharging, motor cycles, high performance turbocharged manufacturers' cars and other specialised applications.

In a subject which is so far-ranging and ever-changing, it is not possible to cover all aspects in every detail, without resorting to writing a volume on each, but wherever possible, facts and figures, together with supporting photographs or diagrams are given.

I originally started compiling information for this book some six years ago, yet even now, such is the rapid development of turbocharging, that more information and details of new developments are coming to hand all the time, so that a new chapter could be written each month.

Unlike most other books concerned with supercharging, I have written in detail about all types of supercharging, whether it be positive displacement mechanically-driven or 'turbo' turbine-driven, showing the relative merits or pitfalls of each and their practical and theoretical application, together with details of design and construction of each type.

As has been said before, one of the most difficult things in producing a book is to sit down and actually write it, but after over twenty years' involvement with the practical application of supercharging and turbocharging, I felt that the time had come when I should put pen to paper. I hope you will find this book as interesting to read as I have to compile and write.

The Allard connection

Those mature readers amongst you who may well remember the past days when my father, Sydney Allard, produced, raced, hillclimbed, rallied and even drag-raced his own

Above *Sydney Allard in the supercharged J1 Allard at Silverstone in August 1949.*

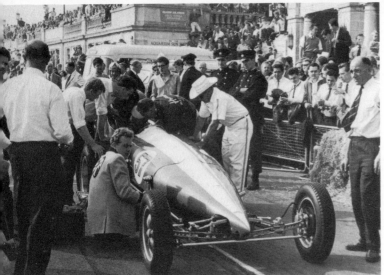

Left *The first Allard Dragster, Brighton speed trials 1962. Built by Sydney Allard, John Hume and Dave Hooper to establish drag racing in this country. Chrysler 350 CI Hemi-head engine with Potvin front mounted blower. Ran on methanol and achieved a best time over the quarter mile of 10.24 seconds. UK rules insisted on front wheel brakes for a 'racing car' in those days. This machine has been carefully restored and is now on display in the National Motor Museum at Beaulieu (Freddie Grevett).*

Left *Alan Allard with co-driver Rob Mackie in the Shorrock Supercharged Allard-ette Anglia on the Col du Turini, Monte Carlo Rally 1963. Finished 56th overall out of nearly 400 starters.*

Above *Goodwood chicane 1963. Alan Allard's Shorrock Supercharged Allardette Anglia sandwiched between the Lotus Cortina of Doc Merfield and the incredibly quick Austin A40 of Willie Cave.*

cars, might be interested to know how it evolved that Allards were to get so involved with supercharging. Indeed, the Allard connection with supercharging dates way back to the days of the J1 Allard, about 1947. My father had two J1 Allards fitted with Marshall superchargers. I believe he was looking for methods to increase substantially power and torque at low and medium engine speeds. There are really only two ways to achieve this: one is by some form of forced induction and the other is by fitting a larger capacity engine. Up until recent times fitting a larger engine had been the normal step, but my father, never a man to tackle a project in a certain manner just because it has always been done that way, decided to supercharge. He always had a passion for engine muscle power, as opposed to what might be termed rpm power, so I suppose supercharging falls quite naturally into this category.

After production of Allard cars had ceased in 1957, the Allard Motor Company branched into engine tuning, motor accessories and various other associated activities. About this time my father met Chris Shorrock of Shorrock Superchargers and came to an agreement to handle the distribution and marketing of these units. Shortly afterwards I too became enthusiastic about supercharging as a method of obtaining big engine performance from a small capacity engine. To both my father and I it seemed the logical way to obtain a 'quart from a pint pot', but generally very few others agreed with this and indeed many of the purists tended to see it almost as a form of cheating, at least when using supercharged cars in competition, even though supercharged cars were often competing in a larger capacity class. I had been convinced that forced induction was the right way to go about it for many years, but until such a time as a larger manufacturer was convinced sufficiently to invest money to develop an efficient supercharging system and the engine to handle it, and by producing in numbers to break through the homologation barrier, it was not possible to bring supercharging back into the limelight.

It may be interesting for readers to know that my father and I competed in the 1960 and

Left *Alan Allard competing in the Allard Dragster at Blackbushe in the 1964 Drag Festival (Geoffrey Willson).*

Below left *The author waits to start his record attempt in Dragon Dragster for the standing-start kilometer. The engine reached maximum revs approximately halfway down the course at a speed of around 145 mph. Even so, the time was a creditable 21.53 seconds.*

Right *Allard Dragon Dragster built to foster the sport of drag racing in the UK. Powered by a Shorrock supercharged Ford Cortina 1,500 cc engine, it produced 175 bhp with a single 2-in SU, running on methanol, and achieved a best elapsed time for the quarter mile of 10.9 seconds with a top speed of 129 mph.*

1961 Monte Carlo rallies with Shorrock supercharged 997 cc Ford Anglia 105Es. I can always remember how the Anglias really got 'into their stride' when hillclimbing. On one such occasion in very thick snow, we had just caught and passed a Russian team (their first event outside Russia) in a Moskvitch, whereupon we got a little too far sideways, a wheel dug into soft snow, the steering was wrenched from my hands and we suddenly found the car on its side blocking the road. Luckily the Russians did not hit us, but we imagined they were somewhat horrified by such wild antics of these capitalists. At least with their help we managed to get the car on its wheels once more.

On another ocasion, when competing in the round-the-town race, which was normal for many years at the end of the Monte Carlo rally, we were racing with—amongst others—Vic Elford and Raymond Baxter in a Sunbeam Talbot and a German-entered Mercedes. I recall following the Mercedes around the circuit. With all his extra power he would pull away on the flat and straighter parts of the course, but when we came to the hill up past the Beau Rivage Hotel on the sea front, the blower really started its characteristic whine and our blown Anglia accelerated past the Mercedes up the hill. It was sweet medicine indeed and left the surrounding crowds of people with a stunned look of amazement on their faces.

About this time my father became interested in the American sport of drag racing. Indeed, most of the fastest dragsters and funny cars were supercharged. Early in 1960 he imported from the Moon Equipment Company of Los Angeles, California, what was probably the first GMC 6-71 supercharger in this country. This, complete with Hillborn Fuel Injection, was fitted on to a specially-prepared Chrysler Hemi engine and installed in the Allard Dragster: the first big-engined American-style dragster outside the USA. This machine was built primarily to establish the sport of drag racing in this country and from this to generate a market for competition and hot rod equipment. The blown Chrysler engine with blower gear driven directly from the nose of the crank churned out about 17.0 psi boost and produced around 750 bhp on straight methanol. The machine turned 10.2 seconds for the standing quarter-mile. No doubt this nowadays sounds slow compared to the times which are being produced in the States, but remember this was back in 1961 and, for the first European dragster produced, was very impressive.

I can recollect driving this projectile for the very first time, I believe, at North Weald airfield. I had obviously driven many fast cars prior to this, but the sheer acceleration of this machine almost took my breath away—and all in top gear too! At that time, dragsters were virtually unknown outside America. In fact, it must have been the fastest-

Left *Allard's Shorrock Super-charged Twin Cam Escort flying high on the 1971 International Scottish Rally* (Foster & Skeffington).

Below left *Allard-Wade Supercharged Escort RS2000 on the 1972 Scottish Rally* (Foster & Skeffington).

Right *Allard J2X2 reborn and now in production in Canada after a lapse of over 25 years. The reason for including this photo is that one or two of the early J-type Allards were supercharged and the latest example is to be available with a turbocharged engine option.*

accelerating vehicle up to 150 mph ever seen in Europe until that time, having a better power-to-weight ratio than the hairiest Auto Union and Mercedes Grand Prix car.

Acceleration in a dragster tends to be the reverse of that in a normal car; or at least, it feels that way. By this I mean the faster you go, the faster it accelerates. So that if you thought 0-100 mph was fast, then 100-200 was faster! With the Mk 2 Allard dragster I held the official world record in 1967 for the standing quarter-mile with a two-direction average of 9.3 seconds. The times could have been in the 8.0 seconds region, but the engine was running on only seven cylinders for one run. The noise of the eight exhausts was deafening and if you stood on the line for too long the exhaust fumes gassed you, or your leg gave out holding the clutch pedal down. All-in-all a definite case of the 'agony and the ecstasy'.

The American dragsters were running in the mid-7.0 seconds region at that time, so obviously they were not interested in quarter-mile records. I competed in the second drag festival which my father organised, in the same machine, and as we were about to take a run it rained. I was staged with Norman Barclay in the ex-Dos Palmas Chevy-engined dragster in the other lane. No-one had ever run slick-shod dragsters in the rain before and I do not for one moment imagine that they have ever tried the same experiment again! Anything but a faint touch on the rather insensitive throttle produced a massive amount of wheel spin; it felt like sliding on sheet ice as I used opposite lock, rally-style, to prevent the dragster slewing from side to side. With each burst of violent wheelspin a high pressure stream of water was shot back into my goggles from the skinny front wheels. At least we both managed to stay on the track and reach the other end, and this was a record in itself.

The Allard Dragon Dragster was designed to foster the drag racing and hot rod market, but although it was not a commercial success, probably due to the fact that the market had not grown sufficiently for that type of equipment at that time, it was successful competitively. Powered by a Shorrock supercharged Ford Cortina 1,500 cc engine, it produced 175 bhp with 12.0 psi boost. It used a 2-in SU carburettor and methanol fuel and accelerated from 0-130 mph in 10.9 seconds over a quarter mile, and also covered the standing-start kilometer in 20.5 seconds.

When the rules permitted supercharging, I always used a supercharged rally car, but homologation regulations stifled much development in this direction. Only large-volume manufacturers are able to make use of these regulations as they are the only people able to produce a sufficient number of identical vehicles to meet the homologation requirements.

As I write this chapter, it appears as though things may have turned a full circle. Arrangements have recently been made with a new Allard Motor Company situated in Mississauga, Canada, to produce a new Allard based on the original J2X model. Outwardly it will appear the same as the original, but under the skin up-to-date mechanicals will give it new refinement in handling and ride. Adequate performance expected of such a machine will be provided by a 318 CID Chrysler V8 and, this is the link with this book, a turbocharged option package will be available to be produced by Allard Turbochargers in the UK.

Indeed, it seems to be the time for nostalgia, but I cannot help but think how very much my father would have approved of such a venture. Generally, with the climate well into turbo-supercharging at this time, I can only imagine my father's comment would be 'what took them so long?'.

Chapter 1

The beginnings of supercharging

At the turn of the century it became evident to several engineers that the power output of an internal combustion engine could be raised by increasing the weight of air charge breathed in by the engine, together with the required amount of fuel. The obvious way to increase the weight of charge entering the cylinder was to use some form of pump to increase mechanically the mass flow, to 'overcharge' or supercharge as the process later became known.

All engines at this time were severely restricted in their breathing ability due largely to very inefficient induction system design, resulting in low power output for a given displacement or swept volume, and low maximum rpm. The power output of a piston engine is determined by the piston area and stroke, the number of engine revs per minute and the mean effective pressure exerted on the pistons. Supercharging is a very effective method of increasing the breathing ability of an engine and thereby the mean effective pressure on the pistons and volumetric efficiency which is directly related to it. It can be seen, therefore, that the basic function of supercharging, by whatever means, is to artificially supply the engine cylinders with more air/fuel mixture than would be taken in under normal atmospheric conditions.

For many years the idea of using a pump or blower to pump air had been employed in the engineering industry, principally in foundry work. However, in 1901 Sir Dugald Clark discovered that if he used a device to increase artificially the volume of air charge entering a cylinder, the engine produced more power. In 1902 Louis Renault used this idea when he patented a system in which a centrifugal fan blew air into the mouth of a carburettor. In 1907 Lee Chadwick, in the USA, developed the idea of putting the carburettor under pressure to increase volumetric efficiency.

Initially a single-stage centrifugal blower was used, driven at nine times engine speed by a flat belt from the flywheel. Because the results were so good, the next development was to install a three-stage blower, again driven at nine times engine speed by a 2-in wide leather belt. Three impellers with 12 blades were employed, each of the same 10-in diameter, but of varying widths to provide the three-stage compression. The carburettor received air under pressure. (It is interesting to note that the use of a blower driven by the engine's exhaust gas was also considered, although the idea of using an exhaust gas-driven supercharger is usually credited to Buchi, a Swiss engineer who applied it to a diesel engine in 1909.)

On May 30 1908, Chadwick's car entered the Wilkes Barr hillclimb, this being the first event in which a blown car was entered—and it won. Over the next two years the car won many events, the most notable being the 200-mile road race at Fairmont Park in 1910. Replicas of this car, which was capable of well over 100 mph, were sold to the public and it became the first catalogued car to exceed 100 mph.

In 1911 Chadwick abandoned his automobile interest despite his obvious success and it is surprising that such a good idea was not developed further in the USA until taken up by Miller and Duesenberg in 1923. In Europe in 1911 and 1912 Sizaire and Birkigt in Paris carried out experiments with centrifugal blower and piston-type displacer, respectively.

The 1914-18 war terminated all racing in Europe and therefore any further super-charging development in this field. At that time the development of aviation was gaining momentum and the war highlighted the need for more power from aero engines. It soon became apparent that the power output of a normally aspirated engine decreased as altitude increased, so that at approximately 18,000 ft above sea level, the full throttle power output is reduced by 50 per cent and this is progressively reduced further as altitude increases. This is simply due to the decrease in atmospheric pressure and therefore air density with the resultant reduction in mass of air being drawn into the engine, so that there is less available for combustion with the fuel. This in turn leads to a decrease in cylinder pressures and corresponding decrease in engine power output.

As supercharging is purely a mechanical means of artificially increasing the air density drawn into the cylinders, it did not take long for the idea to be taken up by the newly

The renowned 1928 4½-litre 'blower' Bentley with 'roots' type supercharger drawing through two 2-in SUs, mounted between dumb irons and gear driven from the nose of the crankshaft (National Motor Museum).

emerged aviation industry, and the development of supercharging was most rapid in this field during the 1914-18 war years. Apart from the use of supercharging as a means of regaining the power lost due to a reduction in air density with an increase in altitude, there were other benefits of importance. More power could be developed for take-off which meant that higher payloads could be carried; while once airborne, the supercharger enabled the aircraft to cruise at higher altitude where the atmosphere was less dense, leading to a reduction in air drag and consequently reduced fuel consumption per mile, which extended the range of the aircraft.

Initially, development of supercharged aviation engines centred on the use of roots-type superchargers, but these were quickly replaced by the potentially more efficient centrifugal superchargers. Because of the necessity to drive this type of supercharger at high speed to obtain optimum pumping efficiency, a very high drive ratio from engine to supercharger was required. This presented a problem with the early gear drives and extensive development work was done to evolve suitable drive mechanisms. Due to the high speed of the centrifugal impeller, it gained considerable rotational inertia and when connected directly to the engine crankshaft would be subjected to excessive stress because the high drive ratio between engine and supercharger would cause even a small change in engine speed to result in a large change in supercharger speed, with tremendous loading on the impeller and shaft.

Many drive systems were tried, including spring drives, various flexible drives, fluid couplings and centrifugal clutches. The Germans were the first to develop supercharged combat aircraft in the 1914-18 war, but the Bristol Jupiter 7 was the first supercharged engine to go into large series production in 1927.

The turbocharger was originally developed by Buchi to boost diesel engine power output, but when fitted to petrol-burning aero engines, with their inherently higher exhaust gas temperatures, it soon became apparent (as early as 1914) that suitable materials to withstand constant running temperatures of 800°C or more were not available and, as a consequence, turbine life was far too short to realise the potential benefits of turbocharging as opposed to supercharging with gear-driven centrifugal superchargers. It is not surprising, therefore, in view of the relatively advanced state of development of the positive displacement supercharger, that the main line of development in Europe continued with this type of supercharger. Nevertheless, the Americans took up the idea of the turbo-supercharger and were able eventually to develop it to its full potential.

At the end of the First World War Mercedes were the first to apply the knowledge gained from supercharging aero engines to automobiles. In 1921 a supercharged 6-cylinder Mercedes 28/95 driven by Max Sailer won the Coppa Florio race. As a result of this success with their first supercharged model, Mercedes designed a supercharged 1½-litre sports car which competed in the 1922 Targa Florio.

All the early Mercedes supercharging systems employed a roots-type blower, mounted vertically and driven by bevel gears from the nose of the crankshaft, feeding pressurised air to the carburettor. The blower drive incorporated a cone-type clutch arrangement connected to the throttle, so that the drive between supercharger and engine was only engaged at full throttle. These early installations used a relatively modest boost of approximately 6-7 psi, yet were able to increase power output by up to 50 per cent.

1929 Mercedes Benz showing 'roots' blower, mounted vertically and typical of early Mercedes practice, blowing into the carburettors (National Motor Museum).

Fiat were the first to supercharge a Grand Prix racing car in 1923, when they ran a 2-litre car fitted with a Wittig vane-type supercharger. Following Mercedes practice, the supercharger was equipped with a hinged flap arrangement which allowed the engine to run normally aspirated, and it was supercharged only when required; as with the Mercedes system, the carburettor received pressurised air.

Mechanical and lubrication problems with the Wittig blower, as well as an apparently low adiabatic efficiency, led quickly to the adaption of a roots-type supercharger, with an intercooler between blower and carburettor.

By the spring of 1924 both Sunbeam and Alfa Romeo also appeared with supercharged Grand Prix cars, each using a roots-type blower driven directly from the nose of the crankshaft. In the USA, following a lapse of some 12 years since Chadwick's work with centrifugal superchargers, the Duesenberg engine appeared in 1924 and won the Indianapolis race. The 2-litre Duesenberg engine followed the practice adopted by Chadwick and used a centrifugal blower with the impeller mounted at right angles to the crankshaft. It was also the first supercharging system to suck air from a carburettor, an arrangement which was subsequently shown to give improved power output with positive displacement blowers due to the fact that the latent heat of vapourisation of the fuel could be used to cool the blower and also the fuel air mixture, resulting in a greater mass of mixture being forced into the engine. From this point on, the widespread use of alcohol fuel mixtures was adopted. It was because of its high latent heat of vapourisation that alcohol fuel was so effective in cooling the ingoing charge and, to a lesser extent, in reducing the tendency towards detonation. Up to this time fuel mixtures had contained percentages of benzole and tetra-ethyl lead mixed with the petrol.

In Europe the 1924 Sunbeam GP cars were the first to appear with the carburettor mounted upstream of the supercharger, and some interesting engine power output figures were taken with the carburettor mounted downstream and, alternatively, upstream of the supercharger. With the carburettor mounted upstream, brake mean effective pressure increased dramatically over the whole rpm range, with an increase in maximum BMEP from 155 lb/ft to 170 lb/ft at the same rpm. With the sole exception of Mercedes, who persisted with their downstream arrangement until 1937, the practice of mounting the carburettor ahead of the supercharger became the normal layout for supercharging systems of this period.

During the years 1925-38, due to the Formulae then prevailing, all competitive Grand Prix racing engines, whether built by Delage, Bugatti, Alfa Romeo, Auto Union or Mercedes, were supercharged. There was a steady increase in power output, coupled with increased boost pressure and the use of alcohol fuel. In the final four years of this period, only two makes dominated the Grand Prix racing scene, namely Auto Union and

1936 Auto Union supercharged V16 Grand Prix with a capacity of 6.0 litres produced 520 bhp at 5,000 rpm on methanol, with a compression ratio of 9.2:1 and supercharge pressure of 27 psi. Notice also the enormous carburettor (National Motor Museum).

Mercedes. The development of their supercharged engines culminated in the 520 bhp Auto Union with 6-litre engine and the M125 Mercedes with a colossal 646 bhp. With a change in Formulae for the 1938 racing season, supercharged engines were limited to 3 litres capacity. In order to obtain maximum power from the smaller engines it was necessary to increase manifold pressure from the already high figure of 2.2 atms (18.0 psi) for a single-stage roots-type blower. To maintain a reasonable adiabatic efficiency, it was necessary therefore to employ 2-stage supercharging for the first time.

When dealing with aero engine applications, a supercharger driven from the engine crankshaft with a fixed gear ratio suffers from a severe handicap as opposed to one with an infinitely-variable drive ratio, such as might be obtained with a fluid drive system. In order to achieve maximum boost, and therefore power output at maximum altitude, it is necessary to employ a drive ratio which will give too much boost at take-off altitude if serious detonation and consequent damage to the engine is to be avoided. For example, a boost of 14.7 psi at 18,000 ft becomes 30.0 psi at sea level.

The onset of detonation is mainly a reflection of the supercharger's thermal efficiency, demonstrated by the degree of temperature rise from the time the air charge enters the compressor inlet port until it emerges from the outlet port. The heating of the compressed mixture can be considerable as can be seen from the chart (Fig 1). Since an increase in charge temperature can considerably reduce the amount of boost which can be employed before the onset of detonation, it is obvious that the boost must be limited at low altitudes in some way, either by throttling or by variable gear ratio drive. The best example of variable gear drive was the 3-speed system of the Rolls-Royce Griffon.

By the 1930s Rolls-Royce were well into supercharging aero engines, and developed the principle of using one supercharger working in series with another to produce a high pressure ratio, yet still absorb less power than achieving the same pressure with a single-stage supercharger. This arrangement became known as two-stage supercharging and permitted the use of higher boost pressure ratios. Both Auto Union and Mercedes Grand Prix cars adopted two-stage supercharging in 1939 with two roots blowers providing up to 2.65 atms manifold pressure.

As a consequence of using higher pressure ratios, the problem of temperature rise of the induced charge became even more evident. In order to combat these problems, two main lines of development were pursued: firstly, the use of intercoolers or aftercoolers to reduce inlet charge temperature; and secondly, the injection of various additives such as water, water and alcohol mixtures, nitrous oxide and nitromethane. The idea of using water injection to cool the charge entering the engine was by no means new, having been patented in 1920 by Hobson.

A turbocharger, which is a supercharger driven by engine exhaust gas heat energy, is undoubtedly the most efficient type of supercharger in terms of both mechanical and thermal efficiency.

The turbine speed, and consequently the compressor speed, is determined by the pressure differential existing across the turbine. The greater the difference between the pressure in the exhaust manifold and the atmospheric pressure, the faster the turbine will turn. It can be seen therefore that, as the ambient air pressure decreases due to an increase in altitude, the turbine will automatically speed up, as the pressure in the exhaust manifold remains substantially the same, but the pressure on the turbine discharge side

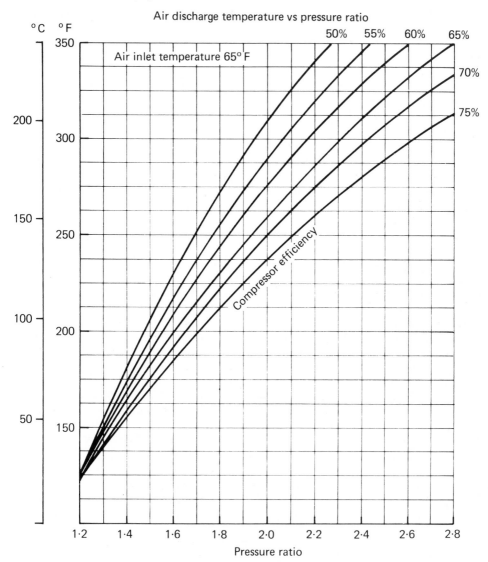

Fig 1: *All superchargers or compressors increase the inlet charge temperature in proportion to the boost pressure and adiabatic efficiency of the supercharger. This chart shows the degree of temperature increase.*

will drop relative to the ambient air pressure. A turbo-supercharger is, therefore, largely self-compensating as far as turbine speed is concerned as altitude increases.

As has been explained earlier, it had long been the practice in the USA to use gear-driven centrifugal superchargers. As a turbocharger combines a centrifugal supercharger driven by an exhaust gas turbine, it is not surprising that most early turbo development work took place in America. Serious development of the turbocharger began in the early 1940s on aero engines but, despite the theoretical advantages of the turbo, it was not without its own particular problems which delayed its early development and adoption on a wider scale, these principally being metallurgical and lubrication problems. It must be remembered that the turbine had to spin continuously at speeds in excess of 30,000 rpm and run at temperatures as high as 850-950°C. To counteract these high temperature problems, early turbos had their turbine wheels set up in the open air with only the turbine inlet nozzle set into a cowling.

It was not until 1940 when a special alloy, Vitallium (previously used in dentistry), was modified and developed as Haynes Stellite 21 alloy and used to manufacture the turbine blades, that the turbocharger heat problem was largely cured. But despite this, it was to be another 15 or more years before manufacturing processes were evolved which would allow the production of turbine and compressor wheel assemblies of sufficiently small diameter and structural quality to make them really suitable for everyday high volume automobile applications.

During the 1945-50 period it became apparent that the gas turbine engine would replace the piston engine as the power unit for all but light aircraft. However, before the final eclipse of the large supercharged piston engine in favour of the gas turbine or jet, there were one or two supercharging developments which should be mentioned.

First is the practice of compound turbocharging. This involves linking a mechanical drive to drive a compressor and employing exhaust energy to spin a turbine, thereby obtaining the benefits of maximum efficiency from each. Two of the most impressive examples were the Wright R3350 Cyclone 18-cylinder radial engine which employed a gear-driven two-speed centrifugal supercharger and three exhaust gas turbines, each linked to the crankshaft by a fluid coupling fed with engine oil. In its most powerful form, this engine developed 3,700 hp. The second, and probably the most complex and highly developed supercharged engine ever built, was the Napier Nomad. The basic specification was as follows: 12-cylinder horizontally-opposed two-stroke liquid-cooled diesel engine, compounded with an axial-flow three-stage exhaust gas turbine and a 12-stage axial-flow compressor, supplying air at a very high pressure of 8.25 atmospheres (equivalent to a maximum boost pressure of 106 psi). Compression ratio was 8:1, but that is not the end of it. An intercooler was added, together with water injection and, in order to burn up the remaining air in the exhaust gases, extra fuel was injected into the exhaust manifold as an afterburner. The final result was a diesel engine of relatively modest weight and overall dimensions which produced 4,500 hp, equivalent to .83 lb per hp.

Unfortunately, as far as supercharging is concerned, further exploitation of this and other supercharged piston aero engines, with the exception of some light aircraft, was completely eclipsed with the arrival and takeover by the jet engine in the early 1950s.

In Europe, the use of supercharged automobile engines during the 1947-53 period was confined to the Grand Prix racing scene and some experimental specialist conversions such as the vane-type blowers fitted to record-breaking MGs, in particular the MG XPAG engine, with which Goldie Gardner broke the class G record, achieving over 200 mph with the 1,500 cc Shorrock supercharged engine. Incidentally, this engine produced over 300 bhp which was similar to the best 1.5-litre supercharged Grand Prix engine then in use.

After the Second World War, when racing was resumed in 1947, Formula One Grand Prix racing came into existence with engine capacities of 4½ litres unsupercharged and 1½ litres supercharged. Initially the supercharged engines remained supreme, but in 1950-51 the 4½-litre unsupercharged Ferrari became dominant, and thus began the decline of the supercharged engine.

In 1952, the adoption of a 2.0-litre unsupercharged class, and a reduction to 500 cc for supercharged engines, together with the general use of normal pump fuel, saw an end to the supercharged engine era. A supercharged or turbocharged engine was not to appear in Formula 1 Grand Prix racing again for another 23 years.

In the USA virtually no use had ever been made of positive displacement blowers and there had been very little development of the favoured centrifugal superchargers in the automobile world, although such belt-driven centrifugal superchargers as the Paxton and McCullough were in evidence in the 1950-55 period, and the Judson vane-type a little later. In Europe long before the emergence of the Wankel rotary engine, it had been used as a very efficient positive displacement supercharger, without the spark plug of course. Some other examples of vane and roots-type positive displacement superchargers were Zoller, Cozette, Arnott, Marshall, Wade and Shorrock.

By the late 1950s and early '60s, both in Europe and the USA, turbochargers began to appear on the larger diesels fitted to trucks, buses and industrial engines. As the techniques for mass-production of smaller turbines and the technology to make the best use of turbochargers were developed, the range of diesel engine applications, particularly in the field of tractors and agricultural equipment, grew rapidly from about 1960. In 1962 the first turbocharged petrol-engined mass-production saloon car was announced, this being the Oldsmobile Jetfire, followed by the turbocharged Corvair Spider in 1964.

Although it was accepted practice by this time to turbocharge the larger commercial vehicles, automobile manufacturers generally still preferred to fit a larger capacity engine rather than get involved in this still relatively unknown area. In general, the rules in motor sport were still heavily loaded against any form of forced induction and therefore there was no feedback or spin-off from the competition departments of the various manufacturers, which could have stimulated more interest in turbocharging development. However, the last six to eight years have seen a rapid rise in the technology and use of turbocharging, as the best means of obtaining high power output with low fuel consumption. This trend has been given additional impetus by the search for cleaner exhaust emissions and with the world fuel crisis hastening the move towards smaller and generally more efficient engines.

Chapter 2

Volumetric and thermal efficiency

Thermal efficiency of an internal combustion engine can be defined as a measure of the quantity of fuel burned, compared to the amount of power produced. Even the most thermally-efficient normally-aspirated engines can do no better than convert approximately 30 per cent of the fuel consumed into useful power. With a positive displacement supercharged engine this figure may drop to 25 per cent or less, but a turbocharged engine, by extracting some of the waste heat energy from the exhaust and returning this to the engine in the form of increased power output, can approach the thermal efficiency of a normally-aspirated engine.

In the normally-aspirated engine, when the piston descends on the power stroke, the gases are expanded and therefore cooled, a process which is defined as the expansion ratio, the resultant heat loss being converted into power at the flywheel. Generally, the expansion ratio is similar to the geometric compression ratio in a normally-aspirated engine. However, when an engine is supercharged, the greatly increased volumetric efficiency results in a substantial increase in effective compression ratio, but at the same time the effective expansion ratio remains similar to that of a normally-aspirated engine.

It can, therefore, be seen that, although a substantial power increase can be obtained through increasing the volumetric efficiency—and thereby the effective compression ratio—a similar opportunity to extract more power does not arise during the expansion period because, unlike the effective compression ratio, the expansion ratio remains unchanged whether the engine is normally-aspirated or supercharged. Therefore it is not possible to extract additional heat energy and in consequence the thermal efficiency of a supercharged engine is lower than that of an unsupercharged engine.

The degree of temperature increase of the charge when passing through the compressor is a true measure of the adiabatic efficiency of the supercharger. As an example, if air entered the compressor at 20°C and, after passing through the compressor, the compressed air was delivered from the outlet port at a pressure of 1.5 atmospheres at 20°C, the compressor would be 100 per cent adiabatically efficient. In practice, current automobile compressors are more likely to have an overall efficiency of 65 per cent, in which case the air delivery at the same pressure would be at a temperature of 75°C, the temperature rise being a measure of the pumping losses through the compressor.

Another measure of efficiency of any form of air pump—and all turbochargers and superchargers are basically air pumps—is the volume of air output at a given rpm compared to the energy input.

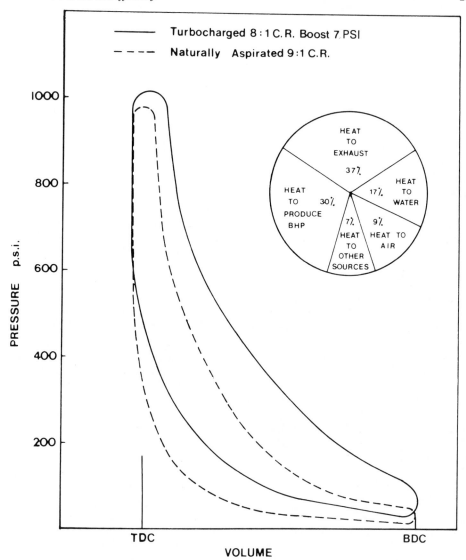

Fig 2: *Cylinder Pressure Indicator diagram: pressurised induction flattens the cylinder pressure curve as shown, by maintaining a greater pressure on the pistons during each power stroke. In consequence the torque of a supercharged engine is substantially increased over a wide rpm range. The diagram also shows that with boost pressures of up to 7.0 psi (0.5 BAR) and modest reduction in compression ratio, peak cylinder pressures are not increased as much as might be expected. Approximately 37 per cent of the heat produced when burning the fuel in a normally aspirated engine is wasted down the exhaust pipe. With modern low inertia turbochargers there is more than enough heat energy available, from as low as 1,500 rpm, to give several psi of boost.*

The pumping (adiabatic) efficiency is determined by the amount of energy required to drive the compressor and the degree of temperature rise of the air across the compressor from the inlet to the outlet port for a given pressure flow. Fig 3 shows the typical hp consumption or power to drive some positive displacement superchargers.

In their normal working range (ie, 3-10 psi boost, 1,500-5,000 engine rpm) vane type superchargers usually have an efficiency of 55-60 per cent, normal roots types 50-55 per cent and turbo-superchargers 60-70 per cent. Once boost pressure exceeds 10-12 psi, the roots types show a steady drop in efficiency, with a steeply rising power consumption curve. The vane types can maintain reasonable efficiency up to 20 psi (2.3:1 pressure ratio), but the turbochargers really excel when high pressures are required and pressure ratios of up to 3.0:1 can be maintained with 65 per cent efficiency. The relative efficiencies of the various types of superchargers are demonstrated by the charts, maps and diagrams which follow.

It is often assumed that the turbocharger, because it has no mechanical drive system, does not consume any power to drive it. In practice this is not so, as the back pressure in the exhaust manifold, which is a necessary function of turbine operating speed, does

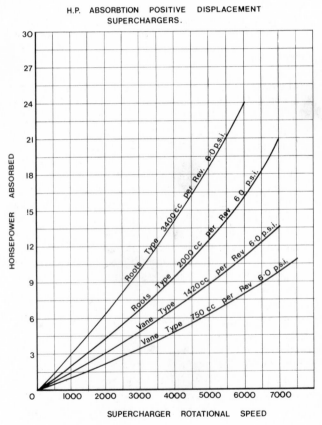

Fig 3: *Positive displacement superchargers as typified by the roots and vane types consume hp from the crankshaft. Nevertheless, on-the-road performance can be impressive. It must be remembered too that under cruise and light throttle conditions the amount of power consumed will be comparatively small.*

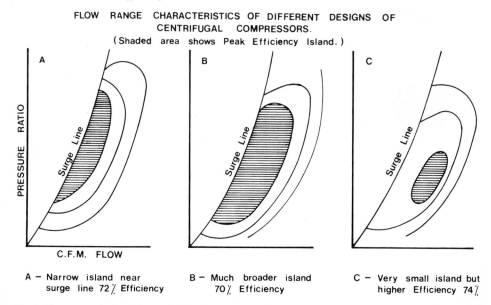

FLOW RANGE CHARACTERISTICS OF DIFFERENT DESIGNS OF CENTRIFUGAL COMPRESSORS.
(Shaded area shows Peak Efficiency Island.)

A – Narrow island near surge line 72% Efficiency

B – Much broader island 70% Efficiency

C – Very small island but higher Efficiency 74%

Fig 4: *Flow range characteristics of different designs of centrifugal compressors.*

reduce the maximum power output which could be achieved at the same boost and rpm if there were no back pressure in the manifold. Obviously this loss of power in driving the turbine is relatively small in relation to the power increase obtained at the flywheel, however, and under light load conditions the loss is commendably low, which is part of the reason for the good overall fuel consumption and specific performance.

It is also often stated that the turbocharger is driven entirely by exhaust heat energy which otherwise would have gone to waste. This is, in fact, not entirely true, in the sense that only a small percentage of the standard engine's exhaust heat energy can be extracted by the turbine to produce extra power without the addition of extra fuel. To gain a power and torque increase of more than approximately ten per cent it is necessary to inject extra fuel with the increased mass air inlet flow, which in turn creates more heat energy to drive the turbine faster. Therefore, although the turbine does extract a substantial amount of waste heat (exhaust enthalpy), there still remains a large percentage of the original waste heat. Interestingly, it has been calculated that there can be an excess of up to 70 per cent heat energy available at maximum engine speed. This means that, of the total heat rejected to atmosphere through the exhaust, the turbocharger only needs 30 per cent. It can be seen, therefore, that there is always more than enough heat energy available at medium to maximum engine speed, but the situation is reversed at low engine speeds, where it is more difficult to obtain the required torque back-up.

It is when a turbocharged engine runs with a positive pressure relationship between boost and exhaust manifold back pressure ('in crossover') that a high specific performance can be achieved, and this is a major reason why most manufacturers have favoured turbochargers as opposed to superchargers. A positive displacement supercharger can excel in

Left *C75B and C142B Shorrock 'vane' type, Wade 4R020 and 4R034 'roots' type superchargers and Holset 3LD turbocharger.*

Right Fig 5: *'Roots' type positive displacement supercharger.*

Far right Fig 6: *'Vane' type positive displacement supercharger.*

Below right Fig 7: *Sliding vane supercharger.*

Below far right Fig 8: *Rotary superchargers used a three-sided rotor with seals, which revolved inside a specially designed casing, similar to the principle of the Wankel rotary engine.*

Bottom right Fig 9: *Lysholm supercharger. The specially designed multilobed rotors are able to produce a high adiabatic efficiency, but make the cost of the unit very high.*

Bottom far right Fig 10: *The reciprocating piston compressor was one of the earliest methods of applying supercharge pressure to the cylinders of an engine, but proved too bulky and lacked high speed efficiency.*

providing low speed boost and instant response at the expense of much lower specific engine performance, although the situation could be considerably improved if the drive to the blower could be disengaged and the supercharger bypassed when not required.

Generally, at high or full load the specific fuel consumption of a turbocharged engine will be better than for a comparable normally-aspirated engine unless, of course, as with competition engines, the mixture is deliberately richened to act as a cooling agent. At low loads and idle there will be very little difference, unless there has been a substantial reduction in compression ratio. In fact, engine displacement has more influence on fuel consumption than compression ratio at low speeds. Tests indicate that for a reduction of one ratio in compression, there is four to five per cent increase in fuel consumption at low and medium speeds.

Another form of efficiency in an internal combustion engine is mechanical efficiency and in this respect a supercharged engine is superior to a normally-aspirated one since the power consumed by frictional losses, friction horse power (FHP) remains substantially the same, even though the power output of the supercharged engine may be considerably greater.

Superchargers—types and characteristics

There are two distinct categories of superchargers or compressors. The first is the positive displacement type, typified by the 'roots' lobe or vane type with eccentric rotor, which displaces substantially the same volume of air per revolution irrespective of engine speed. In the second category are the dynamic types, which include centrifugal, radial and axial flow

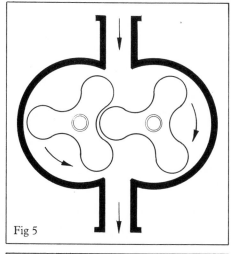

Fig 5

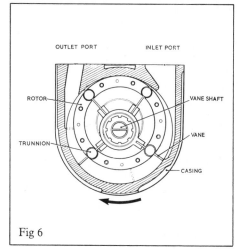

OUTLET PORT   INLET PORT

ROTOR

TRUNNION

VANE SHAFT

VANE

CASING

Fig 6

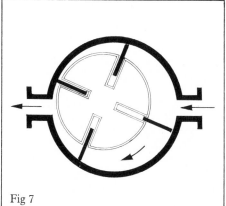

Fig 7

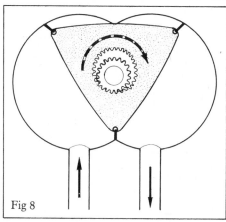

Fig 8

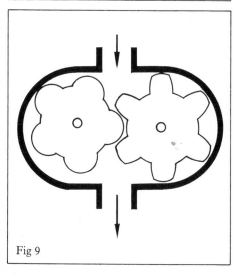

Fig 9

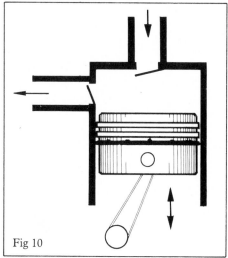

Fig 10

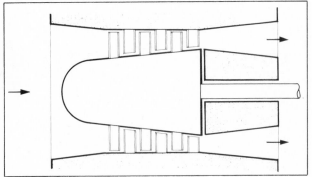

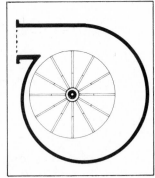

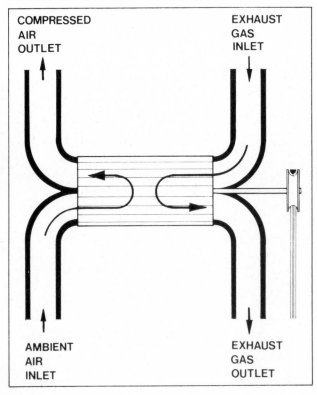

COMPRESSED
AIR
OUTLET

EXHAUST
GAS
INLET

AMBIENT
AIR
INLET

EXHAUST
GAS
OUTLET

Above left Fig 11: *Axial compressor provides high efficiency over a comparatively narrow pressure range. Therefore several stages of compression are normally used, which in turn makes this type rather bulky.*

Above Fig 12: *Centrifugal supercharger. This is similar to the compressor section of a turbo-supercharger, but unlike the turbocharger is mechanically driven. The supercharger-to-engine drive ratio is as high as 10:1.*

Left Fig 13: *Simplified diagram of the Comprex pressure wave supercharger, which features a belt-driven multi-vaned rotor assembly, to obtain instant throttle response, and utilises the pressure waves created by the expanding exhaust gases to compress the inlet charge. In doing so it combines the immediate throttle response advantage of a positive displacement supercharger with the thermodynamic efficiency of a turbocharger.*

compressors and the turbine-driven centrifugal compressor as typified by the turbo-supercharger. I will deal with the positive displacement types first in this chapter as they were, particularly in Europe, the first types to be widely used.

Some of the better known makes were as follows:

Roots type: Fiat (OM); Mercedes; Auto-Union; Rolls-Royce; GMC; Lysholm;

Above *Sectional view of Wade 4R020 supercharger, showing typical construction of a 'roots' type with intermeshing rotors and helical phasing gears.*

Above right *Magnacharger (roots type) blower with toothed pulley drive kit.*

Right *Stirling Moss discussing a GMC supercharged Chrysler-engined Willys Coupé, which competed in the 1964 Drag Festival at Blackbushe.*

Whitfield; Marshall Nordec; Marshall Drew; Wade; Broome Wade; Amhurst-Villiers; and Italmeccanica S.C.O.T.

Vane type: Whittig; Zoller; Cozette; Arnott; Centric; Reveal; Powerplus; Shorrock; Constantine; and Judson.

One of the earliest positive displacement-type compressors was the reciprocating piston type, which used the pumping action of a piston sliding in a cylinder connected to the engine crankshaft by a connecting rod in the same way as a normal engine piston in cylinder arrangement. Because of its inherent high frictional losses, its overall efficiency was rather low even though its volumetric efficiency was relatively high; additionally, a pump of this design is far too bulky for all but stationary engine applications.

The 'roots'-type supercharger

The 'roots'-type supercharger is a positive displacement pump, normally driven from the crankshaft by toothed or 'V' belts. There are two internal rotors phased to prevent clashing of the lobes on the rotors by gears. The driving rotor, which is the one linked directly to the engine by the drive belt system, will be turned in the direction of engine rotation, and as it does so the other rotor will be turned in the opposite direction due to the action of the gears, as can be seen in Fig 5. As the rotors turn, air is drawn in through the inlet port and carried round between the casing and the chamber formed by the hollow in the rotor, both rotors contributing to the pumping action.

The length and diameter of the rotor determines the volume of air which will be pumped per revolution and, together with the lobe profile and port shape, controls the flow rate pattern over the rpm operating range.

All roots-type superchargers have a pulsing flow which can be particularly noticeable at low rpm. This surging or pulsing delivery can be reduced by using three lobed rotors with lobes 120° apart instead of the two-lobed design. The use of helical-shaped rotors, as in the American GMC roots-type blower, provides a further improvement in pumping efficiency by adding some compression to the charge and more even delivery of air.

In the case of the Wade blower, it employs three-lobed straight rotors of extruded aluminium section, but with helical-shaped ports to achieve a more progressive air delivery and at the same time reduce the noise caused by the churning of the air entering the inlet port.

Two-lobed designs are much cheaper to produce and can have a greater delivery volume per revolution for a given length and diameter, but this advantage is more than offset by the more violent pulsing air delivery characteristics.

The GMC blower, like almost all the roots-type blowers used in the last 50 years, was originally developed as a pump to scavenge two-stroke diesel engines. The use of modified versions of these basically very simple units to supercharge 250 mph, 2,500 bhp dragsters, shows just what experimentation and engineering can achieve given sufficient time and money. The two sizes of GMC blower most used on petrol engines are the 4-71 and 6-71, although smaller and larger sizes are manufactured, these being the 3-71 and 8-71 respectively. The number designation is derived from the number of cylinders of the engine to which the supercharger was originally fitted and the displacement of each cylinder (eg, the 6-71 was fitted to a 6-cylinder engine, with an individual cylinder capacity of 71 cu in).

When pumping dry air, as when used on a diesel engine, the supercharger unit will operate at relatively high temperature, hence these blowers were built with large clearances which are reduced when every possible percentage of pumping capacity is required for competition use, and by fitting Teflon sealing strips to the tips of the rotors.

The roots-type blowers, with the exception of the Lysholm type with specially-designed

Above *A superbly engineered 'roots' type supercharger installation fitted to a Ferrari 365 GTB no less. Installation carried out by Weslake. Classic blending of the old and the new. Probably the only Ferrari fitted with SU carburettors.*

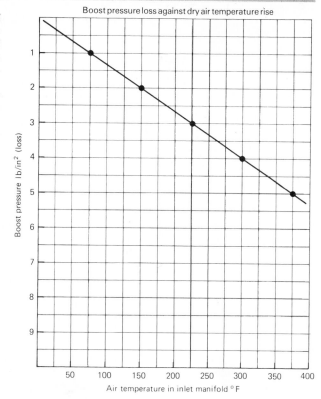

Boost pressure loss against dry air temperature rise

Boost pressure lb/in² (loss)

Air temperature in inlet manifold °F

Right Fig 14: *The effect of compressing air is to raise its temperature. For every 150°F (65.5°C) increase there will be an effective loss in air density equivalent to 2.0 psi boost.*

intermeshing helical rotors, impart little or no compression to the charge within the air chest and should correctly be termed air displacers, not compressors.

One of the most commonly seen roots-type blowers in Europe is the Wade. Two sizes were specially manufactured for petrol-engined applications, these being the RO20 and RO34. The larger RO34 unit was originally designed for use on the two-stroke Commer TS3 diesel as a scavenge pump intended to run at a maximum of 4,350 rpm. Wade Engineering adapted this unit for automobile petrol engine use, principally by fitting steel shafts to support the rotors, as opposed to aluminium used in the diesel units. This eliminated flexing of the rotors under rapid acceleration and deceleration and high gas loadings. It also allowed a safe maximum rpm of up to 7,500 for short bursts.

The RO34 unit is suitable for up to 4,000 cc engines, having a maximum delivery of 450 CFM at 5.0 psi boost and speed of 5,000 rpm. The smaller RO20 unit is suitable for engines ranging in capacity from 1,300-3,500 cc and is a shortened version of the RO34 unit. It is again fitted with steel-shafted rotors.

The Wade supercharger, although somewhat more complicated in construction than the GMC types, does not require special clearances and strengthening work for competition use when fitted with steel-shafted rotors, as is the case with most GMC types.

It has been common practice among people looking for an apparently cheap route to a large power increase for their motor, to obtain a well-worn diesel type 4RO34/1400 unit. It is as well to point out here that, unless a unit is carefully checked over, found to be in sound condition and driven at a maximum of 5,000 rpm, failure may occur in a short time.

The roots positive-displacement supercharger has relatively low frictional losses and the design and mounting of the rotors means that there are no out of balance forces to contend with, as found in vane types. Therefore the maximum rpm at which it can be driven can be as high as 10,000 rpm with a carefully-prepared unit. The limitations are usually brought about by rotor flexing causing clashing of the rotor lobes, or by excessive thrust loadings through the helical phasing gears, causing the rotors to move out of phase or bearings to spin in their housings.

Except when running high nitro percentages in the fuel, backfire or pressure relief valves are not as critical as when using a vane-type supercharger.

The pumping efficiency at very low speeds suffers in relation to the vane types due to the relatively high gas leakage areas round the rotors, resulting in some back flow of air. The use of Teflon sealing strips and spraying of the rotors with an anti-scuff coating can be of great benefit to the pumping efficiency throughout the operating range.

The Magnacharger

Now recognised as one of the leading examples of roots-type blower currently being manufactured in the USA, the Magnacharger is produced in three popular sizes—an 80 cubic inch unit (1,300 cc) to suit engines of 1,300-2,500 cc approximately; 110 cubic inch unit for most 6-cylinder engines; and a 220 cubic inch unit for larger capacity engines. The last is in fact two 110 cubic inch units siamesed together. By designing the blower this way a high air flow capacity unit is produced. The rotors being smaller and lighter allows higher speed rotation, without severe fall in pumping efficiency. It also permits easier installation in a cramped under-bonnet area.

Unlike the GMC blower, the Magnacharger has straight cut gears which reduce axial thrust in the blower and simplify rotor phasing, albeit with some additional blower whine. The rotors too, unlike the GMC unit, are straight three-lobed type, similar in fact to the Wade blower. As previously stated, three-lobed rotors as opposed to two-lobed, reduce the air flow pulsations which are a characteristic of the roots blower, particularly noticeable at low speeds. They also allow a straighter air flow path through the blower and a large air inlet port.

An interesting feature of the Magnacharger is the air flow bar across the inlet port which is designed to direct the air into the rotor air chamber formed in the rotors. This reduces turbulence, back flow and pumping losses.

In addition to the blower just described, there are currently several other makes of roots blower being marketed in the USA, largely based on remanufactured GMC units; as well as centrifugal types, most notably the Paxton centrifugal blower.

The vane-type supercharger
It is not generally known that the principal elements of the Wankel rotary engine were used

Right *Shorrock supercharged MG Magnette, showing how outrigger housing for extended drive shaft allows repositioning of supercharger in a tight space.*

Below Fig 15: *The Shorrock supercharger is a positive displacement vane type with eccentric rotor, incorporating four radially-mounted vanes attached to a vane shaft. Such a system allows fine vane to casing clearances, providing low friction and high efficiency.*

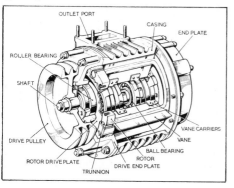

as a vane-type supercharger by NSU to supercharge some record-breaking motor cycle engines.

Many examples of vane-type superchargers were produced in the 1920-1939 period and the Shorrock survived until the 1970s. Most designs, although varying in detail construction, employed the same principle. The Shorrock is a typical example with four vanes mounted radially and secured to eight vane carriers running on a vane shaft with carriers supported by ball bearings. Each vane is anchored to two carriers and does not, therefore, come into contact with the casing, as is the case with the sliding vane type. A minimum of .004 in vane tip to casing clearance is maintained. The vanes slide over or through a trunnion bush or block, in order to accommodate the angular motion of the vane. The trunnion in turn is carried in a longitudinal drilling in an aluminium rotor. Characteristically, the rotor is mounted eccentrically and the vane shaft assembly centrally to the casing, so that as the rotor rotates, its action opens a chamber between the extremities of two of the vanes, so creating a vacuum and drawing air in through the inlet port. As the supercharger continues to rotate, the chamber begins to reduce in size again, thus compressing the air before releasing it through the outlet port and into the inlet manifold.

This internal compression is the main advantage that this type of supercharger has over the roots-type. The effect of the internal compression is to increase the density and therefore the weight of charge per revolution and consequently the temperature rise for a given weight of charge (boost) is reduced. The contra pressure of the mixture in the inlet manifold is reduced also, thereby improving the pumping efficiency by reducing power consumed in driving the supercharger for a given pressure ratio.

Below left *Sprintex S82 supercharger designed and manufactured by Fleming Thermodynamics in Glasgow. Its 'screw' type intermeshing rotors are expensive to produce, but provide very high thermodynamic performance.*

Below right *Compact Del-charge 'roots' type supercharger manufactured in the UK.*

Sprintex supercharged Manta 1.8S.

Positive-displacement superchargers

Despite the fact that in recent years the turbo-supercharger has been the pre-eminent type of supercharger, there are indications that there may be a revival of the positive displacement supercharger, particularly for applications where low speed torque and throttle response are the most important factors.

For many years from the early 1920s, superchargers as opposed to turbochargers proved the effectiveness of forced induction, particularly on the European motor racing circuits. Although the peak mechanical and thermal efficiency of the turbocharger can be substantially higher, in practice—even with relatively highly developed turbochargers—the difference is not that apparent in road or track performance, partly due to the fact that the peak efficiency of a turbocharger is confined to a relatively narrow band. Once the compressor is operating out of its highest efficiency island, it may almost be matched by the more efficient types of supercharger. It should be borne in mind too that over the last 30 years or so there has been minimal development of the supercharger as opposed to the turbcharger.

There are now indications that other designs of supercharger and compressor are being experimented with, or older designs being re-engineered with modern materials and manufacturing techniques. It could be, therefore, that a new generation of superchargers could emerge, possibly linking the best features of a positive displacement compressor with an exhaust-driven turbine.

The FTD 'Sprintex' screw-type supercharger has been developed by Fleming Thermo

Rotomaster turbocharger components, showing mechanical face type seal on compressor side. This turbocharger therefore can be used with carburettor mounted upstream of the compressor.

Dynamics in Glasgow, and is based on some design principles previously proven over many years in industrial compressors, but now adapted specifically for automobile applications. The Sprintex supercharger provides high thermodynamic performance due to the internal compression of the charge combined with sophisticated manufacturing techniques which allow very fine clearances rotor to rotor and between casing and rotors.

Two sizes of unit are available, these being the S82 and S102, both being suitable for petrol and diesel engines ranging in capacity from 1,000-2,000 cc for the S82 and 2,000-3,500 cc for the S102 unit. Units are manufactured with short or extended drive shafts, to suit various applications. A range of after market conversions are available from appointed distributors.

Supercharging

Unlike a turbo-supercharger, the positive displacement supercharger by definition requires some form of mechanical drive arrangement. A supercharger is usually driven from the engine crankshaft by 'V' belts or toothed belts, or directly coupled to the nose of the crankshaft. The power absorbed by the supercharger and drive system when it is not supplying boost pressure to the engine, as under cruise conditions, can be compared to the power absorbed by the additional back pressure reflected back to the engine by the turbine of a turbocharger. If some form of electromagnetic clutch arrangement is incorporated in the drive system and a bypass manifold provided, this power loss can be eliminated altogether. Again, this could be compared to a turbocharger part throttle open wastegate valve arrangement.

Whereas a turbocharger is supported by the exhaust manifold, a supercharger needs either to be bolted directly to a specially-designed inlet manifold as seen on many V8 supercharged engines, or to be securely attached to the engine by substantial front and rear mounting brackets, with the drive shaft parallel to the crankshaft axis.

The requirements for carburation and inlet manifold design, as well as the engine build specifications, are generally similar to a turbo-supercharged engine, so need not be discussed again here. However, a free-flow fabricated exhaust manifold and a large bore exhaust with low back pressure will greatly enhance the engine power curve. This is also true of such modifications as fitting a camshaft with a greater lift and duration. Such a 'competition' type camshaft will usually have a similar effect on the power curve as it would if fitted to an unsupercharged engine. The additional scavenging such a camshaft creates leads to a considerable drop in exhaust valve and cylinder temperature due to the blow-through of partly-burnt mixture, but at the same time this loss will cause a significant increase in fuel consumption. If valve overlap is excessive, there can be a sizeable drop in boost pressure too, which may more than offset the benefits from the scavenging effect. In such a case the supercharger-to-engine drive ratio may need to be increased to compensate for this loss of boost.

The centrifugal compressor

All centrifugal compressors (superchargers) are intrinsically high speed devices which, unlike the positive-displacement types, do not displace the same volume of air per revolution. In practice the air flow delivery from this type of supercharger increases as the square of the speed of rotation of the compressor, and a speed of up to 25,000 rpm may be necessary before a positive pressure above atmospheric is apparent.

As an example of the rpm vs boost curve characteristics of this type of compressor, if we take a compressor which develops a pressure ratio of say 1.3 (4.5 psi boost) with a

The larger C142B Shorrock supercharger fitted to a Ford 1600 GT increased power output from 85 to 110 bhp at 6,000 rpm with 7.0 psi boost.

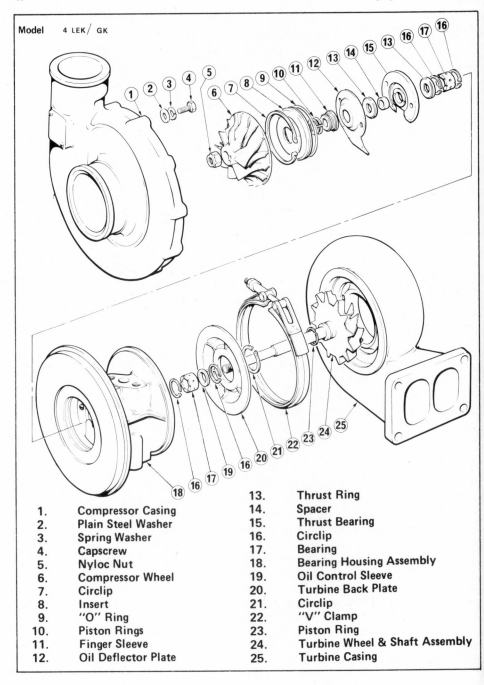

Model   4 LEK / GK

1.	Compressor Casing	13.	Thrust Ring
2.	Plain Steel Washer	14.	Spacer
3.	Spring Washer	15.	Thrust Bearing
4.	Capscrew	16.	Circlip
5.	Nyloc Nut	17.	Bearing
6.	Compressor Wheel	18.	Bearing Housing Assembly
7.	Circlip	19.	Oil Control Sleeve
8.	Insert	20.	Turbine Back Plate
9.	"O" Ring	21.	Circlip
10.	Piston Rings	22.	"V" Clamp
11.	Finger Sleeve	23.	Piston Ring
12.	Oil Deflector Plate	24.	Turbine Wheel & Shaft Assembly
		25.	Turbine Casing

Left Fig 16: *Exploded view of a typical turbocharger. This one is a Holset 4 LEK which would usually be fitted to diesel engines.*

Right *Cutaway of Holset H2 turbocharger, showing construction typical of small and medium sized radial flow turbochargers* (Holset Engineering).

compressor speed of 50,000 rpm, by doubling the compressor speed to 100,000 rpm the pressure ratio has increased to 2.5 (22.0 psi boost). Yet this may correspond to an increase in engine speed of only 3,000 rpm.

Perhaps a classic example which vividly illustrates this point was the V16 BRM which was supercharged with a two-stage centrifugal supercharger designed and manufactured by Rolls-Royce. At 5,000 rpm the 1.5-litre engine produced only 100 bhp, yet at 8,000 rpm this had increased to 330 bhp, backed by a similar rapidly-rising torque curve.

Turbo-superchargers

The principles of turbo-superchargers, although devised way back in the early 1900s by a Swiss engineer, were not sufficiently developed for reasons already explained, to make them suitable for passenger car applications until about 1960. During the last eight to ten years, the application of turbo-superchargers to a wide range of diesel and petrol engines has been seen.

The turbocharger, as this type of supercharger is commonly known, has several advantages over other types and also one or two disadvantages. Its weight, including installation components, in relation to its air pumping capacity, is considerably less than for an equivalent positive-displacement supercharger. In other words, if an engine requires 250 CFM of air at 1.5 pressure ratio, a turbocharger capable of delivering this could only weigh 8-10 lb. In contrast, a supercharger of similar air pumping capacity might weigh 35-40 lb including its drive system and, because of its weight, additional mountings will be necessary to support it.

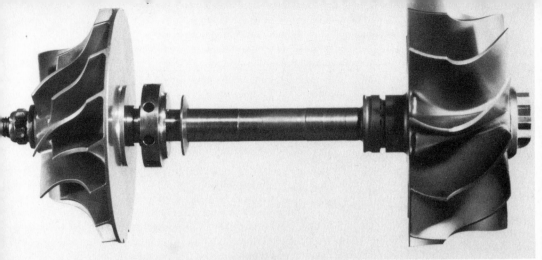

Above *Turbocharger typical 'wheel assembly' comprising compressor, shaft and turbine wheel.*

Left *Turbocharger compressor wheel showing disastrous results of some solid object entering the compressor. Demonstrates the desirability of always using effective air filters.*

The turbocharger has a higher adiabatic pumping efficiency, as high as 75 per cent at its peak efficiency, although the overall figure is more likely to be in the region of 60-65 per cent. The term adiabatic is defined as a process in which work is carried out with no gain or loss of heat to or from an external source. Such a process would be 100 per cent adiabatically efficient, which unfortunately is not possible in practice.

The current automobile turbo-supercharger comprises a centrifugal compressor with radial outflow through a vaneless diffuser housing with a tapered constant-velocity volute collector, leading to a diffusing outlet pipe. The turbine end comprises a centripetal radial inflow exhaust gas turbine, surrounded by a vaneless turbine housing. The compressor and turbine wheels are mounted at each end of a common shaft and this assembly is balanced to very fine limits. In between the two wheels is a bearing housing which, as its name implies, houses the bearing or bearings upon which the wheel assembly runs, with a thrust ring and an oil seal at each end. The unit is completed with an aluminium housing for the compressor and a cast iron housing for the turbine end.

Right Fig 17: *In the naturally aspirated engine about 40 per cent of the energy generated from fuel consumption is discharged into the atmosphere as heat in the exhaust gases. A turbocharger utilises a portion of this energy to drive the turbine and the compressor which is attached to the same shaft. The compressor increases the pressure of the engine intake air which enables the engine effectively to use a greater mixture of air and fuel. This produces an increase in power output over the naturally aspirated engine.*

Below Fig 18: *Diagram to show the effect of compressor blade profile on pressure ratio/air flow curves.*

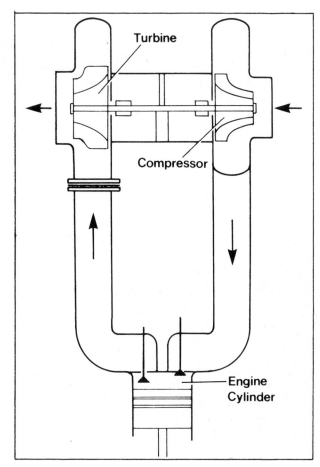

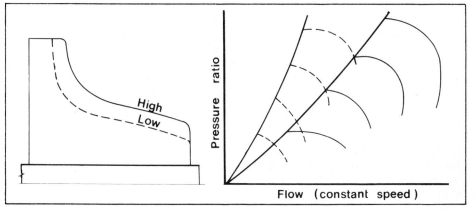

The centrifugal compressor

The design of the typical automobile compressor in current use has been evolved over many years to a very high degree of thermodynamic efficiency. Some units have a maximum design speed of up to 180,000 rpm at 3.5:1 pressure ratio and with a wide flow range. The compressor must spin at very high speed so that the impeller section of the compressor can accelerate the air and so impart a high velocity to it by centrifugal force. The diffuser section of the compressor then reduces the velocity, so causing it to build up pressure in the process. The increase in pressure causes an increase in the air temperature also, in proportion to the adiabatic efficiency of the compressor. The compressor housing incorporates a vaneless diffuser section with a gradually increasing cross sectional area to increase the static pressure.

There are various designs of compressor, each having its advantages and disadvantages. The simplest design has straight blades, but has relatively low efficiency due to the shock waves created at the blade tips. To reduce the loss through shock waves, another design, which is one of the most common in current use, has curved inducer blades with the angle of curvature at the leading edge at the same angle as the air entering the compressor.

Another type has backward-curved inducer blades. Currently the type with highest efficiency is the backward-curved impeller, in which the blades are curved backwards from the direction of rotation, from the root of the blade. The resistance to the centrifugal loadings is somewhat lower with this design and consequently the maximum compressor speed—and, therefore, the pressure ratio—is normally less than for other designs. In addition, pressure ratio is less for a given speed than the radial designs.

Lotus Esprit rolling chassis. Note twin stainless steel exhaust pipes, one for wastegate and one for turbine discharge (Focalpoint).

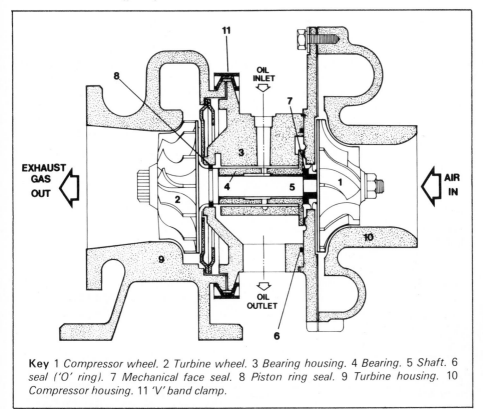

Key 1 *Compressor wheel.* 2 *Turbine wheel.* 3 *Bearing housing.* 4 *Bearing.* 5 *Shaft.* 6 *seal ('O' ring).* 7 *Mechanical face seal.* 8 *Piston ring seal.* 9 *Turbine housing.* 10 *Compressor housing.* 11 *'V' band clamp.*

Fig 19: *Rajay turbo sectional view.*

There are several types of diffuser housing, the two main categories being the vaned and vaneless designs. The vaneless type, with a broader flow range, is now used exclusively for automobile applications, usually of the parallel wall design with a gradually increasing area proportional to the inside and outside diameter of the diffuser. The internal finish should be as smooth as possible to reduce frictional losses which could be caused by a rough casting. Most housings are, therefore, diecast to obtain the desired smooth internal finish.

The exhaust gas radial inflow turbine

There are two types of exhaust gas turbine, the axial flow which is generally confined to relatively large capacity engines, and the radial flow which is now used exclusively in automobile applications. In the radial design, the turbine housing can be of vaned type with a series of nozzle vanes, but current practice is to use a vaneless housing which is far cheaper to produce. The turbine inlet throat area, measured at its narrowest point divided by the distance from the centre of this area to the centre of the turbine wheel, controls the speed at which the turbine will spin relative to a given gas pressure. A more detailed explanation is given later in the section dealing with sizing and matching.

To obtain an increase in turbine speed at low engine speeds, a turbine housing with a twin entry and axially-divided gas passages is sometimes used to harness the exhaust gas pulses present in the engine's exhaust system.

By machining different profiles on both compressor and turbine wheels, the same basic castings can be used for turbochargers of several flow ratings. The contour of the compressor wheel profile is more critical to obtain optimum flow characteristics than it is for the turbine, which is much less sensitive, three or four trims covering the whole flow range.

Compressor wheels are cast aluminium, but as the turbine may have to withstand continued running temperatures as high as 1,000°C, it is cast from a high nickel alloy such as GMR 235 or Inco 713C. Sometimes the wheel is cast complete with the shaft. When the wheel is cast separately, various processes are or have been used by manufacturers to attach the turbine wheel to the shaft, including brazing, inertia or friction welding, shielded sigma-arc welding and electron beam welding.

The turbine housing must have sufficient strength to contain a bursting wheel and have resistance to corrosion and cracking. The majority of housings are cast in spheroidal graphite (SG) nodular iron which is suitable for constant running temperatures of around 700°C.

For high boost, competition or other heavy duty applications where higher exhaust temperatures may be encountered, a high-nickel cast iron such as Niresist D2 or 2B will have to be used. It also has a higher resistance to sea water corrosion, so is recommended for marine use. Most turbochargers are also fitted with a heatshield between the rear face of the turbine wheel and the bearing housing.

The bearing housing assembly

This component is the centre section which supports the compressor and turbine housing and the shaft to which the compressor and turbine wheels are attached. It is usually cast in grey iron or, as with the Rajay turbocharger, in aluminium. As its name implies the bearing housing contains the bearing or bearings. Although early designs used ball bearings, current practice is to use almost exclusively two fully-floating plain bearings lubricated and cooled by a continuous supply of oil from the engine's lubrication system.

These bearings can be manufactured from aluminium or bronze with a leaded tin coating. Bearing frictional losses account for about five per cent of turbine power and because of the square law* the effects on turbine speed can be quite significant at higher turbine speeds. The bearings, which are a comparatively loose fit in the housing and on the shaft journal, are allowed to turn within the housing: this is to allow a cushion of oil to build up between shaft and bearing and the housing to damp out any tendency for a whirling motion to develop. Such a motion or vibration which might develop due to some imbalance in the rotor assembly is thereby virtually eliminated, as is any contact between journal and bearing. This factor considerably extends the life of the turbocharger, which may cover up to 100,000 miles before overhaul.

---

*In this context, 'square law' means doubling the speed of the turbine increases frictional loss four times.

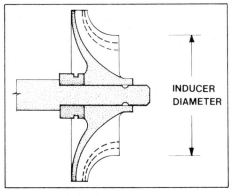

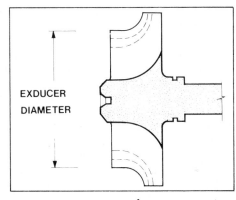

Above Fig 20: *High, medium and low blade profiles of the turbocharger compressor wheel as shown here control the volume of air flow for a given rotational speed.*

Above right Fig 21: *Turbine wheel, showing high, medium and low flow turbine blade profiles.*

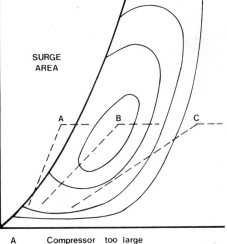

Right Fig 22: *Typical compressor map showing compressor sizing to an engine.*

A	Compressor too large
B	Compressor correct size
C	Compressor too small

Some oil is also directed to lubricate the thrust ring, which is designed to control axial movement of the rotating assembly.

Because the gas pressure behind the turbine and compressor wheels will be much higher than the pressure inside the bearing housing (and also at times much lower), effective seals are necessary on both compressor and turbine ends of the housing to stop oil leaking out from the bearing area, or hot gases getting into it.

Normal practice at the turbine end is to fit a tightly fitting piston ring or labyrinth type seal. At the compressor end, where at times there may be a vacuum, in addition to a piston ring seal some control is necessary to stop oil entering the compressor housing. This usually takes the form of an oil slinger with a machined section like a screw thread, which acts as a pump to transport oil away from this area when the shaft turns. On petrol engines which use a non-pressurised draw-through type of carburation system, the problem is a little more difficult as a very much higher vacuum will be experienced at times during the operating range, such as when the engine is shut down from high speed. If a turbocharger with the normal 'diesel' type of compressor seal is fitted with this carburation arrangement, the engine is liable to suck in quantities of oil, which will show as clouds of light blue smoke coming from the exhaust. Turbochargers designed for use with draw-through carburation (that is, mounting the carburettor upstream of the compressor), are fitted with a mechanical face seal which incorporates a spring behind the seal to hold the seal face to a mating ring. Some increase in friction is noticeable in this design.

When an aluminium bearing housing is used, such as on the Rajay turbocharger, it is preferable to fit a semi-floating bearing to reduce wear in the housing. In this design the bearing is held by a flange and not allowed to rotate.

Sizing and matching turbochargers for petrol engines

The information in this section is intended to give a general guide so that some understanding of how to match a turbocharger to an engine can be achieved. If these principles are followed, it will be found in practice that a good working match can be obtained.

To match the turbocharger exactly as would be required on a production-designed installation requires a considerable amount of detailed development work for each engine, which may extend over several years. It involves far more than just sizing and matching the turbocharger to an engine. Every component in the turbocharging system and many in the engine will have to be considered as well as the overall engine duty requirements, if long-term reliability is to be maintained.

As has been explained earlier in this chapter, the characteristics of a centrifugal compressor driven by an exhaust gas turbine are such that if a reasonable boost of, say, 7.0 psi (1.5 PR) is required at 3,000 rpm, then the corresponding boost at 6,000 rpm could be more than 20.0 psi. With a correctly matched turbo, controls are therefore necessary to limit the top end boost compatible with engine reliability and the performance increase required.

With an incorrectly matched unit, it may be 4,500 rpm before any appreciable boost is obtained and exhaust back pressure too may be excessively high. If the compressor is working in an inefficient range, overheating could be experienced causing engine damage or poor overall performance.

Sizing means choosing a compressor with adequate air flow capacity which will meet the engine power output requirements at or near peak compressor efficiency over as wide an engine operating range as possible. In order to achieve the required engine power curve with torque back-up, a turbine housing has to be chosen which will allow the compressor to be driven at sufficient speed to provide the necessary air flow and boost pressure. This is called matching. If the sizing and matching is carried out correctly, the turbocharger compressor should be working within, or very near to, the maximum efficiency island throughout the greater part of the engine's normal working range. (As shown on the compressor map, Fig 22.)

It should be realised therefore, that it is no good just picking up any old turbo from a diesel truck and bolting it on to your motor. You might just be lucky and have picked a unit which is somewhere near correct, but the chances are you will be wasting your time

Fig 23: *Garrett-AiResearch T3 turbocharger unit with integral wastegate. This turbocharger unit is now the most widely used model by the car manufacturers, being fitted by Saab, Mercedes, Ford, GMC, Renault, Volvo and Peugeot.*

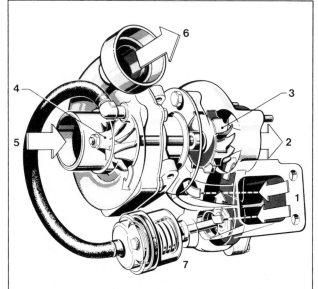

Key 1 *Exhaust gases to turbine of turbocharger.* 2 *Exhaust gas outlet.* 3 *Turbine wheel.* 4 *Compressor wheel.* 5 *Intake air to compressor.* 6 *Compressed air to engine.* 7 *Wastegate boost control.*

and money and it could involve you in expensive turbo or engine repair bills later.

Since, unlike a positive-displacement supercharger, the turbocharger has no mechanical connection with the engine and is sensitive to both engine speed and load, it relies on being driven by the heat and pulse energy which it can extract from the exhaust gases. The speed at which the turbine turns is a function of the differential pressure existing across the turbine which is influenced by the gas temperature/velocity and expansion ratio acting on the turbine combined with the inertia of the turbine and compressor wheel assembly and the A/R ratio of the housing.

One often hears mention of throttle lag when discussing turbochargers. Throttle lag, or more correctly turbine lag, which has the effect of delaying the delivery of full engine power when the throttle is opened, is primarily caused by the time needed for the turbine and compressor assembly to accelerate in response to the increased exhaust gas flow caused by opening the throttle. The response, therefore, of the turbocharger is directly related to changes in load and speed of the engine and rotational inertia of the wheel assembly.

Let us take an example as follows:

The car may be cruising at, say, 50 mph on a very small throttle opening with the engine inlet manifolding working with a vacuum reading of 10 in hg. When the throttle is opened wide more fuel will be drawn into the engine, which when burned produces more hot gas in the exhaust manifold. The additional heat energy accelerates the turbine and compressor wheel assembly. The speed with which the turbine accelerates and thereby causes the compressor to supply pressurised air to the engine, is determined by the moment of inertia of the wheel assembly, also the A/R ratio of the housing which surrounds the turbine and the mass of heat energy available. The moment of inertia increases at the square of the radius of gyration, moment of inertia being the resistance of a rotating body to a change in speed. Therefore it is essential to have a turbine wheel designed with a small diameter and a minimum of weight at its outside diameter to reduce the moment of inertia.

Calculations show that, by increasing the turbine diameter from three to 3.5 in and its weight from 1.5 to 2 lb, the turbine moment of inertia is increased by almost two and a half times. This is why it is sometimes preferable to fit two small turbos rather than one large one. However, even with the smallest turbines currently available, fitting two turbos to an engine of under 2.0 litres is likely to give worse throttle response, as consideration has to be given to the fact that when two turbines are fitted to, say, a 2-litre engine, each turbine is in effect only receiving heat energy equivalent to an engine of 1,000 cc at best. Thus the gains from having less turbine inertia per turbo are more than offset by having only 50 per cent of the total heat energy available for each turbine.

There is another factor to consider. As the turbine wheel gets smaller, so in percentage terms the gas leakage area around the profile of the turbine blades increases. Since allowance has to be made for expansion and some radial and axial movements of the wheel assemblies, the necessary relatively large clearances between wheel and housing must be maintained.

Such a factor could wipe out any gains from using turbine wheels of less inertia. It has been generally accepted that if turbine wheels with even less inertia could be produced, this would improve throttle response (ie, the time it takes to reach maximum power output at any given rpm upon opening the throttle). However, the smaller the turbine wheel, the faster it needs to turn to allow a sufficient flow of exhaust gas, so unless the minimum turbine speed under cruise conditions can be maintained, a very small turbine wheel assembly may not reduce throttle lag.

To illustrate this, assume that, with a conventional-sized turbocharger, the turbine is rotating at 25,000 rpm under cruise conditions. Upon opening the throttle the turbine accelerates to 85,000 rpm, the turbine speed being controlled by a wastegate valve which limits maximum boost to 0.5 pressure ratio. Under the same light load conditions, with a smaller turbine wheel assembly, let us assume that the compressor and wheel assembly rotates at 30,000 rpm, but it needs to accelerate to 110,000 rpm to achieve the same boost as the larger unit. It can be seen, therefore, that the smaller assembly has to accelerate by 80,000 rpm as opposed to the larger unit which accelerated by 60,000 rpm, so that although the smaller assembly may accelerate more rapidly, it has a wider range to accelerate over.

Other factors which can cause turbine lag are poor manifolding and carburation and ignition advance curves which are not optimised, but all of these can be engineered out of the system with sufficient development.

A/R ratio

As already explained, turbine speed and acceleration is a function of several factors, but the most critical as far as small petrol or diesel engines which operate over a wide rpm range are concerned, is turbine housing A/R ratio.

The A/R ratio is the ratio of the area of the turbine inlet nozzle or throat at its narrowest point to the distance from this point to the axis of the turbine shaft. The turbine housing A/R ratio determines the speed of rotation of the compressor and turbine wheel assembly for a given exhaust gas energy input (enthalpy).

A larger A/R ratio allows the turbine to spin more slowly for a given mass gas flow, by reducing the angle at which exhaust gases impinge on the turbine vanes. A smaller A/R ratio will have the opposite effect. Changing the turbine A/R ratio can be considered as comparable to changing the pulley drive ratio in a mechanically driven supercharger. Some turbocharger manufacturers use the throat area only to size a turbine housing.

The turbine housing on a small turbocharger is normally designed with a single or twin entry internal volute tract which directs and accelerates the gas through the turbine, gradually changing the angle of gas flow from tangential to axial in the process. With the twin-entry design, it is possible to improve low speed turbine response by harnessing the natural exhaust pulses.

Because turbochargers have no mechanical drive from the engine and are therefore free-running devices employing a centrifugal compressor, it is usual for them to be spinning at at least 25,000 rpm before any manifold pressure can be supplied to the engine, and on most road-going systems under boost conditions, turbine rpm will range between 30-110,000 rpm for the smallest turbochargers currently in use.

The chart (Fig 26) shows how matching of the turbine and housing A/R ratio affects the efficiency of the system. Fig 26 line 'D' shows a mis-match because turbine speed is higher than it need be for a given boost as the A/R ratio is too low, which can lead to very high exhaust temperature and increased inlet air temperatures. Line 'C' is an optimum match as the engine is operating with the compressor within the island of peak efficiency over a wide rpm range. Line 'B' shows that the turbine A/R ratio is too high, consequently boost is not available from low rpm as the compressor is not being driven at sufficient speed to obtain the necessary boost versus rpm curve, and without sufficient speed the compressor is working at lower efficiency.

In Fig 27 we can see the effect matching the turbine and housing A/R to give the optimum compressor speed has on the engine power curve. Line 'A' is a typical normally-aspirated engine power curve. Line 'B' shows a mis-match due to the high A/R ratio. Line 'C' shows a good match for normal road use. Although line 'D' may seem to show a good power curve, in terms of thermal efficiency it is low and therefore will put unnecessary additional thermal loading on the engine.

The required air flow over the entire load and speed range of the engine can be established and then plotted on a compressor flow map to see if it falls within the desired operating efficiency envelope. Fig 28 shows just such a typical engine air flow requirement plotted on a compressor map.

There are many factors which will have an influence on the field of air flow, but those with the greatest influence are intercooling, use of a wastegate, the effect of altitude and the speed range and torque backup requirements of the engine.

Because a car engine operates over a relatively wide range with frequent fluctuations in both speed and load, the turbocharger must also be matched to cover this field of

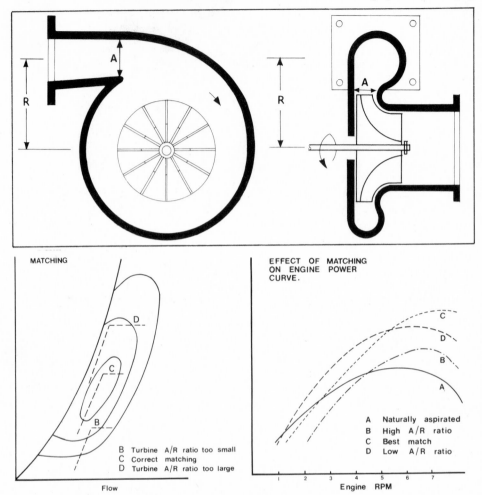

operation as efficiently as possible. If we look at Fig 28 we can see a typical compressor with an area bounded by a dotted line and with the letter A, B, C, D at each corner. This area denotes the complete range of air flow requirements of an engine. The line A-D-C denotes the path followed during full throttle acceleration. Point D is at an engine speed of 4,000 rpm when the wastegate comes into operation and point C the engine's maximum rpm. The engine idle is shown at point A and maximum speed no load at point B. If an intercooler is to be used, a broader flow range will be required and point C on the map is moved to the right towards the choke or less efficient area.

The air flow requirements must never be allowed to pass to the left of the surge line. Surge can cause violent reversals of flow within the compressor causing serious damage. Fundamentally, surge is a condition which can occur when the compressor is too large for

Left Fig 24: *Turbine housing A/R ratio.*

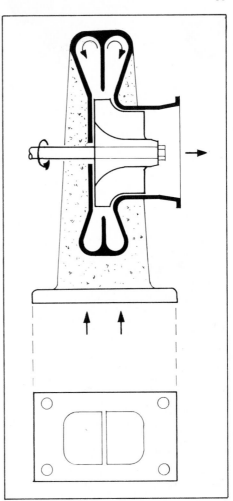

Right Fig 25: *Twin entry turbine housings are designed to harness the exhaust gas pulse energy present in each exhaust tract when the exhaust valve opens. In doing so it is possible to increase turbine speed at low rpm.*

Left and far left Figs 26 & 27: *Matching curves.*

the engine or builds up too much pressure at too low a compressor flow, leading to a condition of instability with a tendency for the flow to stall and flow back in the opposite direction.

To size and match a turbocharger to an engine the following requirements must be determined and then used to obtain a suitable match: the total volume of aspirated air; density of the aspirated air; engine displacement; engine speed; and supercharger efficiency.

To determine the air flow required by an engine when turbocharged:

Take as an example an engine of 2.0 litres producing 100 bhp naturally aspirated, and a power increase to 140 bhp at 6,000 rpm is required. From previous data it is known that

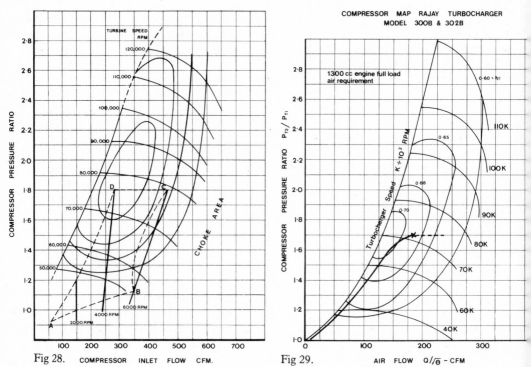

Fig 28. COMPRESSOR INLET FLOW CFM.

Fig 29. AIR FLOW Q/√θ - CFM

7.0 psi should give between 35-50 per cent power increase depending on the efficiency of the original engine and turbocharging system. We now need to know the compressor efficiency. This will usually be in the range of 60-70 per cent, so an average figure of 65 per cent will not be too optimistic or pessimistic.

The density ratio is now required and to use this chart, boost pressure must be converted to pressure ratio.

$$\text{Pressure Ratio} = \frac{\text{Boost pressure} + \text{Atmospheric Pressure (sea level)}}{\text{Atmospheric Pressure (sea level)}}$$

Example: $7.0 \text{ psi boost} = \dfrac{7.0 + 14.7}{14.7} = 1.47$ pressure ratio.

If we now look at the density ratio chart (Fig 30) and plot 1.47 PR against 65 per cent compressor efficiency, the density ratio will be 1.27 as shown by the dotted line. Turning to the engine volume flow chart (Fig 31), the dotted line shows the air flow requirement for a 2,000 cc naturally aspirated engine.

Right Fig 30: *Compressor air density ratio vs pressure ratio. Example: at pressure ratio of 1.5, air density ratio is increased to 1.275, with a compressor efficiency of 65 per cent.*

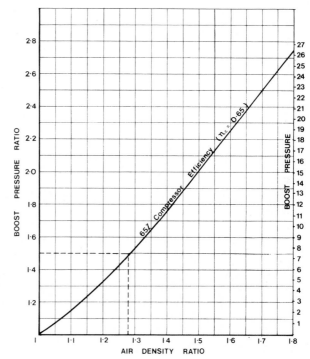

Below Fig 31: *This chart shows the air flow requirement of naturally aspirated four-stroke engines at various rpms. Because a supercharged engine compresses the charge, the air flow requirement taken from this chart must be multiplied by the air density ratio from Fig 30 to obtain the correct volume for a supercharged engine.*

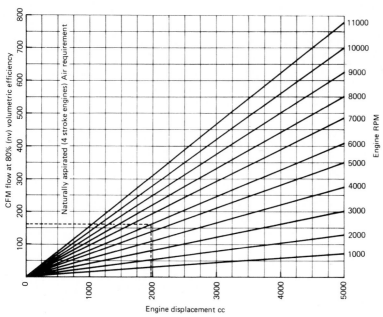

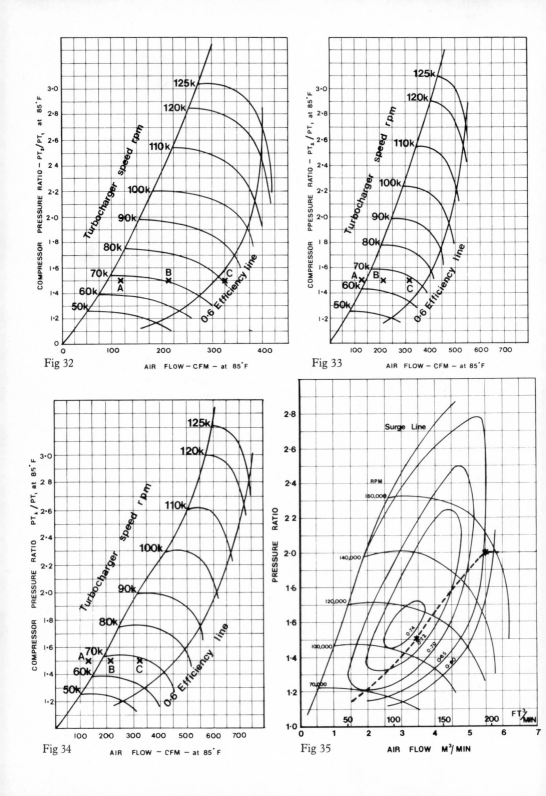

Fig 32

AIR FLOW — CFM — at 85°F

Fig 33

AIR FLOW — CFM — at 85°F

Fig 34

AIR FLOW — CFM — at 85°F

Fig 35

AIR FLOW   M³/ MIN

Far left Fig 32: *Y4 Turbocharger compressor map. In this and the following two figures A represents a 1,300 cc engine, B a 2,000 cc engine, and C a 3,000 cc engine.*
Left Fig 33: *S4 Turbocharger compressor map.*
Below far left Fig 34: *V2 Turbocharger compressor map.*
Below left Fig 35: *High performance 1,300 cc engine's full throttle air flow requirements plotted on IHI RH05 compressor map, with wastegate opening at 15 psi boost.*

To determine the turbocharged air flow, the NA air flow must be multiplied by the density ratio—eg, turbocharged air flow = NA air flow 165 CFM at 6,000 rpm × 1.27 DR = 209.5 CFM. (For every 1,000 ft above sea level subtract 0.5 psi; for draw-through carburettor systems subtract an additional 1.5 psi.)

This figure can now be plotted on the compressor flow maps (Figs 32-34) as shown by the letter 'B'. Similar calculations have been made for 1,300 cc ('A') and 3,000 cc ('C') engines and plotted on the maps. In Fig 32 it can be seen that the compressor is a good match for engines 'A' and 'B' but too small for engine 'C', as the plot falls to the right of the 60 per cent efficiency line and will have a choking effect on a 3-litre engine due to the lesser compressor efficiency. Figs 33 and 34 show that these compressors are too large for engine 'A' as the plot falls to the left of the surge line.

Chart showing possible applications for turbocharging/supercharging, together with system requirements

Application and category	Maximum Boost psi	Power requirements
Car/van (petrol), road use	5-9	Maximum low speed torque, 35 per cent power increase
Car/van (diesel), road use	9-12	Maximum low speed torque, 35 per cent power increase
Mild competition (rally), etc	7-15	Maximum low and mid-range power, 40-50 per cent power increase
Competition autocross, hillclimb, sprint, etc	10-25	Good mid-range and top end power with quick throttle response; up to 250 bhp per litre
Competition circuit racing (petrol)	15-35	Maximum top end power compatible with reliability; up to 400 bhp per litre
Competition drag racing (methanol), tractor pulling	20-75	As much power as possible using special fuel blends; 450 bhp per litre

Boost control

The function of a supercharger of whatever type is to fill the engine cylinders with air/ fuel mixture at higher than normal atmospheric air pressure. We call this supercharger pressure, boost pressure or more accurately pressure ratio above one atmosphere (14.7 psi at sea level).

The use of boost pressure can be divided into two main categories.

The use of relatively low boost of up to 10 psi (petrol engines) or 15 psi for small diesels for normal road applications; or the use of higher pressures such as in racing or other special purpose applications where the maximum amount of power output is required from a given engine displacement. In the latter case, two- or even three-stage supercharging may be used to achieve boosts in excess of 100 psi for short durations.

In almost all petrol engine applications, some form of boost limitation is necessary to keep an excess of boost from destroying an engine. Some control is also often necessary to limit the rpm of a positive displacement supercharger to avoid damage to the internals of the unit through excessive centrifugal forces.

As the rpm/boost curves of the turbocharger, and positive displacement supercharger types and their associated controls are so different, I will deal with the positive displace-

Below left Fig 36: *Typical boost vs rpm curves for turbochargers and superchargers.*
Below right Fig 37: *Typical turbocharger boost vs engine rpm curves with various controls and without control: A Boost with no controls; B Wastegate operated by pressure from exhaust manifold; C Wastegate operated by pressure from inlet manifold; D With fixed exhaust restriction downstream of turbine.*

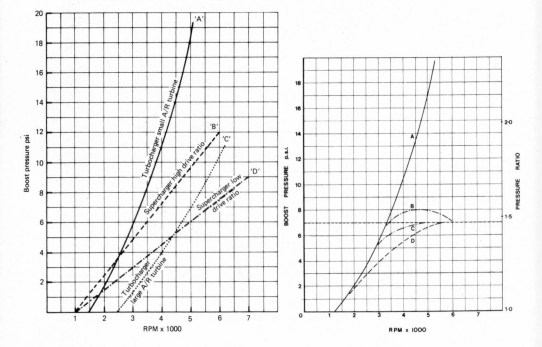

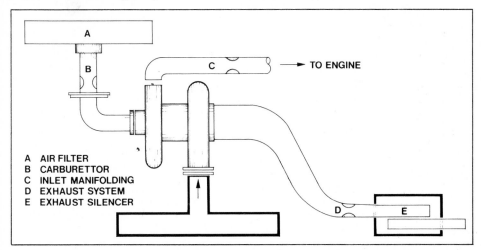

A AIR FILTER
B CARBURETTOR
C INLET MANIFOLDING
D EXHAUST SYSTEM
E EXHAUST SILENCER

Fig 38: *Diagram showing various restrictors to control boost pressure on both inlet and exhaust manifolding.*

ment types separately except when showing the typical comparative boost/rpm curve characteristics of each type (Fig 36).

Turbocharger controls for low boost (up to 10.0 psi) applications are essentially required to prevent too much boost causing detonation, leading to engine damage through excessive cylinder temperatures. A typical uncontrolled boost rpm curve for a modern turbocharger would be as shown in Fig 37'A'.

If the typical production engine has a compression ratio of 8.5-9.5:1 and is using 98 octane petrol, and assuming that carburation, ignition and the general turbocharger system are accurately set up, detonation may start with approximately 3-4 psi boost for the least efficient or highest compression engines, rising to over 12 psi boost for the more efficient or lowest compression ones. Even a small amount of detonation cannot be sustained for more than a very short period without resulting in engine damage. The detonation factor cannot be emphasised too much. When detonation occurs it is either necessary to use less boost, lower the compression ratio or ensure that the peak cylinder temperatures are reduced by some other method.

On a production engine it is normally desirable to aim to increase torque and power output from as low rpm as possible in order to achieve maximum performance where it is most needed in everyday use. Therefore a relatively low match A/R ratio turbine housing will be required, coupled to a compressor of adequate flow capacity. This will result in a boost rpm curve as shown in Fig 37. It is obvious from previous statements therefore that *boost control is essential.*

The types of boost controls which have been experimented with are quite numerous, but I shall deal largely only with those which are readily adaptable to our requirements in the automobile field. Controls can be fixed or adjustable in nature and fitted to either inlet or exhaust side of the turbo. One of the simplest methods is to use fixed restrictions such

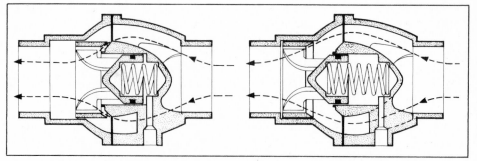

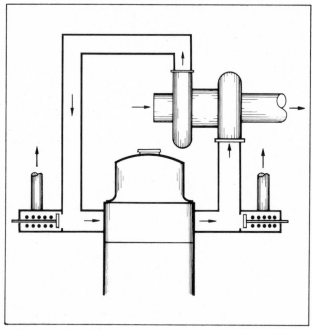

Above Figs 39 & 40: *Impco boost pressure valve. As the boost pressure forces against the cone-shaped face of the piston, the pressure reaches a point when it compresses the spring behind the piston. When this happens, the air flow is restricted and consequently the boost pressure also is stopped from rising further. The maximum pressure will depend on the strength of spring fitted.*

Left Fig 41: *Boost pressure control by inlet manifold and exhaust dump valve.*

as air filter, carburettor choke size, inlet restriction or exhaust pipe restrictor. These can be used singly or in combination.

The problem with fixed restrictors is that their effect is progressive, giving an increasing restriction with increasing exhaust flow as a square law, which means in practice that in order to limit boost to a maximum of say 6.0 psi at 4,000 rpm, they have to start restricting the breathing ability of the engine from much lower rpm, with the result that the engine is less efficient and has poorer throttle response and overall road performance. This is particularly true with a fixed exhaust restrictor downstream of the turbine, which should only be considered as a device to give a small reduction in exhaust gas flow at full throttle, in conjunction with some inlet restriction. Remember, an increase in exhaust system back pressure can cause a progressive rise in cylinder temperature which is just what we need to avoid if possible. An adjustable or variable exhaust restrictor would be a much better proposition as it could be designed to have little or no restrictive effect until maximum boost was reached.

On blow-through pressurised carburettor systems where the compresor is pumping only dry air, a simple blow-off valve can be used (see Fig 41), although this will produce a lower engine thermal efficiency, as work done in compressing the air being dumped has not been put to use. However again, as its operation is of a progressive nature, it will give a progressive restriction with some limitation of power output before the boost limit is reached. A valve which only came into effect at or near the maximum desired boost would be much more efficient, although it would increase the charge temperature when in operation and would reduce the speed of the compressor.

It has been demonstrated that up to 80 per cent more air flow can be drawn through a carburettor of given choke size when an engine is supercharged or turbocharged without excessive throttling and a consequent tailing off of boost, although with a reduction in overall efficiency. This means in practice that up to 120 bhp can be obtained with an 1½-in SU without resorting to excessive rpm. Likewise up to approximately 185 bhp can be obtained with an 1¾-in SU and approximately 250 bhp with a single 2-in SU. However, the choke size will eventually restrict the engine breathing and as the charge temperature is a function of the difference in pressure before and after the compressor coupled with compressor efficiency, excessively restrictive air filters and carburation should be avoided. A mildly restrictive air filter and exhaust silencer can be quite effective in controlling maximum boost pressure.

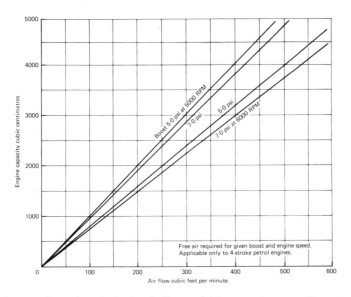

Fig 42: *This chart can be used to obtain the air flow needed by an engine to produce a manifold boost pressure as shown for a given rpm. This figure can then be plotted on a compressor flow map to ascertain its suitability.*

Supercharged engines.

Maximum BHP obtainable with each size of SU carburettor (on petrol)

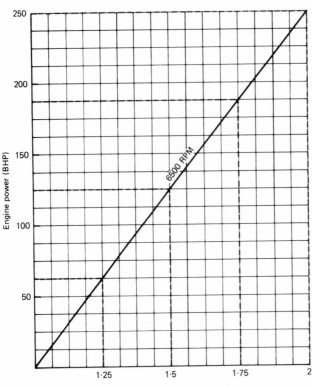

Engine power (BHP)

6500 RPM

SU carburettor size (inches)
(Allow for up to 20% power increase with methanol)

Left Fig 43: *Due to the pumping effect of superchargers, it is possible for a considerably greater volume of air to pass through a given choke diameter, compared with a naturally aspirated engine. However, small carburettors will cause drop in peak efficiency which will be seen as a pressure drop across the compressor.*

Right Fig 44: *Typical 'wastegate' exhaust gas turbine bypass system.*

The 'wastegate' exhaust gas bypass valve

The wastegate is mounted on or near the exhaust manifold or turbine housing with its bypass outlet directed into the turbine discharge exhaust pipe. A common form is the poppet valve type in which the valve stem is connected to a diaphragm above which a spring is enclosed. A boost pressure feed line is fitted between the inlet manifolding and the diaphragm chamber. When the boost pressure fills the chamber on one side of the diaphragm, the spring is compressed. The amount of boost required to compress the spring will depend on the spring strength or cracking pressure. Springs are normally colour-coded to denote the maximum boost at which the valve will open. As the spring starts to be compressed, the bypass valve in the wastegate will start to open, thereby letting an increasing percentage of exhaust gas reach the exhaust pipe without passing through the turbine. The resulting effect is to halt the rapid increase in turbine and compressor speed with a consequent limitation of boost pressure.

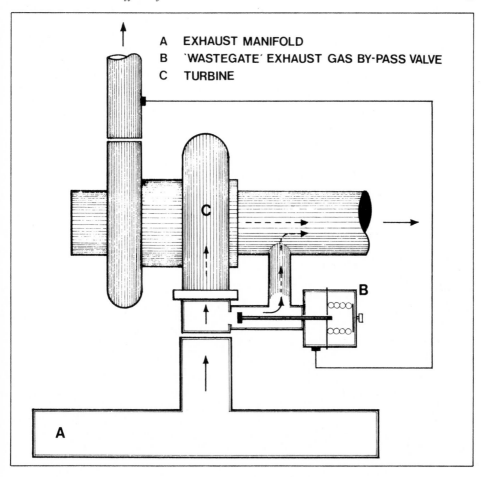

A   EXHAUST MANIFOLD
B   'WASTEGATE' EXHAUST GAS BY-PASS VALVE
C   TURBINE

Some valves, usually the more expensive types, have a built-in adjustment to increase the spring force and therefore the maximum boost at which the valve opens will be higher. In practice, some over-ride may be experienced allowing a higher boost to be indicated. To control this it is sometimes necessary to adjust the spring tension or fit a spring requiring slightly less cracking pressure. If over boost still occurs it may be necessary to increase the diameter of the connection from the exhaust manifold to wastegate valve, or from the wastegate outlet to turbine discharge pipe, or reposition the wastegate. Although it is possible on some engines to use one or two branches of the exhaust manifold from which exhaust gas is bypassed, generally best results are obtained by mounting the wastegate with the inlet port close to the turbine inlet flange, so that gas is bypassed equally from all manifold branches. Failure to do this may cause some cylinders to run hotter than others due to the variations in back pressure before the turbine. This may have an adverse affect on the long term durability of the exhaust valves and pistons. If surging is experienced, this is caused by the valve opening too far too fast, thereby dropping the manifold back pressure too drastically, then when the valve snaps shut boost surges back again. This effect can be virtually eliminated by experimenting with the pipe diameter to and from the wastegate valve or by using a spring with a more progressive compression rate.

Some turbochargers, usually the smallest types used on petrol engines, are designed with an integral wastegate. In this design the wastegate valve and turbine bypass are built into the turbine housing and actuated by a mechanical linkage connected to a diaphragm capsule. The valve can be of swinging or poppet design. Boost is fed directly to one side of the diaphragm from the compressor housing volute. The position in the housing or the inlet manifolding from which the boost sensing line is taken, can have a significant influence on the effectiveness of the wastegate system and on the actual engine power and torque curve.

Sectional view of IHI turbocharger showing internal construction. In this design the wastegate, exhaust bypass valve is built into the turbine housing and actuated by a rod linkage which is connected to a boost sensitive diaphragm capsule which is bolted to the compressor housing.

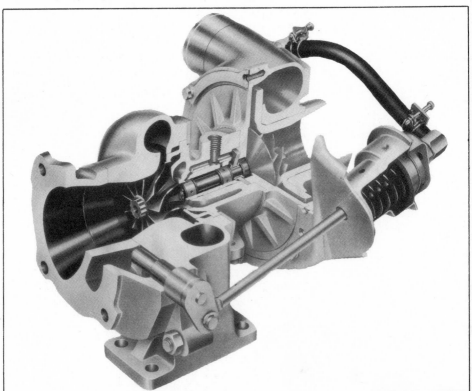

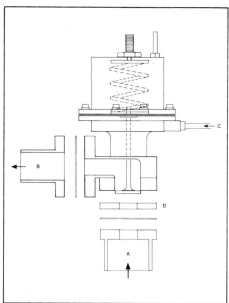

Above left *Rajay 'wastegate' exhaust gas bypass valve. Limits turbine speed by bypassing some of the exhaust gas round the turbine. Pressure at which valve opens is primarily determined by strength of spring inside capsule, although some adjustment is possible by loosening or tightening screw on top of the housing.*

Above right Fig 45: *Sectional view of Rajay wastegate showing: A Exhaust flow from manifold, B exhaust gas outlet to exhaust system downstream of the turbine. The valve is lifted from its seat plate (D) when boost pressure entering at C lifts the diaphragm and overcomes spring pressure.*

Depending on the design of the inlet manifolding, the indicated pressure gauge reading taken at various positions on the inlet manifolding between compressor housing volute and inlet ports, can vary considerably according to engine speed and load. It is possible to have an indicated over boost condition with the wastegate bypass operating correctly if the boost sensor feed pipe to the wastegate is taken from a different point on the inlet manifolding than that used to feed the boost gauge. This could be caused by a pressure build-up at certain points in the inlet manifold due to restrictions in the manifold, or in the inlet ports.

The point from which the wastegate control pressure line is taken can have a considerable influence on the rpm vs boost curve. The optimum position is usually on the compressor housing outlet or near to it. The control line need only be a small bore pipe.

The wastegate can be operated by exhaust manifold pressure instead of inlet manifold pressure. Saab used this system. This can have the advantage of producing a boost peak at around 50-70 per cent of maximum engine speed with boost falling thereafter. A limited improvement can be obtained in engine response, but the engine must be designed to handle the higher peak boost. This system, as would be expected, gives a corresponding increase in torque, but in order to obtain a sufficiently rapid opening response from the wastegate, a comparatively large connection is required between the exhaust manifold and the wastegate diaphragm chamber. Consequently, the thermal loading on the wastegate diaphragm can be substantially increased when employing exhaust manifold gas pressure as opposed to inlet manifold boost pressure to open the wastegate.

By using pressure differential to control boost—that is, using the pressure differential existing between compressor inlet and compressor outlet—the exhaust back pressure under part load operation in the 4,000-5,000 rpm range can be reduced together with the turbine speed. Also, a reduction in thermal loading on valves and pistons and improved fuel consumption at higher speed cruise conditions can be expected. Renault have recently introduced this method in their R18 Turbo. When using a blow-off valve or any type of inlet restrictor to control maximum boost, the exhaust back pressure will be higher

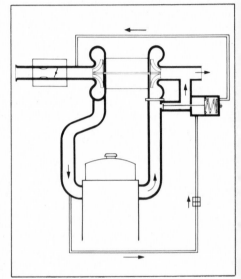

Right Fig 46: *This diagram shows a wastegate which is opened under cruise conditions by the high vacuum existing between the carburettor and the compressor, and also in the normal way by boost pressure. A wastegate operated in this way will be subject to high thermal loadings.*

Below Fig 47: *In this system the opening of the wastegate is controlled by sensing the differential pressure across the carburettor. With this system it is possible to obtain the highest boost pressure at lower engine speed, so obtaining maximum low speed torque back-up.*

Below right Fig 48: *With pressurised carburation systems, boost pressure can be controlled by recycling some of the pressurised air back to the compressor inlet as shown in this diagram. It is also possible with this arrangement to reduce back pressure on the compressor, and so maintain a higher turbine speed when the throttle is closed.*

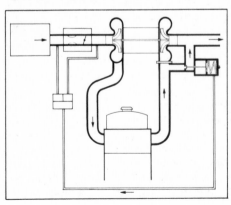

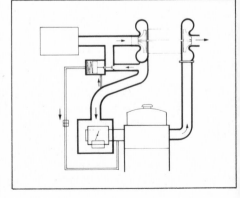

than with a wastegated system, and this can lead to an expansion ratio of 3:1 or more. Consequently, the thermal loading on the valves and pistons will be higher than for a wastegated system.

Under the same conditions, a wastegated system will normally generate only as much crossover at full engine speed and load as a typical car exhaust system back pressure, usually less than 2:1 expansion ratio. (Crossover being in this case the point at which pre-turbine pressure exceeds ambient pressure.)

Generally, at least on road-going turbo systems requiring maximum boost to be limited to 1.8 pressure ratio or less, up to 20 per cent of the total exhaust gases will need to be bypassed through the wastegate at full load and speed, to control turbine speed and thereby limit the boost pressure.

It is not always necessary to use a wastegate system on a diesel engine, unless a very large power increase or high pressure ratio is required. There are several reasons for this. As the amount of diesel fuel injected directly determines the engine power output, the amount of additional fuel can be limited, thereby also limiting maximum cylinder temperature and pressure. Therefore to a large extent, any overboost will have little effect on cylinder temperature and will, in fact, be useful in scavenging any unburnt fuel and possibly lowering the cylinder temperature. The pressure ratio used can be up to 50 per cent higher than would be employed on a petrol engine and still the percentage increase on an already much higher maximum cylinder pressure would be approximately the same as a petrol engine. Also, due to the relatively low maximum engine speed, maximum boost is to a certain extent rev-limited.

Design of supercharger drives

I have included details of supercharger drives here because the drive ratio of supercharger to engine can be compared to matching a turbocharger in that the pulley ratio determines the boost vs rpm curve for a given supercharger and engine combination.

Supercharger drives usually take the form of 'V' or internally toothed rubber belts, direct drive from the nose of the crankshaft or by gears.

For the smaller, lighter units where a maximum boost of no more than 7.0 psi is required, a twin 'A' section, 'V' belt arrangement or a single duplex belt can be used with some form of belt tensioning device. The use of a supercharger pulley with a taper fitting does assist in reducing the amount of adjustment necessary. Toothed drive belts of the power grip design with nylon reinforcement provide a more positive and efficient drive system without a high degree of tensioning, but if fitted to Shorrock vane-type superchargers, some form of inertia absorbing device should be included in the drive system as excessive torsional loads can lead to premature rotor drive plate failure and cause the vanes to contact the casing.

The diameter of the crankshaft drive pulley, in relation to the diameter of the supercharger pulley, determines the supercharger-to-engine drive ratio and therefore the speed at which the supercharger turns in relation to the engine. Most supercharger conversions would employ a drive ratio of from 0.8:1 (supercharger-to-engine speed) to 1.25:1; in the latter case, therefore, the supercharger would be being driven 25 per cent faster than the engine. Higher drive speeds are not normally practicable, due to drive system and supercharger limitations, mainly because of the high centrifugal loads and the

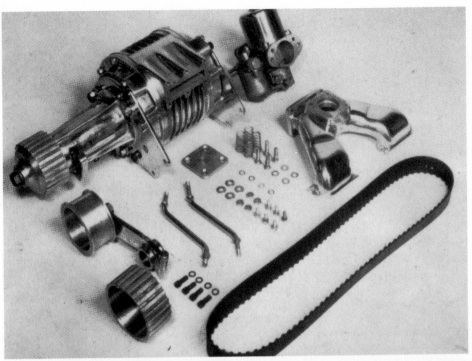

Left *Typical supercharger toothed drive system components.*

Below left *Large GMC 8-71 Dragster blower as used by Dennis Priddle, complete with Crane manifold and triple inlet port injector assembly.*

Right *Power grip toothed rubber belt, usually with steel or nylon reinforcement, is used in the majority of supercharger drives. In this Dragon Anglia drag racer, a 1,650 cc Ford pushrod motor developed 220 bhp on methanol. A centric blower produced a maximum of 17.0 psi boost. The car covered the quarter mile in 12.5 seconds with a terminal speed of 115 mph. Injection was Hilborn.*

rapidly increasing amount of power consumed in driving the supercharger.

The alignment of the pulleys is particularly important with toothed belt drives to avoid the belt winding itself off the pulleys. A typical toothed belt drive system for a supercharger such as a Wade RO20 type fitted to a 2.0-litre engine would have a 1½-in wide ½-in pitch toothed belt, with supercharger and crankshaft pulleys of 30 teeth each. The same supercharger fitted to a 3.0-litre engine would require a smaller supercharger pulley and a larger crankshaft pulley of 28 and 32 teeth respectively to provide a similar maximum boost of approximately 7.0 psi on each engine.

Excessive tensioning of 'V' or toothed belts is not required. Too much tension can cause excessive side loading on the supercharger bearings leading to premature failure of these items. As an approximate guide, the belt tension should be similar to a well-tensioned fan belt.

All belt tensioners must tension the slack unloaded side of the drive belt and should preferably be mounted on the inside of the belt, provided the pulleys are large enough to maintain sufficient belt wrap around the pulley. If there are too few teeth in contact with the pulley, the belt will soon be stripped of its teeth. For this reason, very small pulleys should be avoided. Tensioning the belt from the outside pushing inwards is acceptable if the bending of the belt is not too severe.

On the largest blowers such as the GMC 6 or 8-71 used on dragsters, a similar drive pulley system is normal practice, but of course in order to transmit possibly as much as

250 bhp in driving the supercharger, a 3-4-in wide belt and corresponding pulleys with 8 mm pitch teeth are essential. Additional belt loading capacity in the order of 50 per cent should be allowed for withstanding inertia stresses.

Changing the drive pulley ratio is similar to changing the turbine housing A/R ratio of a turbocharger and determines the speed at which the supercharger will turn and therefore the boost delivered to the engine. Unlike a turbocharger, however, the boost pressure delivery is almost linear over the normal engine rpm range, assuming that there are no restrictions such as an excessively small carburettor. Because of this characteristic and the fact that it is linked directly to the engine, full power is available instantly from almost tick-over speed, but in order to achieve this level of boost, say 2.0 psi at 1,000 rpm, a high supercharger-to-engine ratio is necessary; consequently, just as with a turbo-supercharger, maximum boost may be too high at peak engine speed. Additionally, the supercharger system efficiency will be tailing off due to the high speed involved. This could, of course, be solved by incorporating some form of clutch device to disengage the supercharger when a predetermined speed or manifold pressure is reached.

Chapter 3

Low-pressure supercharging

Turbocharger and supercharger system requirements for everyday road use

This chapter sets out the basic requirements for turbocharging or supercharging for normal road use, with information on some typical conversions. It also shows how to install and set up your own turbo system, and gives basic explanations of sizing and matching, engine modifications, together with maintenance and trouble shooting advice. More detailed technical information on particular aspects such as compression ratio, lubrication, sizing and matching, etc, can be found in other chapters. This chapter serves only to give the basic facts as a background to the more detailed information.

Basic engine modifications

One thing is certain, turbocharging will not cure a sick engine. Be sure your engine is in good condition before installing a turbocharging system. If the engine has completed more than 30,000 miles since new, or rebuilding, a very close examination of cylinder head, pistons, rings, cylinder bores and crankshaft assembly is called for. Even on lower mileage engines, careful checks should be made prior to installing your turbocharger.

Mention has already been made of the necessity or otherwise of a reduction in compression ratio, so here I will just mention that as a general rule it is best not to start with a compression ratio of more than 8.5:1. Also as a general rule, fuel with a minimum octane rating of 98 should be used. In some countries this may not be possible, in which case a further reduction in compression ratio is required and/or the use of water injection and ignition retard.

Although with sufficient time and money it would no doubt be possible to develop a camshaft to suit the characteristics of the turbocharged engine more closely than the standard component, as a rule it is best not to change the standard camshaft for normal road use.

No other internal engine modifications should be necessary for normal road use provided the engine is in good condition and no more than 6.0 psi boost is used, apart from an alteration in the ignition timing and the fitting of a slightly colder grade of spark plug.

The effect of the boost pressure is similar to increasing the swept volume or cubic capacity of an engine and thereby the power output in proportion to the pumping efficiency and pressure of the supercharging system.

Strictly, there are two distinct types of supercharging. The first is for normal road applications where a maximum pressure of 5-8 psi is used, with limited modifications necessary to the internals of the basic engine to gain a medium power and torque increase. Perhaps this should be called 'pressure charging' rather than supercharging. The second method is supercharging to obtain maximum power output from a given engine displacement, when supercharge pressures of from one to over six atmospheres (90 psi) are employed.

Over the last ten years or so, turbochargers for small-capacity engines have been improved considerably in both design and efficiency, as has the knowledge of matching, sizing and installation to make them work correctly. Now that turbochargers are available for small-capacity engines, they have almost entirely eclipsed the manufacture of mechanically-driven superchargers for automotive applications. The manufacturing costs involved in building this type of supercharger in small batches would make them more expensive than a turbocharger. Although in the USA there is a sufficiently large market to make producing some roots-type units worthwhile, generally the larger blowers, as seen on most dragsters, are rebuilt versions originally used on GMC diesel engines. However, there are signs that there is a resurgence of interest in superchargers and several new units are under test or being produced in small numbers.

The turbo system
Most standard inlet manifolds can be retained when fitting a turbocharger. If the standard manifold is for a twin carburettor arrangement, an additional 'log type' manifold with

Left *PAO-Allard turbocharger conversion on Range Rover with only 5.0 psi boost raises power by up to 35 per cent with no sacrifice in fuel consumption.*

Right Fig 49: *A common layout for an 'add-on' turbocharging conversion, with single SU carburettor mounted upstream of the turbocharger and the wastegate opened by inlet manifold 'boost' pressure.*

Far right *Allard Escort XR3 Turbocharging system. IHI RHB6 turbocharger with integral wastegate and HIF6 SU carburettor.*

single central entry from the turbocharger at right angles to the longitudinal pipe will be required. If designed for a single carburettor then a single pipe entering at 90° can be bolted in place of the carburettor. On turbo systems with pressurised carburation, the standard manifold and carburettor can normally remain unaltered except for a specially designed fuel system.

A cast iron exhaust manifold is usually preferable to a fabricated one, partly because it is usually easier to adapt by either fitting a 'J' pipe or by welding or bolting on a turbo mounting flange, and also for the reason that it is comparatively strong and retains heat which is good for turbine performance. A good fabricated exhaust manifold is satisfactory, but generally normal thin gauge fabricated free flow multi-branched types are unsuitable for normal road turbo systems.

Listed below are the main components which comprise a typical low-pressure turbocharging system:

System components using 'suck-through' carburation

Air filter

Carburettor (or carburettor modifications)

Carburettor manifold

Turbocharger

Exhaust manifold

System components using 'blow-through' carburation

Air filter

Trunking and adaptor

Turbocharger

Compressor discharge pipe

Compressor discharge hoses

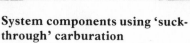

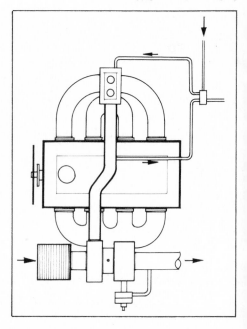

System components using 'suck-through' carburation

Wastegate

Compressor discharge manifold

Compressor discharge hoses

Inlet manifold adaptor

Oil feed pipe

Oil drain pipe

Turbine discharge pipe

Boost gauge

Spark plugs

Oil cooler

Turbine heatshield

System components using 'blow-through' carburation

Carburettor modifications

Oil feed pipe

Oil drain pipe

Turbine discharge pipe

Boost gauge

Spark plugs

Oil cooler

Turbine heatshield

High pressure fuel pump

Fuel piping and control valves

Additional items which may be required include: inlet manifold; set of lower compression pistons; lower compression cylinder head; special cylinder head gasket; electronic ignition; engine speed and boost limiter; ignition retard system; free-flow exhaust; intercooler; and water-injection system.

As far as an 'add-on' turbo conversion is concerned, equally good results can be obtained with either of these systems, so if such conversions are available for your vehicle, deciding which type to purchase may come down to that which offers the best value in

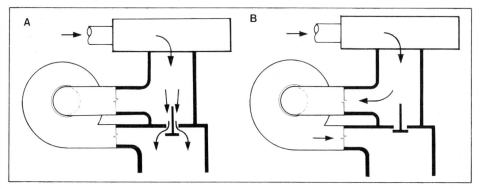

Far left *Escort XR3 turbocharging system with pressurised Weber carburettor. Power output is increased from 95 to 127 bhp with maximum boost of 6.5 psi.*

Left Fig 50: *Typical turbocharging system with carburettor being fed with pressurised air from turbocharger compressor.*

Above Fig 51: *The priority valve system, particularly suited to many V8 engine layouts. In diagram A air is passing from the carburettor through the open priority valve directly into the inlet manifold, and in doing so bypasses the turbocharger. As the compressor speed increases the pressure in the inlet manifold rises above the pressure existing below the carburettor and the valve closes, as shown in B. The priority valve system is designed to improve throttle response and low speed pick-up.*

terms of price, performance, quality in design and construction, back-up assistance and advice. If you are building up your own conversion—and, after all, this particular chapter is primarily devoted to this subject—then the choice may not be so easy. With a 'blow-through' pressurised carburettor set-up, you can use a normal small diesel type turbocharger, providing not more than 15 psi boost is to be used. These turbochargers are not built with a special mechanical face seal on the compressor side. However, the necessary high pressure fuel system can present problems.

On engines with crossflow manifold configuration, the 'blow-through' set-up may well be the most attractive. However, on engines with both inlet and exhaust on one side of the head, the 'suck-through' carburettor arrangement will usually be simpler to design and install, particularly if space is limited.

When reading this chapter, it should be borne in mind that add-on supercharging systems necessarily have to compromise in certain areas and, although usually giving good value for money, should not be compared directly to the manufacturer's product which may have had several £100,000s spent on development.

When considering supercharging with whatever type of supercharger, as a means of increasing the power output of a production engine, the following criteria should be the essential characteristics to aim for:

1 To obtain a substantial power increase, but to keep well within the thermal and mechanical design limits of the engine, with the smallest increase in overall fuel consumption; **2** To obtain a torque increase over the widest rpm range, yet to obtain these increases within the standard engine's maximum rpm limit; **3** To maintain or reduce overall noise levels; **4** To maintain or reduce overall exhaust NOX and CO^2 emissions; **5**

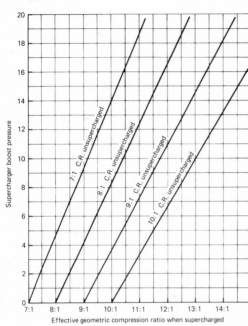

Effective geometric compression ratio when supercharged

Left Fig 52: *The compression ratio is effectively increased as boost pressure increases, as shown in this graph. However, allowances may be necessary for any additional heat build-up within the cylinder.*

Right Fig 53: *Typical maximum and minimum power increases which can be expected from a given boost pressure. Generally the least volumetrically efficient normally aspirated engines will show the largest gains for a given boost pressure.*

Far right Fig 54: *Power and torque curves for Allard Turbocharged Capri 2.8i.*

Not to affect starting or slow-running ability under all conditions or town driving characteristics.

To achieve these results, the lowest boost required should be used, compatible with the highest compression ratio, in order to maintain maximum thermal efficiency when the engine is running without boost pressure, such as experienced under cruising and light throttle conditions. However, when running with maximum boost, the effective compression ratio should be no higher than 9.5:1 or well below the detonation point. In practice therefore, it can be seen from Fig 52 that if the basic standard compression ratio is 9.0:1, only 2.0 psi can be used before exceeding the 9.5:1 limit. Correspondingly, with a reduction to 7.0:1 in compression ratio, the maximum boost can be increased to 13.0 psi.

Certain engines, particularly those with aluminium cylinder heads, can tolerate higher compression ratios. This also applies where road conditions and the speed of the vehicle are such that full throttle boost cannot be held for more than a few seconds.

Generally, particularly on engines of under 2.0 litres, it is preferable to keep the basic compression ratio relatively high to avoid rather a 'flat' motor in the lower rpm ranges before the turbo is working effectively. The lower the basic compression ratio and the higher the maximum boost pressure used, the more noticeable will be the change from no boost to full boost, together with a correspondingly increased time interval before obtaining maximum power output (ie, the time it takes to go from zero to maximum boost at any given rpm). When a manufacturer produces a turbocharged car, these conditions can to a large extent be engineered out of the system. However, as regards an almost bolt-

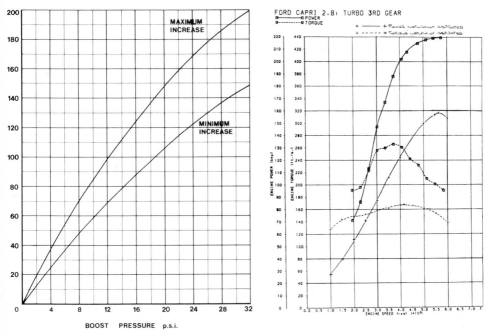

BOOST PRESSURE p.s.i.

on conversion, these comments are largely born out in practice. It should be remembered that engines with a low breathing ability in normally-aspirated form will usually give a larger power increase for a given boost than those starting with a higher volumetric efficiency.

When you decide that you want to turbocharge your engine there are a number of basic requirements for normal road use. A maximum power increase of 25-35 per cent and a similar torque increase is all that is necessary to give a substantial performance boost, without impairing reliability or necessitating extensive internal engine modifications. For good all-round road performance, a broad, comparatively flat torque curve is far more important than a high maximum power output, and this can be achieved with a modest boost of from 4-7 psi.

Even with a power increase of up to 30 per cent the overall fuel consumption increase should be less than ten per cent, and be better than that of a larger-capacity unturbocharged engine giving a similar performance.

As a general rule, a maximum of 5-6 psi boost will increase power output by 20-35 per cent, after allowing for a reduction in compression ratio. With 6-7 psi the increase will be between 30-45 per cent.

Some engines will tolerate a relatively high boost and high compression ratio combination for short bursts of full throttle power output. However, the optimum compression ratio for most road-going engines is in the range 7.5-8.5:1 when using a maximum boost pressure of 5-7.0 psi with 97-98 octane fuel, when no intercooler is fitted.

A turbocharger is the most efficient form of supercharger both mechanically and

Sprintex S82 supercharger on Manta GTE. Designed and developed by Allard Superchargers.

thermally in its optimum working range and if correctly matched to an engine, can give a power and torque output equal to that of a normally aspirated engine of at least 50 per cent greater capacity and with a better overall fuel consumption than the larger engine.

In practical terms, if the overall fuel consumption was 30 mpg before turbocharging, it may drop to 27-28 mpg when turbocharged under similar conditions, for a power increase of 30 per cent. These are, of course, approximate figures, but can be used as a guide.

The turbo-supercharger is a free-running device using heat energy contained in the expanding exhaust gas, as the energy source to drive it. With the throttle partially closed, it will almost free-wheel in effect and there will still be vacuum in the induction tract. Under these conditions, with a well-designed and matched turbo system, the turbocharged engine should have a similar fuel consumption to the normally-aspirated engine. It has been shown under normal road conditions that, even when driven hard, the turbo will not be applying boost to the engine for more than 20 per cent of the journey time. Therefore for the remaining 80 per cent of the time the engine's overall fuel consumption should not be affected, except to the extent by which it has been necessary to reduce the compression ratio and the effect of the slightly higher exhaust manifold back pressure.

Turbochargers are now available in sizes suitable for matching to engines of down to around 25 bhp. Such is the advance of turbocharger design in recent years. Therefore a turbocharger can be fitted to virtually any automobile engine, whether petrol or diesel. The degree of complication or ease of fitting will obviously vary considerably, depending on the basic engine specification and engine bay layout. Some makes commonly used are AiResearch T04B and T3, Schwitzer 3LD, Holset 3LD and HIA, Rajay 300/375/377 series, Rotomaster T04B, IHI RHB5 and RHB6.

As a turbocharger is relatively small in relation to its pumping capacity, and most units

Golf IHI turbocharging system with maximum boost of 6.5 psi—gives vivid performance to GTI models.

for cars weigh less than 17 lb, finding room for the turbocharger, particularly the new small series, should not present too much of a problem in most engine bays. The heat which it generates can, however, cause problems if the layout of the turbo system is not carefully designed. Shielding of the turbine housing is usually necessary, as well as various ancillaries which are in the vicinity of the exhaust manifold turbine and turbine discharge pipe.

As far as overall road performance is concerned, equally good results can be obtained with the carburettor before or after the turbocharger. It is also true that most types of carburation can be adapted to give good results (for full details see pages 106-114 on carburation), although some are much easier than others to adapt successfully.

If the carburettor is mounted in front of the compressor, some heating of the manifolding between carburettor and compressor inlet is essential for good slow running, particularly when starting from cold when the air temperature is below approximately 50°F (10°C). A hot air pick-up may also be required to feed exhaust-heated air into the carburettor in very cold conditions. However, when the ambient air is warm it is better to duct cool air to the air filter as this improves the overall effectiveness of the turbocharger boost by lowering the charge temperature and thereby increasing its density and weight. In this regard it is worthwhile keeping the underbonnet temperature as low as possible.

In the interests of long-term turbo and engine life, a paper element or oil bath-type air filter of adequate air flow capacity is essential. The critical feature of any add-on turbo-charging system is the exhaust manifold. The prime consideration is strength to carry the weight of the turbo, combined with the very high (up to 1,000°C) exhaust gas temperature as well as the ability to withstand the frequent rapid expansion and contraction caused by the heating and then cooling down of the manifold. These conditions can cause internal scaling and corrosion leading to cracking.

Left *Suzuki SJ410 Allard IHI turbo system with pressurised carburettor and air-to-air intercooler. Power and torque increases by up to 50% and turns it into a lively performer.*

Below left *Renault 5 TS. Rajay turbocharger conversion for Renault 5 TS by Allard Turbochargers, raises power output to the Gordini version of this engine. Fed by an SU carburettor. Maximum boost 6.0 psi; compression ratio is lowered to 8.2:1 with cylinder head modifications. Capable of 0-60 mph in 10.7 seconds (Autocar).*

Above left *Shorrock supercharger installation on a VW Beetle 1300 flat-four air-cooled engine layout made installation rather difficult, but nevertheless, it was very effective.*

Above right *Allard-Wade supercharged Capri V6; gave 156 bhp at the wheels with maximum boost of only 6.5 psi.*

When the exhaust manifold is designed to support the turbo, a cast manifold specially designed for the job is the most satisfactory answer. When this is not possible, then good results can usually be obtained with a modified standard cast iron manifold with a strong extension and flange welded on, or a thick walled steel fabricated type, provided a relatively low maximum boost is used. Although strength is the prime consideration, flow is important too and the turbo should be mounted as close to the exhaust ports as possible compatible with reasonable flow. The manifold should be designed to keep the gas velocity as high as possible between exhaust ports and turbine, but without causing excessive restriction as this will lead to higher cylinder temperatures.

The turbine gas outlet pipe should have an inside diameter equal to, or slightly larger than, the turbine outlet port (exducer) diameter for at least the first few inches, reducing progressively to two inches for the remainder of the down pipe. Thereafter the standard exhaust system can often be used and, although most standard systems will cause some restriction, this can be useful in controlling maximum boost, providing the restriction is not too severe. If possible, the turbine outlet pipe should be secured to the engine to reduce piping loads being transmitted to the turbo and/or a flexible coupling incorporated in the system. Optimum performance can usually be obtained by removing the silencer and fitting a straight through type of slightly larger diameter, or by simply fitting an expansion box in place of the silencer. The silencing effect of the turbine is often sufficient to keep the exhaust quiet when used in conjunction with one or two non-restrictive expansion boxes.

As explained earlier, it is essential that the maximum boost is limited to 5-7.0 psi for long-term reliability. For optimum thermal efficiency, the use of a 'wastegate' exhaust bypass valve is the most efficient system, but a small carburettor, dump valve or compressor flow restrictor on the inlet side, or restriction in the exhaust downstream of the turbine, can be very effective when used as a means to limit the maximum boost by a relatively small amount.

Turbochargers require a continuous flow of clean oil with a minimum pressure under load of 25 psi and a minimum flow of 0.5 gallon per minute. An oil feed is normally taken from the point on the cylinder block where the sender for the oil pressure warning light is fitted. A tee piece is used, the warning light being connected to one side and the oil feed pipe to the other.

As the oil is drained away from the turbo by gravity, an unrestricted flow is important. The pipe should slope downwards throughout its length and have a minimum inside diameter of ½ in and re-enter the engine, normally the sump, well above the oil level. Crankcase breathers may need increasing in size to cater for any increased piston blow by. Crankcase pressurisation can cause oil leaks in the turbo by restricting the oil from draining back to the sump and at various engine gaskets. Feed breather pipes back into the air filter or to a separate catch tank; it is sometimes necessary to fit an oil trap or control valve in the pipe to prevent oil saturating the air filter element.

Because a relatively large quantity of the engine oil is being used to cool and lubricate the turbocharger, an oil cooler is essential for almost all applications, preferably fitted with a thermostat temperature control. Failure to maintain the oil at a reasonable temperature, or to change the oil and oil filter regularly, can lead to premature turbocharger or engine bearing wear or associated symptoms.

The belt-driven positive displacement supercharger

Despite what the theoretical engineers and pro-turbocharger lobby may say, in sheer 'get-up-and-go' and general all round performance on the road, as opposed to the drawing board, the supercharged engine compares very favourably with the turbocharged one. Having developed both supercharging and turbocharging systems on similar engines and driven them on the road for many thousands of miles, practical experience shows this to be true. Had each of these cars been handed to an average driver, and had he been asked to say which performed best on the road, as opposed to the test house, he may well have picked the supercharged vehicle.

It must be remembered too that supercharger design for road-going vehicles has hardly progressed since the 1930s and minimal development has gone into the 'enthusiasts'' blown engines, so it is technically unsound to assume that this is the best that can be achieved with a supercharging system as opposed to turbocharging. There are signs that not all manufacturers have been hooked on the turbocharger route, without at least exploring the possibilities of other forms of supercharging.

When fitting a supercharger for normal road use, all the information in the preceding part of this chapter on turbocharging applies to the supercharged engine. The details at the end of this chapter are specific to positive displacement supercharger installations.

Testing

Ideally some testing should be done on a rolling road, in particular to establish the total ignition advance requirement and mixture strength at full load. Full load mixture should be on the rich side, approximately 12.5-13.0:1 fuel:air ratio and maximum ignition advance under the same conditions, usually not more than 30-32° BTDC. However, careful road testing can achieve acceptable results in some cases.

When running the engine up in the workshop, check for oil leaks. You may notice that no boost shows on the boost gauge (a boost/vacuum gauge should always be fitted on such a do-it-yourself installation). This is normal, as the engine is merely revving and is not consuming much air in an unloaded condition. On the road, boost should show by 1,800-2,300 rpm in top gear, even lower on some systems. If the boost comes in much higher, this may mean that a lower A/R housing is needed, but other factors could include incorrect mixture, ignition timing, excessive exhaust system or inlet restrictions. Below are listed some symptoms, causes and cures to assist in setting up your engine.

Trouble shooting

Symptom	Cause	Cure
Flat spot at low speed	Mixture too lean. Incorrect ignition timing. Fuel condensing in overcooled manifolding.	Heavier damping in dashpot (SU). Larger pump jet. More ignition advance at low rpm required. Additional heating to charge air.
Hesitation at full throttle	Restrictive air filter or trunking.	Increase air flow to engine.
Engine cuts out at full throttle or backfires	Lean mixture, fuel starvation, excessive ignition advance.	Enrich full throttle mixture. Fit larger float needle valve. Check fuel pipes and pump capacity. Reduce total ignition advance.
Surging or lumpy running at idle	Carburettor flooding. Mixture too rich. Fuel condensing on manifold walls.	Reset float level. Cure carburettor vibration. Adjust mixture, improve heating of air/fuel mixture before entry to manifold.
Running on	Air leak into exhaust, cracked exhaust manifold.	Cure leaks by repairing or fitting new manifold.
Overheating	Incorrect ignition timing. Insufficient cooling capacity in cooling system. Restricted exhaust system. Turbine A/R ratio too small.	Adjust ignition timing. Increase cooling system capacity and air flow through engine compartment generally. Fit less restrictive exhaust system. Fit higher ratio housing or larger turbine wheel.
Stalling, lumpy idle	Overcooled inlet manifolding. Air leak in manifolding. Incorrect fuel level. Incorrect mixture. Incorrect ignition timing.	Cure air leaks. Adjust mixture and fuel level. Adjust ignition timing.

Symptom	Cause	Cure
Poor fuel consumption	Mixture too rich. Overcooled engine. Engine not warming up sufficiently quickly. Restrictive air filter. Incorrect timing. Generally worn engine.	Adjust mixture. Fit hot air pick-up to carburettor. Change thermostat. Fit new air filter. Adjust timing. Rebuild engine as necessary.
Low boost	Restricted air filter. Turbine A/R ratio too high. Leak in exhaust manifold. Carburettor too small. Throttle not opening fully. Restricted exhaust system after turbine. Generally worn engine. Wastegate not seating correctly.	Fit new air filter. Fit lower A/R ratio turbine housing. Cure exhaust leak. Fit larger carburettor. Adjust throttle. Use free flow system. Rebuild engine. Check wastegate seating.
High boost	Wastegate outlet pipe of insufficient diameter. Faulty wastegate sensor pipe. Incorrect wastegate setting. Turbine A/R ratio too low.	Fit larger diameter outlet pipe. Fit new sensor pipe. Reset wastegate. Fit higher A/R ratio housing.
Exhaust manifold overheating at light or medium load	Retarded ignition timing. Restricted exhaust. Turbine A/R match too low.	Reset ignition timing. Reduce exhaust restriction. Fit higher A/R ratio housing.
Misfire	Incorrect plug gap. Burnt plug lead. Damaged plug. Incorrect timing. Excessive temperature or pressure in cylinder. Voltage at plug too low. Plug wet or oiled.	Set plugs to correct gap. Fit silicon rubber leads, fit colder grade of spark plug. Fit C.D. ignition. Adjust mixture, check for engine wear, oil leak from compressor back plate seal.
Oil smoke from exhaust	Restricted oil drain. Gummed up turbo seals. Damaged seal. Turbine body mounted at incorrect angle for oil drain away.	Cure restriction by re-routing or fitting larger bore pipe. Re-position connection to sump. Increase crankcase breathing. Clean or replace seals.
Wet or oiled plugs, oil in inlet manifold.	Mixture too rich. Engine not warming up sufficiently quickly. Plug grade too cold. Damaged or dirty compressor seal.	Adjust mixture, change plugs, change thermostat. Replace seal.
Fuel smell under acceleration	Leak on inlet manifolding or compressor housing. Carburettor vibration.	Fit new gasket or sealing compound to housing. Fit 'O' ring between carburettor and manifold.

Poor starting	Incorrect timing. Incorrect points gap/dwell. Fouled plugs. Incorrect mixture. Bad air leak in manifold.	Adjust timing and points. Change plugs. Adjust mixture, tighten manifold hoses and cure any leaks.
Burnt spark plug	Plug of too soft a grade fitted. Ignition over-advanced. Excessive boost or compression ratio. Ignition excessively retarded.	Fit colder plugs. Adjust timing. Reduce boost or compression ratio. Reduce cylinder temperatures by improving cooling.
Engine will not start	Split hose or loose joint on inlet manifolding. Incorrect ignition or valve timing. Very lean mixture.	Find air leak and cure. Adjust as necessary.

Obviously this is a very brief resumé of the general principles to follow for many engines, but it is not practical to attempt to try to cover the detail variations which may well be necessary to get the optimum settings for each engine.

Choosing the turbocharger/supercharger and system

The most satisfactory way of having your vehicle turbocharged or supercharged is to have a system fitted by the company which developed it. The next best way is to purchase a tried and tested conversion kit for your vehicle and fit it yourself, following carefully the instructions supplied. However, if you have a good general understanding and some practical experience of auto engineering, and if no conversion is available for your particular vehicle, then it can be a practical proposition to build up your own system with advice from the experts.

Engine build requirements

As has been said before, there are turbocharger units now available which make it theoretically practical to turbocharge any automobile engine from approximately 500 cc upwards. However, there are several factors to bear in mind before deciding to turbocharge. It is no good just hanging any old turbo on the side of an already worn out or sick motor, expecting the turbo to give it a new lease of life. There is one sure result from this type of approach and it certainly will not be happy motoring. The engine must be in sound mechanical condition, within the manufacturer's recommended tolerances. The compression ratio should be no higher than 8.5:1 and maximum boost limited to 6.0 psi. If the compression ratio is reduced to 8.0:1 a maximum of 7.0 psi can be used safely with a correctly-engineered turbocharging system.

The compression ratio can be reduced by several methods, such as fitting a set of pistons with a lower crown height or larger dish, by machining out the cylinder head to enlarge the combustion chamber volume, by fitting a decompression plate or by a combination of these methods. Fitting of two cylinder head gaskets is not recommended.

Generally, a turbocharged engine responds to modifications such as higher lift and longer duration camshafts, larger valves and ports in a similar way to an unsupercharged

Left *I.H.I. RHB6 turbocharger and system on Ford Sierra XR4 × 4. Produces 210 bhp.*

Below left *Rotomaster turbocharging system on Capri 2.8i by Janspeed.*

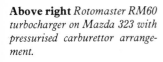

Above right *Rotomaster RM60 turbocharger on Mazda 323 with pressurised carburettor arrangement.*

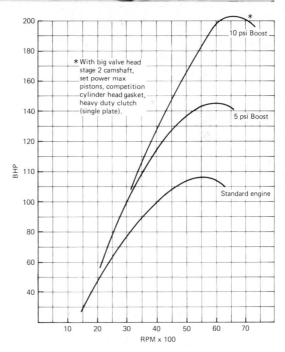

* With big valve head stage 2 camshaft, set power max pistons, competition cylinder head gasket, heavy duty clutch (single plate).

10 psi Boost

5 psi Boost

Standard engine

BHP

RPM x 100

Right Fig 55: *Ford 2,000 SOHC turbocharged engine power curve.*

Above *Rayjay-turbocharged Escort RS2000 with H1F6 SU carburation. Compression ratio must be reduced by fitting lower compression pistons and/or by machining the cylinder head.*

Left *IHI RHB6 turbocharger on Ford Transit 2.0-litre automatic.*

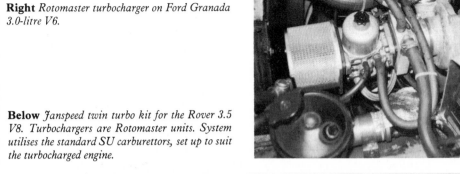

Right *Rotomaster turbocharger on Ford Granada 3.0-litre V6.*

Below *Janspeed twin turbo kit for the Rover 3.5 V8. Turbochargers are Rotomaster units. System utilises the standard SU carburettors, set up to suit the turbocharged engine.*

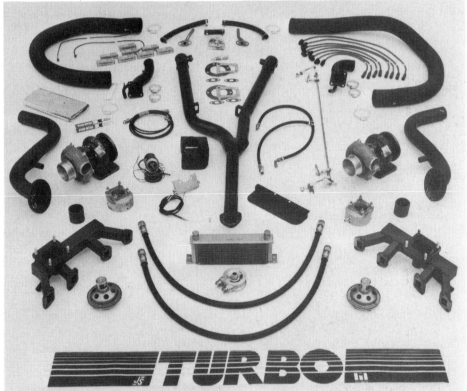

engine. A wilder camshaft will therefore tend to move the useful torque curve higher up the rpm range and may also raise the rpm at which the turbo becomes effective, by allowing overcooling of the exhaust gases. At the same time fuel consumption will suffer too, as some partially burnt mixture is blown out through the exhaust port during the valve overlap period. As the required 30-35 per cent power increase can be obtained

Above *Early 1980 turbocharger kit by Janspeed for Datsun 240, 260Z and 280C. Turbocharger and waste-gate are Rotomaster items.*

Below *The IHI RHB51 turbocharger on this Mini engine is one of the smallest turbochargers currently available in the world, although other small units are due to be released shortly. Allard produced this system for the Mini and Metro and a competition version producing up to 175 bhp.*

without resorting to alternative camshaft timing, it is normally considered unnecessary to change the camshaft. This also avoids an additional expense which is not essential for normal road use.

Of particular importance is the condition of the cylinder head, its face, valves and valve seats. The condition of the pistons, rings and cylinder bore are also vital to the turbocharged engine, but provided they are within manufacturing tolerances, no special modifications should be necessary, except insofar as may be necessary to obtain a lower geometric compression ratio. Nor should it be necessary to modify the cylinder block or crankshaft assembly provided that these components are within the manufacturer's specifications and the normal maximum rpm as specified for the engine in standard form is not exceeded. Even the standard clutch, which you might think would not stand a 35-45 per cent increase in torque, can usually be used without a problem.

Testing, tuning and maintenance after conversion

After you have fitted your turbocharging system, final setting up, testing and adjusting can make the difference between success or failure, so make sure all settings are correct before using full boost.

Adjust points, spark plugs and tappets to the manufacturer's standard specifications. The ignition timing may need some alteration from standard (consult Chapter 2 for details). Before starting the engine, remove the high tension lead from the coil and earth

Fig 56: *Mini 1,275 GT power curves.*

Fig 57: *'A' Series 1,293 cc power curves.*

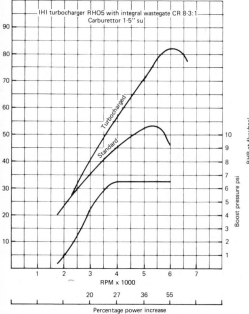

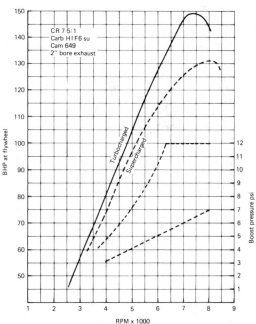

and loosen the union nut on the oil feed pipe where it enters the turbocharger. Spin the engine over on the starter until oil starts to run from the oil pipe union, then tighten the union and crank again. The oil pressure warning light should go out almost immediately.

As far as carburation is concerned, the idle and low speed settings should be virtually unchanged from the standard engine if you are using a modified version of the standard carburettor, although more choke may be required when starting up from cold due to the extra length of manifolding. If you are using a new carburettor, then unless you have previous experience, you will have to do it by a process of trial and error. With SU carburettors, it is best to start with the jet adjusted so that the jet face is approximately 1/32-in below the bridge. This is easily checked by removing the dashpot and piston assembly.

The engine can now be started. If it will not start, check the turbo system to see that all connections are tight. It must be realised that just because the engine is turbocharged, does not mean that it needs any different technique in tracing a fault, other than that there are more joints and hoses for potential air leaks. Check that there is a spark and that fuel is reaching the plugs.

Right *Allard 'Turbomaster' turbocharging system for the Land Rover 2¼-litre petrol boosts performance to that of the Land Rover 3.5 V8.*

Left *VW Beetle flat-four with neat turbo system employing the Japanese IHI RH05 turbo; designed for use in a Dune Buggy by Shelby Spearco.*

After fitting a new turbocharger, carry out a general check of the system when it has completed 100-200 km approximately. In particular check all hose connections and tighten as necessary. Check exhaust manifold bolts.

At 5,000 miles (8,000 km), check installation generally and for signs of chafing on hoses and tightness of hose clips in particular. Check plug leads, plugs and points. Adjust as necessary. If there is any sign of erosion of electrodes, fit new plugs and if it is serious, fit a colder grade of plug. Change oil and filter. Check air filter and clean if necessary. Top up dashpot (SU) with 3 in 1 or SAE 20 oil.

Every 10,000 miles change spark plugs, oil filter and air filter element.

Turbocharger maintenance

There are two questions which I am often asked. Firstly, what is the life expectancy of a turbocharger, and secondly what maintenance does a turbocharger need?

If due attention is paid to the practical information detailed in this book, the answer to the first question is that a turbocharger should last at least as long as might be expected of a normal engine. It is not uncommon for diesel engine turbochargers to run for 200,000 miles before overhaul.

The answer to the second question will depend to a substantial extent on the standard of workmanship of the turbocharger installation, and maintenance of the engine itself. It should be pointed out that modern turbochargers are highly developed and precisely-engineered products which, if treated correctly, are very reliable.

There are two main causes of turbocharger failure. Dirty oil or an inadequate oil supply, and foreign objects entering the turbocharger. The first condition can be eliminated by changing the oil and filter regularly and following the instructions given on lubrication in Chapter 4. Additional oil filters should not be necessary.

If any dirt or objects of significant size are allowed to enter the compressor when it is rotating at high speed, damage can be extensive, both to the turbo and engine if one or more blades break off through contact with a solid object and pass through the engine. Likewise, damage can also be caused to the turbine.

The shaft and wheel assembly is very finely balanced and can be put out of balance by damage to one or more blades. Subsequently, rapid journal bearing wear will occur if nothing worse. In fact, any foreign object entering the turbine will have great difficulty in passing through until it has been smashed to tiny particles and in the process the tips of the turbine blades will take a severe battering. The short answer, therefore, is always keep the air and oil supply clean and the turbocharger unit should need no attention.

Compressors are designed with a maximum safe operating speed. If the turbocharger is incorrectly sized and matched to the engine, the maximum design speed may be exceeded with disastrous results. Dirty oil can also be responsible for clogging up the shaft seals both on compressor and turbine ends, leading to oil leaks and coking up at the turbine end.

IHI RHB52 turbocharger on Hyundai Stellar 1.6—gives an impressive improvement in performance.

Chapter 4

Carburation, induction and exhaust systems

Carburation

Any type of carburettor can be adapted to operate reasonably well, at least in 'suck-through' mode, provided it has adequate air and fuel flow capacity to meet the maximum requirement of the supercharged engine. However, as far as an after market conversion is concerned, an SU is probably the most forgiving and adaptable and, being of a side draught design, it fits in under the bonnet when clearance would be a problem with a downdraught carburettor. On engines of over approximately 3,000 cc (215 cubic inches) or producing 250 bhp or more, single or twin carburettor arrangements, with an air flow capacity in excess of 350 CFM will be necessary. Alternatively, a fuel injection system with sufficient air and fuel flow capacity could be incorporated. There are three basic systems for supplying fuel to the supercharged engine. First, the 'suck-through' carburettor arrangement with the carburettor mounted ahead of the compressor; second, the pressurised carburettor arrangement with the carburettor mounted downstream of the compressor; and third, fuel injection. Each system has its advantages and disadvantages. The main advantages and disadvantages of each system are listed briefly as follows:

Suck-through advantages
A standard type of carburettor can be used with standard fuel system, therefore the carburation and fuel system can be far more simple.

Not subject to hot fuel handling problems.

Simplifies design of turbo system on non-crossflow headed engines.

Disadvantages
Extra manifolding and the vacuum before the compressor can cause fuel to condense on the cool manifold walls, leading to poor mixture distribution and generally lumpy low speed running with icing and stalling under extreme conditions.

Extra manifolding can lead to inferior throttle response, particularly if fuel is condensing on the manifold walls.

A pocket of fuel can collect in the compressor housing volute, or manifold, causing a slug of fuel to enter the engine, leading to unstable fuel/air ratio.

The centrifuge effect of the high-speed compressor can cause the fuel to form into laminar flow with resultant unstable fuel/air ratio and mixture distribution.

Left *Small Block Chevrolet turbo installation by Shelby-Spearco, a popular motor in the USA.*

Right *Janspeed turbocharged Jaguar 4.2-litre XJ6 with fuel injection.*

Below right Fig 58: *Turbo system with fuel injection.*

As latent heat of evaporating cooling effect of the fuel is being imparted to the air flow at a point where the inlet air is still quite cool, its intercooling effect on the ingoing charge is less effective than it would be with a pressurised carburettor working at a higher initial air inlet temperature, and the greater pressure differential across the compressor can increase the temperature of the compressed charge. Due to the pressure drop through the carburettor, a positive shaft seal is required at the compressor end. This does make this design of turbocharger more expensive than those without this type of seal.

Blow-through advantages

A positive shaft seal is not required on the compressor end, so the turbocharger can be cheaper to manufacture.

The standard carburettor, its location and controls, can often remain substantially standard.

Good air/fuel distribution and fuel vapourisation under cold start conditions.

Slightly better intercooling effect through carburettor due to the high inlet air temperatures, and reduced pressure differential across the compressor.

Disadvantages

The constantly changing air density can upset the fuel/air ratio.

Carburettor requires sealing.

Requires relatively complex high-pressure fuel system with fuel pressure regulator and associated pipework.

Hot fuel handling problems after heavy load operation, particularly with high under-bonnet temperatures.

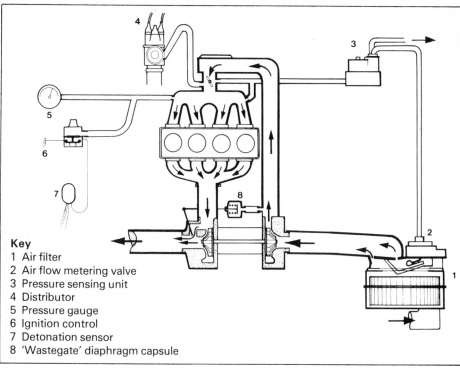

Key
1 Air filter
2 Air flow metering valve
3 Pressure sensing unit
4 Distributor
5 Pressure gauge
6 Ignition control
7 Detonation sensor
8 'Wastegate' diaphragm capsule

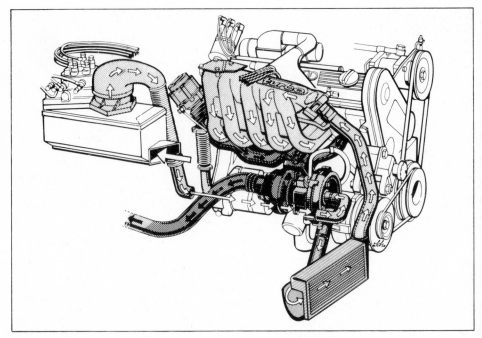

Fig 59: *Audi Quattro 5-cylinder in-line engine with fuel injection, KKK turbocharger, air charge cooler which lowers charge temperature by 50°C approximately and all-electronic ignition.*

Fuel injection advantages

This method should give the best all-round results for the same reasons as with a normally-aspirated engine. This is the most accurate fuel metering and distribution system, resulting in the best economy and lowest emissions.

Disadvantages

This method is normally rather expensive, due to the number of sophisticated components required to make the system operate at peak efficiency.

Many years ago, when positive displacement supercharged engines came to the fore in Grand Prix racing, it was found that up to 20 per cent more peak power and torque was obtained by placing the carburettor before the supercharger, as opposed to after it, primarily due to the latent heat evaporation cooling effect of the alcohol fuel cooling the supercharger unit and dropping the air delivery charge temperature.

Turbochargers, with their somewhat higher thermal eficiency, are not so dramatically affected, although a significant drop in charge temperatures is still obtained by the suck-through system, resulting in improved BMEP and torque. The other advantages of the suck-through, or upstream carburettor system, are that it simplifies the turbo layout, in that a high pressure fuel pump is not required and the carburettor can operate under conditions similar to those for which it was originally designed.

Above *Honda turbo engine in Spirit Formula 1 car.*

Below *McLaren MP4/2 turbocharged Formula 1 car.*

As has been mentioned in the summary of advantages and disadvantages, the disadvantages are that the carburettor and carburettor manifold can be overcooled, causing poor cold starting and running, stalling and lumpy tickover, due to fuel droplets condensing on to cold manifold walls, causing 'slugs' of raw fuel to enter the engine and at other times causing an over-lean mixture. In extreme conditions icing of the carburettor caused by the pressure drop between carburettor and compressor can jam the throttle butterfly causing the engine to race or to stall.

Having developed many turbo systems using either blow- or suck-through carburation set-ups, I have found that this potential problem can usually be eliminated by fitting a water-heated carburettor manifold, linked into the car heater water pipes and adapting the standard car's 'summer' cold air and 'winter' hot air pick-up trunking from the engine's exhaust manifold or turbine housing which will provide warmed air within a minute of start-up from cold. With this arrangement there should be no idling and warm-up problems even in the most severe conditions.

It should be mentioned here that the use of an intercooler without a thermostatically controlled by-pass arrangement can lead to icing on pressurised carburettors as well, unless some care is taken to see that hot air is taken from above the exhaust manifold and fed to the air filter air intake. There should also be a facility for the air inlet to pick up cool air, particularly in hot weather.

Another point to remember when positioning the turbo compressor, if the engine bay layout allows, is to position the housing and manifolding so that as little fuel as possible can collect in the pocket formed in the volute of the housing or in the inlet manifolding.

Even at very low engine rpm the turbocharger compressor will still be spinning at at least 5,000-10,000 rpm and acts as a very efficient cocktail shaker, causing a very even air/fuel charge with improved combustion and smoother engine running.

With the carburettor upstream, the compressor end of the turbo can be subjected to vacuum of up to 29-in hg, and therefore a turbocharger which is fitted with a mechanical face oil seal on the compressor end of the turbine shaft will be needed to prevent oil being drawn into the engine from the turbo bearing under high vacuum conditions. If clouds of blue oil smoke are evident at idle or on overrun, then you know the problem. All Rajay turbos are fitted with the mechanical face seal, as are some Rotomaster and IHI units; however, all Holset, Schwitzer and AiResearch units in general use are fitted with a simple piston ring-type oil seal, which seals effectively against only up to 4-5 in hg vacuum.

This problem can be overcome by venting the area in front of the seal to atmosphere, or by fitting a secondary throttle butterfly between compressor outlet and engine. Although this is effective, it is somewhat complicated. I would suggest that you use a blow-through carburettor arrangement if using a turbo without a suitable seal, as in practice, equally good results are obtained with the carburettor mounted in either position.

Under certain conditions with a suck-through carburation system, the volumetric efficiency of the compressor may be reduced, particularly if the carburettor is causing a substantial pressure drop due to too small a choke area.

With the blow-through system, the standard carburettor and mounting position, together with the throttle and choke linkage, can be left as standard. However, this advantage is largely offset by the fact that the carburettors need to be sealed in an airtight

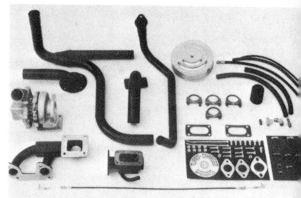

Above and above right *V6 Capri 2.6-litre. This draw-through system uses a modified version of the standard down-draught Weber Carburettor.*

Right *Renault V6 F1 engine in a Lotus.*

Left *A tidy installation by Shelby-Spearco on 350 CID Chevrolet engine, using Rajay turbocharger and wastegate with heatshield around turbine.*

Below right *Broadspeed Capri Bullit turbo featured pressurised carburation and pressurised air recirculation system to control boost. Turbocharger is Holset 3LD with blueprinted 3.0 V6 engine; power output was increased to 215 bhp* (Autocar).

chamber or sealed to prevent a fuel leakage when subjected to boost. In addition, the float chamber must be subjected to boost to equalise the air pressure throughout the carburettor and so avoid fuel being blown back through the jets as boost pressure overcomes fuel pressure. A float which will stand the boost pressure must be used and perhaps the most complicated point is that a high-pressure fuel pump or a modified version of the standard pump is necessary to supply fuel at a constant 3-4 psi above boost pressure, and a regulating valve will be necessary so that excessive fuel pressure is not generated under off boost conditions, which would allow the needle valve to stay off its seat and flood the engine.

General carburation requirements for turbocharged engines

A supercharged engine, whether of the suck-through or blow-through pressurised configuration, does not require a carburettor of larger than standard choke area to produce up to 80 per cent more power than a similar normally-aspirated engine at the same rpm. In fact, where twin carburettors are fitted in normally-aspirated form, it is often possible to use only one of the pair of carburettors when turbocharged.

Choke area is even less critical with a pressurised carburettor as it is working under pressure and therefore senses a denser charge passing through it. With constant depression carburettors such as SU and Stromberg CD, it has been shown that the swallowing capacity of the carburettor is increased by up to 80 per cent when installed upstream of a turbocharger, without seriously throttling the compressor flow capacity. In fact, the first limiting factor often encountered with these carburettors is fuel starvation due primarily to a needle valve which is too small to maintain fuel pressure and mixture strength to match the greatly increased air flow which the supercharger is able to force into the engine. The remedy is to fit a larger needle valve, or in extreme cases, such as when running with methanol fuel, fit an additional float chamber to duplicate the fuel feed.

Fuel flow, as opposed to air flow limitations, can be experienced in other types of carburettor, sometimes promoted by fuel frothing and needle valve bounce due to high-speed engine vibrations. This can be particularly noticeable when the carburettor is mounted a long way from the engine. In such a case a rubber mounted float chamber and/or a neophrene 'O' ring fitted between carburettor and manifold, with double coil spring 'thackery' washers fitted behind the carburettor stud nuts to allow some carburettor flexibility, should cure the problem.

I am often asked which is the best type of carburation to use with a turbocharged engine. For many lower pressure applications, I favour the use of an SU carburettor because it is easily adaptable and because of the variable choke characteristics which give very good low-speed throttle response if correctly set up. However, it is true to say that almost any carburettor which is a reasonable air flow match for the particular engine can be made to work almost equally well. It must be said here, though, that a fully-developed fuel injection system adapted for use with the turbocharged engine offers the best all round flexibility coupled with maximum power and low overall fuel consumption.

The pressurised carburettor (blow-through) arrangement can be applied to most types of carburettor, although it is not practical to attempt this on constant-vacuum carburettors without considerable experimentation.

The essential feature of this system is that the carburettor will experience normal

This AK Miller Ford 360-390 CID Ford turbocharger conversion kit uses an Impco valve to control boost pressure. AK Miller is one of the leading specialists in the USA and markets a wide range of kits.

atmospheric conditions when the turbo is not supplying pressurised air to the engine and boosted or pressurised air when the turbo is raising the air pressure in the inlet manifold above atmospheric pressure. When there is no boost pressure being supplied to the carburettor, the carburation requirements of the turbocharged engine will be similar to those of a normally-aspirated engine; however, in the pressurised condition certain modifications will be required to the carburettor and fuel system. In a normally-aspirated engine, the fuel pressure to the carburettor is normally no more than 4.5 psi and if at any time the pressure drops much below this figure, there is a danger of fuel starvation due to incorrect fuel pressure and fuel level being maintained in the float chamber. The effect of the pressurised air being fed to the carburettors, is to overcome the fuel pressure and cause fuel starvation. To overcome this a high pressure fuel pump is used which will maintain fuel pressure at 4.5 psi above the air pressure being fed to the carburettor. Some form of fuel pressure regulator valve, usually controlled by boost pressure, will be necessary in the fuel line between pump and carburettor to maintain the correct pressure, the excess fuel being returned to the tank. It is also necessary to ensure that the float chamber internally is subjected to the same air delivery pressure, by connecting it to the air delivery pipe, to prevent fuel being blown out of the chambers.

Some types of float can collapse under the increased pressures. Nylon foam-filled types are generally the most satisfactory. Most carburettors will need to be sealed at the throttle butterfly spindle to avoid leakage of boost and fuel at this point. Many carburettors are quite well sealed in standard form for satisfactory operation with boost pressures of up to 7.0 psi. Another way of achieving this is to enclose the complete carburettor in an airtight box with seals for the fuel pipe and throttle linkage.

It is possible to seal the throttle shaft by connecting a pipe to it from above the carburettor venturi which will always be at a slightly higher pressure than below the venturi, and feeding this air directly to the end of the throttle shaft; or by feeding air in via an adaptor plate fitted between carburettor and manifold and a drilling in the base of the carburettor-to-throttle shaft. Alternatively, the shaft can be shortened and the recess plugged.

As a cheaper and more simple alternative, it is often possible to adapt the standard mechanical fuel pump to deliver a higher fuel pressure when running under boost pressure. A pipe is connected between the inlet manifold and the underside of the diaphragm in the pump so that when boost pressure in added to the spring force, the fuel pressure is increased in proportion to the amount of boost. To stop the boost pressure entering the engine crankcase via the fuel pump actuating rod seal, a more substantial seal may be necessary for satisfactory long-term operation.

Progressive twin-choke carburettors are generally the most suitable when used in blow-through (pressurised) applications, for several reasons. Although often a substantially smaller choke area can be used on a supercharged or turbocharged engine to achieve a particular bhp figure without a substantial loss in top end power, the use of a twin-choke carburettor can provide a more correct gas velocity over a wider operating range, resulting in an improved torque curve and throttle response.

Larger than standard chokes in single- or twin-choke non-progressive carburettors where both chokes open simultaneously can cause bad flat spots from low to medium engine rpm, particularly in the suck-through applications due to low gas velocities causing poor atomisation and the inability of the carburettor to supply sufficient fuel under medium to wide open throttle conditions. Modifications to improve the fuel enrichment or power valve circuit and pump jet delivery can improve pickup. In some cases a reduction in choke tube diameter may also be required.

There is another reason for using a twin-choke progressive carburettor. In many cases where little or no boost is seen when the primary choke only is in use, that is under low speed or cruising conditions, the primary choke can be jetted relatively lean for best economy and the secondary choke relatively rich for maximum power output under boost.

Another cause of lean mixtures under initial acceleration with suck-through carburation is an effective power valve circuit. The power valve circuit is normally operated by an internal drilling close to the throttle butterfly. Under acceleration the wide open throttle causes a reduction in vacuum at this point, allowing the power valve to lift from its seat, to open a drilling and provide fuel enrichment for acceleration. With a supercharged engine there may be insufficient drop in vacuum to operate the power valve circuit. To overcome this problem, the power valve circuit should be connected to the manifold downstream of the turbo or supercharger.

Carburettors which have vacuum-operated secondary chokes will have to have their operation converted to mechanical operation, which is feasible on some carburettors.

Induction system design

It is a mistake to assume that, because the induction system is operating under higher than normal atmospheric pressure, liberties may be taken in its design and layout. In practice, under normal road use, turbo boost will in fact only be being generated for between 10-20 per cent of the time the engine is in operation. Therefore it can be seen that for up to 90 per cent of the time the induction system will be working under similar conditions to those of a normally aspirated engine.

To obtain maximum efficiency, as much thought must be given to the design and layout as would be given to the induction system of a normally-aspirated engine. Under boost conditions it is arguable that the internal finish of the inlet pipework is even more important than for an unsupercharged engine. Any lumps, restrictions and sharp edges should be removed. Cast aluminium manifolding is preferable to fabricated mild steel, as its heat dissipation ability is far greater and the greater wall thickness allows a smoother radius at bends and, where hose joins are necessary, will lessen the tendency of the hose connection to chafe under continual flexing, as the hose is subject to frequent variations from vacuum to boost and vice versa.

When using a turbo system with a suck-through carburettor arrangement, I have found that hoses manufactured from silicon reinforced with aramid fibre fabric are of the best types available, having good flexibility, yet with excellent resistance to petrol, oil and high working temperatures.

The induction system on a supercharged engine can be considered as having two sections. One before the compressor or supercharger, which carries the carburettor in the case of suck-through designs, and the section between supercharger and engine.

With the suck-through design some form of heating of the carburettor manifold is normally essential when the ambient air temperature falls below about 50°F (10°C). For optimum idle, slow running and low rpm throttle response under extreme conditions, a hot air pick-up from around the exhaust manifold or turbine housing, to give almost instant inlet air heating once the engine has started, is useful. Without sufficient heating it will be necessary to use considerably more choke for a longer period and may be necessary to run much richer than normal to prevent stalling. The reason for the stalling is that, as the gas velocity is increased as it passes through the carburettor choke, there is a pressure drop and consequent charge temperature drop. This cools the inlet tract and the fine droplets of fuel combine with water vapour in the air and then condense on the cold walls of the inlet tract causing erratic mixture distribution with the attendant problem of stalling, poor idling and slow running generally. Under extreme conditions, the water vapour content will freeze and form a layer of ice which, as well as aggravating the previously mentioned problem, can also cause the throttle to jam by preventing complete closing of the throttle butterfly.

As far as add-on turbo conversions are concerned, the engine's standard inlet manifold should be retained if possible.

Above right *Volkswagen Golf GTI/Rabbit/Scirroco turbo system by Callaway Cars.*
Right *Spearco slope flow module for V8 engine with carburettor such as Holley 4-barrel. Sloping design eliminates pockets for raw fuel collecting in the manifolding and incorporates water jacketing.*

Always, when handling an air/fuel mixture, enter the longitudinal manifold cross tube at the centre at right angles. If the connection is not made at right angles the fuel droplets, which are heavier than the air, will have a tendency to continue in the direction of least resistance, so that if the connection is biased towards the front cylinders, the rear cylinders will run lean or vice versa if the pipe is biased in the other direction. One or two quite sharp bends can be of assistance in breaking up laminar flows in the inlet tract. The inlet stubs should be as short as possible and the manifolding designed in such a way that pockets of excess raw fuel cannot build up in the manifold. A square-section longitudinal rail can help in this respect, but is not so pleasing to the eye. The inside diameter of the inlet stubs should match the inlet port diameter and the remainder of the pipework should have an inside diameter sufficient to allow maximum air flow at the supercharger maximum output without causing excessive pumping losses due to a very high gas velocity. In practice this means that the connection to the compressor outlet should match the compressor outlet pipe inside diameter as closely as possible. Most turbochargers used on engines of up to approximately 6.0 litres have an outlet pipe of 1½-2 in inside diameter.

Ideally, the compressor discharge or diffuser pipe should be designed with a gradually increasing cross sectional area from the point where it connects with the compressor housing outlet until it meets the inlet manifold. The longitudinal manifold rail should have an inside diameter at least equivalent to the carburettor choke area.

Priority when positioning the turbocharger should be given to the turbine as it is preferable on road-going systems for the turbine to be mounted as close to the exhaust ports and centrally on the exhaust manifold as is feasible without undue complication and cost.

Contrary to popular belief, a long inlet tract between compressor outlet and inlet ports does not necessarily cause any noticeable throttle response delay, provided the pipework is correctly designed and the mixture is not allowed to condense on the walls of the manifold. However, the inlet tract should, if feasible, be kept as short as possible with suck-through carburettors, as a long pipe is more likely to cause erratic mixture distribution, mainly through overcooling, and as a consequence poor throttle response at low speed may be the result. As would be the practice with all normally-aspirated engines, all sharp edges inside the manifold should be radiused.

With suck-through systems the carburettor manifold must be kept as short as possible and fitted in such a way as to avoid pockets of fuel collecting under part-throttle conditions.

When unequal mixture distribution does occur under high load conditions, where one or more cylinders goes lean, piston or cylinder head gasket failure is likely to be the result within a matter of seconds.

Observation of most turbo systems will reveal that they do not always adopt all these ideal principles, but it should be borne in mind that there may be other considerations such as development costs, ease of manufacture and fitting, interchangeability with other installations, cost to customer, etc.

Most normally-aspirated engines are designed with an inlet manifold 'hot spot'. Ideally this should, if possible, be eliminated when fitting a turbocharger or supercharger for maximum power with suck-through carburation, and the water hot spot transferred to the

Turbo system for the BMW 320i by Callaway Cars.

compressor inlet side. The inlet manifold should be insulated from excessive heating from the exhaust. Under certain conditions, particularly when the carburettor is pressurised, water heating can, in fact, become in effect water cooling. Such a situation may occur after sustained high speed operation when the heat soak out could, without sufficient cooling, cause vapourisation problems. In these circumstances and at times of high inlet manifold temperature, water circulation through the manifold will act as a heat sink.

Backfire valve
The use of some form of pressure relief valve to release excess inlet manifold pressure caused by an engine backfire is essential in most mechanically-driven supercharger systems to prevent the pressure from the backfire coming into contact with the contra-rotating supercharger vanes or rotors, which may be turning at high speed with considerable inertia. A backfire at this time can cause considerable damage to vane types, although roots types are less critical in this respect unless the manifold happens to be carrying a heavy nitro fuel load as in the case of the fueler dragsters and funny cars of the drag racing scene.

Such a backfire valve, when incorporated in an inlet manifold, should be positioned close to the inlet ports and in line with the charge pulse. The pressure outlet port should be capable of releasing sufficient volume of the charge under full boost to dissipate the

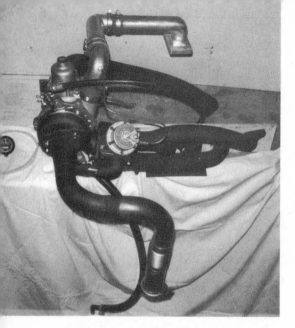

Left *Allard Turbochargers produced this kit for the Renault 5 Gordini. Standard twin outlet exhaust manifold is retained and a specially designed adaptor fitted to hold a Rajay turbocharger. Engine is fitted with lower compression pistons and produces 124 bhp with 7.0 psi boost. Turbocharger and wastegate are Rajay.*

force of the backfire. Two valves may be necessary, one fitted at each end of the inlet manifold, to give sufficient release capacity.

Exhaust

The requirements of a turbocharged engine exhaust manifold and system are different in many ways from those of a normally-aspirated engine. As the exhaust gas turbine of the turbo obtains the power to spin it from the heat energy and velocity of the exhaust gases in the exhaust manifold, it is evident that within the design limits of the various components the hotter we can keep the exhaust manifold and the higher the gas velocity in the manifold, the faster the turbine will spin. The turbine housing is designed to increase considerably the already high velocity of the exhaust gas, since it is necessary to spin the turbine at up to 75,000 rpm even on moderately turbocharged engines. A turbine speed of 75,000 rpm may require a gas velocity of approximately 1,250 feet per second when employing a typical 3-in diameter turbine wheel. For this reason a very large bore exhaust manifold is not necessary and will, in fact, be detrimental to throttle response and overall performance. Nor is a specially flowed manifold necessary for all but highly-turbocharged competition engines.

The main criteria when designing and fabricating an exhaust manifold are: firstly, to build in sufficient strength to take the weight of the turbocharger system and to remain rigid without distortion or fracture even when working at up to 1,000°C; and secondly, to have sufficient wall thickness (3.0 mm minimum is recommended) to withstand the corrosion effects of running up to high temperature over a long period. The considerable amount of expansion and contraction caused by the continual heating and cooling of the manifold, according to the loading of the engine, will soon lead to cracks appearing at the various bends or joints in insufficiently robust manifolds. This point cannot be emphasised too strongly.

Even though, in theory, lagging of the exhaust manifold may be beneficial, in practice it is best avoided, as it can cause rapid burning out through overheating, although some form of heat shielding around the turbine housing will usually be necessary to stop the heat damaging surrounding components or burning the engine cover paintwork. The shielding should have a small air gap between it and the turbine housing to dissipate the radiated heat more gradually.

Various forms of flexible reinforced asbestos sheeting or aluminium foil-backed asbestos cloth are most easily adapted, but a metal shield looks best, although it must be properly supported. When fabricating your own exhaust manifold, use as simple a design as possible; although there is no reason why you should not design an elegant-looking flowed manifold, its advantage is minimal at least when looking for power increases of up to 50 per cent. Nevertheless, some consideration should be given to the gas flow.

I have found that the normal exhaust manifold gaskets are quite adequate providing the

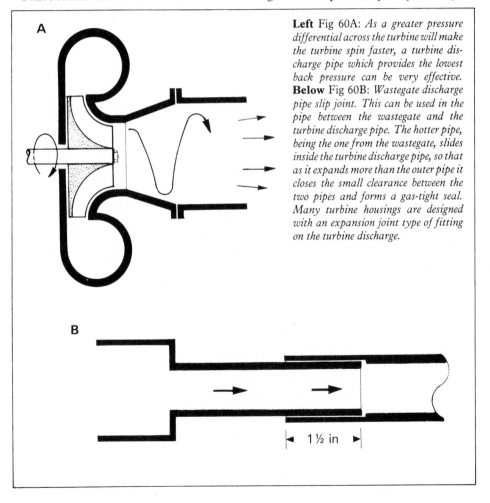

Left Fig 60A: *As a greater pressure differential across the turbine will make the turbine spin faster, a turbine discharge pipe which provides the lowest back pressure can be very effective.*
Below Fig 60B: *Wastegate discharge pipe slip joint. This can be used in the pipe between the wastegate and the turbine discharge pipe. The hotter pipe, being the one from the wastegate, slides inside the turbine discharge pipe, so that as it expands more than the outer pipe it closes the small clearance between the two pipes and forms a gas-tight seal. Many turbine housings are designed with an expansion joint type of fitting on the turbine discharge.*

1½ in

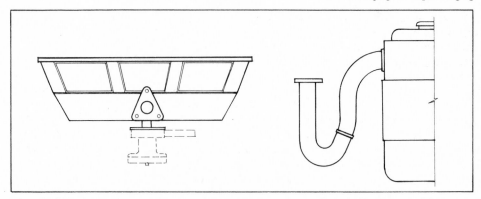

Above left Fig 61: *Fabricated exhaust manifolds can prove quite satisfactory if half-inch thick flanges are used together with thick walled tubing.* **Above right** Fig 62: *'J' pipe. This form of fabricated exhaust manifold is connected as an extension to the standard production cast iron manifold and eliminates the need to modify the existing manifold.*

head and manifold faces are completely flat, and the same applies when no gaskets are fitted as standard. Embossed stainless steel gaskets can also work well.

The exhaust flange should, if possible, be machined from a one-piece plate of 7/16-in minimum thickness to allow for machining if any distortion is evident after welding. Fabrication in mild steel is satisfactory, but stainless steel is better. The outlet stubs should have an inside diameter equal to the exhaust port, be as short as possible, of equal length and enter the longitudinal pipe at right angles or angled in towards the turbine inlet mounting flange (see Fig 60).

The longitudinal pipe can be round or square section with a cross sectional area not more than two and a half times, and not less than double, the area of one exhaust port, for 4-cylinder engines or V8s, increasing to 2½-3 times for 6-cylinder inline engines. The use of square section simplifies the construction and improves the rigidity of the manifold. All flanges and other joints should be electrically welded.

The outlet port from the manifold rail should match the turbine housing inlet port. In the interests of design and strength it is sometimes necessary to compromise and use a pipe of larger cross sectional area than the turbine inlet port; although this will reduce gas velocity somewhat, a pipe of smaller area can cause excessive back pressure and overheating leading to damaged pistons or valves. This is one reason why it is often not good practice to use a 'J' pipe extension to the standard exhaust manifold (see Fig 61). However, this system can be used successfully on some standard cast iron manifolds, providing additional support is given to take the full weight of the turbo assembly off the manifold flange. Failure to do so adequately will lead to the eventual failure of the exhaust manifold at the junction with the 'J' pipe.

The turbine flange and manifold will be subject to considerable expansion and contraction due to the high running temperatures which are a necessary feature of any turbo system. Therefore, all attachment bolts or studs must be of good quality high tensile material, preferably of stainless steel type, and wire or tab locked.

If the turbine flanges have a good mating surface, a perfectly good and long-lasting seal will be obtained without any gasket. The only gasket which I have found to be really satisfactory is the thin stainless steel type with embossed sealing ring.

Without a doubt, a heavy-duty cast iron exhaust manifold designed specially for the turbocharging system is the most satisfactory type. However, it is not always practical to use a specially cast exhaust manifold unless the tooling and pattern cost can be absorbed in a production run of at least fifty units. Such exhaust manifolds would be cast in spheroidal graphite (S.G. Nodular) iron or high silicon molybdenum iron.

Engines of 'V' cylinder arrangement will need to have the flow from both exhaust manifolds directed into the turbine when using a single turbocharger system. Due to the length of exhaust piping between the two manifolds and the varying expansion rates, it is good practice to fit a flexible coupling between the two manifolds.

Below Fig 63: *Two designs of cast iron exhaust manifolds with mounting flange for turbocharger.*

Bottom Fig 64: *Typical exhaust piping arrangement for a V8 engine with single turbocharger. Note expansion joint incorporated in exhaust manifold link pipe to relieve manifolds of stresses caused by pipe expansion.*

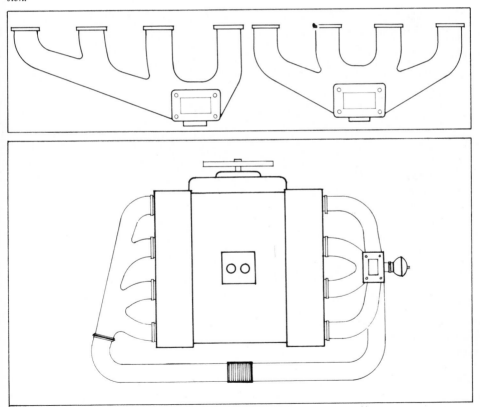

Rotomaster turbo system on Sierra XR4i by Janspeed.

All exhaust systems should incorporate a flexible connection or be supported in such a manner as to relieve the turbine housing of all piping forces emanating from the exhaust system.

The exhaust system from the turbine outlet to the rear of the vehicle also has a great influence on the operating efficiency of the turbocharged engine, as the greater the pressure difference existing across the turbine between the turbine inlet and outlet port, the faster the turbine will spin. It is readily evident, therefore, that anything that can be done to reduce the back pressure in the exhaust pipe after it leaves the turbine should increase the turbine speed for a given pre-turbine pressure.

Ideally, an expansion chamber mounted just after the exhaust gases leave the turbine exducer, with a slightly larger cross sectional area than the exducer bore, should be used if space permits. Some turbine housings have a stepped exducer bore to achieve this effect.

Exhaust systems should be of the big bore free-flow type with low back pressure at full engine load. Suggested minimum diameters are 1½-in up to 1,300 cc; 1 3/8-in up to 2.0 litres; and between 2-3-in, or twin pipes, over 2.0 litres.

Although turbochargers do subdue the typical exhaust noise, some form of silencing is normally necessary. I have found that one silencer of straight-through design of the same bore as the exhaust pipe is often satisfactory, but the addition of an expansion box, again of the same minimum diameter, gives a further reduction in decibels without affecting engine performance.

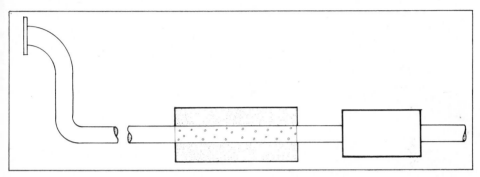

Above Fig 65: *Typical exhaust system requirements of a turbocharged engine. Large bore piping with straight-through silencer and non-restrictive expansion box. In some cases one large or two small expansion boxes are all that are necessary.*

Below left Fig 66A: *Exhaust manifold design to harness the natural exhaust pulses. With an engine firing order of 1/3/4/2, the individual pipes should be connected as shown. This is particularly beneficial with twin-entry turbine housing designs, but the flow through most manifolds can be improved by harnessing the natural exhaust gas pulses in this way.* **Below right** Fig 66B: *Exhaust manifold design for a twin turbocharged V8 engine. Similar layouts are often used on marine applications with water cooling of the exhaust manifolds and turbine housings.*

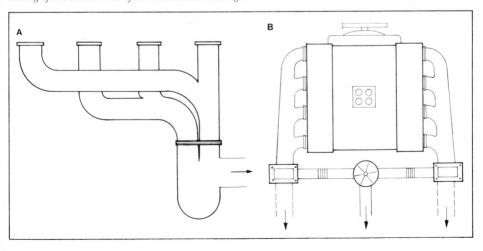

Chapter 5

Compression ratio and ignition systems

Reduction in compression ratio

A reduction in compression ratio from that of a similar naturally aspirated engine is an essential feature of almost all pressure-charged engines, except in cases where other measures such as anti-detonant additives are introduced or low boost pressures are used on an already low compression ratio engine. It is a fact of thermodynamics that when a gas is compressed its temperature rises. The effect, therefore, of the boost is to increase the peak cylinder temperature and bring it closer to the temperature at which detonation commences. (Detonation is the uncontrolled burning of the fuel/air mixture, leading to a further rapid increase in cylinder temperature. If this process continues for more than a few seconds, a cylinder head gasket will blow at best or a piston crown will melt.)

In the range of relatively low boosts, say 4 to 8 psi, the effect of every 3.7 psi boost is to increase the effective compression ratio by 1 ratio approximately. For example, starting with a geometric compression ratio of 9.0:1 and adding a boost of 8.0 psi, the effective compression ratio will have increased to 11.2:1. However, to the increased cylinder temperature caused by the 11.2:1 compression ratio, must be added the general heat build-up around the cylinder walls on the piston crown and valves. This can be a significant factor to a greater or lesser degree, depending on the overall thermal efficiency of the supercharging system and engine, particularly under sustained boost conditions. It also has to be borne in mind that the ambient air inlet charge temperature will have a significant bearing on the final peak cylinder temperature. It is quite possible to work on calculations which show that a certain engine should be safe at full throttle without detonation with an effective compression ratio of say 10.5:1, yet in practice detonation occurs, as the significance of these other facts has not been fully realised and cannot always be accurately calculated in advance.

As an approximate guide a maximum compression ratio of 8.5 is normally permissible with a maximum boost of 6.0 psi and 98 octane fuel, providing the complete system is correctly set up. Some engines, particularly those with an aluminium cylinder head, can run at higher compression ratios for short bursts at full throttle or with some ignition retard under peak load and knock-sensing devices, as now employed in most production turbocharged cars.

The amount by which the geometric compression ratio must be reduced for a particular engine will depend on the following factors: susceptibility of the engine to detonation in normally-aspirated form and its basic compression ratio, the boost pressure to be employed, the overall efficiency of the supercharging system, the fuel octane rating and whether ignition retard or other devices are fitted.

Detonation is a condition which occurs when the progressive burning along a defined flame front of a homogenous air/fuel mixture is interrupted by a small pocket of mixture, usually near the exhaust valve, which reaches a critical temperature and ignites spontaneously along a counter front, causing a rapid rise in cylinder temperature with consequent overheating of pistons and valves leading to failure of these components.

In the case of pre-ignition, hot combustion chamber surfaces or carbon deposits cause the critical temperature to be reached prior to ignition from the spark plug. Both these conditions will produce audible 'pinking' when the process is severe, but often high speed detonation cannot be heard without detonation amplifiers or vibration-sensing devices. Under these conditions a piston can fail with no audible warning or for that matter any indication on water or oil temperature gauges.

Mathwall Engineering specialise in turbocharging the Alfa Romeo and produce this system with AiResearch T04B turbo and pressurised Dellorto carburettors similar to those used on the Lotus Esprit Turbo.

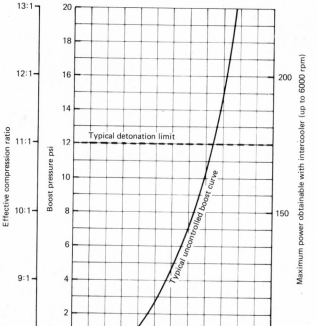

Fig 67: *Chart showing typical turbocharger uncontrolled boost vs rpm curve and the power output which can be achieved on 98 octane petrol, starting with a basic 8.0:1 compression ratio and 100 bhp. Modifications such as change of camshaft and intercooling can give further power increases.*

* Example:- Take an engine (unturbocharged) with a compression ratio of 8:1 and maximum BHP of 100 at 6000 RPM, using 98 octane fuel

The chart (Fig 67) shows the relationship of effective compression ratio to boost pressure. It is interesting to note that tests carried out many years ago by Richardo showed that a reduction in compression ratio from 9.0 to 8.0:1 allowed a 40 per cent increase in IMEP before the onset of detonation. Also, a reduction of this amount generally produces a four to five per cent drop in IMEP.

Too large a reduction in compression ratio will make the engine thermally very inefficient at lower rpm or under part throttle cruise conditions, with poor fuel consumption and a flat feeling to the engine. With a turbocharger it will also have a tendency to exaggerate the off and on boost condition and give less precise throttle response.

The following formula can be used to determine the compression ratio required:

$$r^2 = r_1 \left(\frac{P1}{P2} \right) \times .73$$

where r_1 is the maximum compression ratio (unsupercharged) without detonation, r^2 is the allowable supercharged compression ratio, P1 and P2 are the supercharged and unsupercharged intake pressures (atms absolute).

There are several methods of reducing compression ratio. The simplest and cheapest method, but not the best way, is to fit a decompression plate, usually manufactured from sheet copper with a cylinder head gasket placed either side of it. Good results can be obtained by this method, but it is not always reliable for long-term duty and should be considered only as a short-term expedient.

The second alternative is to have the combustion chambers in the cylinder head enlarged by machining. Many cylinder heads can be modified in this way by removing metal to increase the combustion chamber volume. Up to 5 cc can often be removed without encroaching on the water jacket or drastically reducing the squish effect. During this process, flow can be increased around the valves by removing metal in this area. The same basic principles apply when modifying a cylinder head for normal or supercharged application, apart from the fact that a lower compression ratio is usually required, although the size and, more importantly, the cooling of the exhaust valve can be of benefit.

Usually the most technically correct way of reducing an engine's compression ratio is to build it with pistons which give a lower geometric compression ratio. Usually this is achieved by fitting dished pistons instead of flat topped, by pistons having a deeper dish or bowl, or by reducing piston crown height in relation to cylinder block deck.

Ignition system

As with a normally-aspirated engine, an ignition system which is in top condition is essential for peak engine performance. Indeed, it can be justly argued that with an engine operating under higher pressures and temperatures, such as experienced in a supercharged engine, the condition and capability of the ignition system to function effectively is even more essential.

A supercharged engine has in effect a variable compression ratio. This is brought about by the fact that at low engine revs when boost pressure is not being applied to the engine, the effective compression ratio will be the basic geometric compression ratio, but as the engine speed and load is increased, the cylinder will be subjected to increasing boost pressure with a resultant increase in effective compression ratio.

Because of this characteristic, a supercharged engine requires a different ignition advance curve from that of a normally-aspirated engine. Generally a reduction in geometric compression ratio of an engine will require increased advance of the ignition timing. Putting it very simply, this is due to the slower burn rate of the fuel at lower cylinder pressures. A typical supercharged engine with a compression ratio of 8.0:1 may require a timing of up to 12-14° BTDC at idle, increasing rapidly to a maximum of 28-34° at 2,000 rpm approximately. Thereafter, as the boost takes effect, some retard of the ignition may be necessary, ignition retard increasing in step with rising boost at 1-2° per 1 psi boost increase. Maximum susceptibility to detonation is usually in the area of maximum torque and consequently peak cylinder pressures, usually in the rpm range of 3,500-5,000 rpm. After this point in an engine where the maximum boost is governed, the engine may require more advance again.

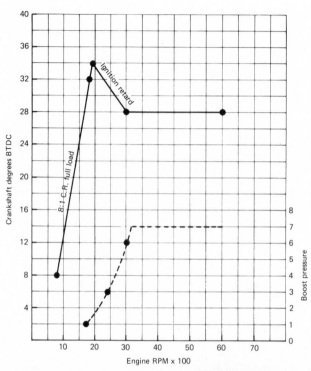

Left Fig 68: *Ignition advance requirements will vary with each engine, being influenced by many factors. This curve, however, indicates a typical requirement with an 8.0:1 compression ratio.*

Below *Micro-Dynamics engine management, electronic ignition system.*

As already stated, the effect of boost pressure in a cylinder is to increase the effective compression ratio with a resultant increase in peak cylinder pressure and temperature. In addition, the boost pressure produces a denser, more rapidly-burning mixture, which needs less ignition advance. These two factors can mean that over-advanced timing can destroy a supercharged engine by producing detonation or pre-ignition or possibly both.

Retarding the ignition, or more accurately reducing the amount of ignition advance at or near full load, will reduce the tendency of the fuel air mixture to detonate by reducing the peak cylinder pressure and temperature. This can be effective up to a maximum of 12-15°, but with further retardation there can be an increasing tendency to pre-ignition and fall in engine power output. Fig 70 shows a typical boost/rpm curve and the associated ignition timing requirements for supercharged and normally aspirated engines, together with the usual compromise advance curve adopted.

Modifications can be made to most distributors to reduce the amount of mechanical advance built into the distributor, by reducing the movement of the advance bob-weights. This can be achieved by reducing the length of the slot in the operating mechanism, putting a sleeve over the stop pegs or altering the position of the pegs. A reduction in advance in this way will allow the engine to operate with more advance at lower rpm, which most relatively low compression turbocharged engines need to obtain optimum low speed performance and throttle response.

Some distributors are now equipped with double-acting diaphragms in the vacuum advance capsules. In some cases it is possible to connect one side of the diaphragm chamber to the inlet manifold, so that under boost the diaphragm will operate in the reverse direction to give the effect of boost retard. Several far more sophisticated ignition systems are now in use on some turbocharged production cars.

It is normally recommended to use spark plugs which are one or two grades 'colder' than would be used in the normally-aspirated version of a particular engine, but this will depend to a large extent on the compression ratio and maximum boost employed. If the spark plugs are too cold, carbon deposits will build up on the electrodes causing misfiring in bad cases, or a general fall off in sparking efficiency with a consequent drop in engine performance. On the other hand, it is safer to run too cold a plug rather than too soft a one. Too soft a plug can overheat very rapidly at full power, leading to a melted electrode. This can lead to a holed piston very quickly since the molten electrode creates a localised hot spot as it rests on the piston crown.

On certain engines, particularly competition ones running a high boost pressure, where plug leads necessarily lie close to the exhaust manifold, some form of plug lead insulation should be fitted, or alternatively silicon leads and connectors used.

Over-revving can be a problem with turbocharged engines, due to the high volumetric or breathing ability which does not necessarily tail off so rapidly as in an equivalent normally-aspirated engine. In these circumstances, it is advisable to use an ignition cut-out to stop over-revving. There are various ways of achieving this. A common method is to fit a distributor rotor arm which mechanically cuts the spark as revs rise past a pre-determined point. The Micro-Dynamics system cuts every other spark to each cylinder with no asymmetric sparks, thus eliminating roughness or misfiring and obtaining a more progressive, less severe rev limiting effect which can be held at the rev limit if necessary, with no backfiring due to partly burned fuel collecting in the exhaust manifold.

Some electronic engine control systems have been developed principally for turbocharged engines, incorporating controls to limit engine revs and over boost: a time delay to allow oil pressure to reach the turbocharger and ignition retard, coupled with a set of warning lights mounted in a display module. These controls can be adjusted to suit a particular engine. The Micro-Dynamics ignition retard system is adjustable and can be set to retard the ignition ½° or 1° per thousand rpm. On another system the retard is not subject to rpm, but can be adjusted or operated by a pressure switch to limit total advance as required by a particular engine. The best system is one which has a detonation sensor or amplifier and retards the ignition in response to sensing detonation. With this system it is possible to achieve optimum engine performance and economy.

Chapter 6

Lubrication

All types of supercharger require a continuous and adequate supply of clean oil to give reliable long-term service. A correctly designed lubricating system is particularly critical for turbo superchargers, which operate at far higher speeds and temperatures than the positive displacement types.

Turbocharger lubrication systems

All automobile turbochargers require a pressurised oil feed which will maintain a minimum pressure of 15-30 psi depending on the particular design of turbocharger and turbocharging system.

The oil is required to lubricate and cool the bearings which support the turbine and compressor shaft and wheel assembly. Most automobile turbochargers use a single or twin bearing design which allows the oil to pass around both the inner and outer surfaces of the bearing. By passing between shaft and bearing, the oil acts as a wedge and, in doing so, centres the shaft in the bearing cavity at the same time as almost eliminating any mechanical contact of the working surfaces, except when used to absorb axial thrust.

Even the most lightly loaded turbocharger will be turning at a speed of not less than 25,000 rpm for most of its working life, with a turbine temperature in excess of 500°C. It can be readily realised, therefore, that should the oil supply be inadequate, because of an insufficient or dirty supply, rapid wear, or in severe cases destruction of the whole turbocharger, can result.

Even the smallest turbochargers require an oil flow to the bearing under load of not less than half a gallon per minute. However, the actual amount of oil consumed by the turbocharger should be negligible.

Flexible oil piping of ¼-in bore is required, with elbows and fittings having not less than 1/8-in inside diameter and preferably 3/16-in. Occasionally, usually on the smallest-capacity engines, a slight restriction at the oil feed take-off point may be necessary to avoid too much reduction in oil pressure at engine idle. If this means insufficient oil supply to the turbo at full load, a higher capacity oil pump must be fitted. Some engines may show a drop of 2-3 psi in oil pressure at idle due to the oil supply to the turbo.

Normally, a suitable method of providing lubrication is to fit an oil tee piece in place of the oil sender unit, which is usually screwed into a tapping in the engine block or oil filter housing. The oil sender is fitted to one side of the tee piece and the oil feed pipe to the turbo to the other.

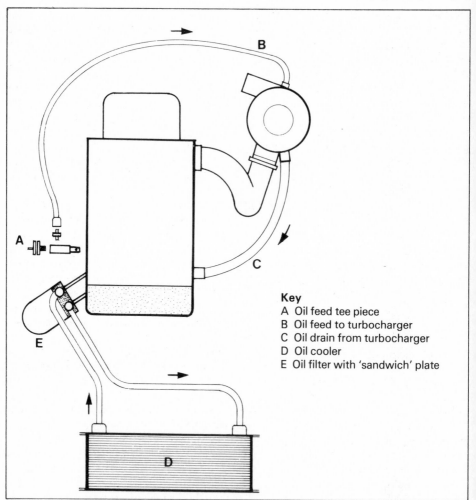

Key
A Oil feed tee piece
B Oil feed to turbocharger
C Oil drain from turbocharger
D Oil cooler
E Oil filter with 'sandwich' plate

Fig 69: *Typical turbocharger lubrication system. Diagram shows oil pressure feed from the tee piece tapped into engine oil gallery. Free flow oil drain by gravity back to the sump with oil entering above the level of oil in the sump.*

The oil feed inlet to the turbocharger, which is located in the bearing housing, should be positioned at the top not more than 35° from vertical. On twin-turbo systems, a single take-off point from the engine will usually be sufficient, but it is best to use two separate pipes from the oil feed tee piece, one to each turbocharger.

All turbochargers also require an oil drain system which is equally important to maintain correct turbocharger functioning. Unlike the oil supply, the oil is drained from the bearing housing cavity by gravity. For this reason, and because the high speed rotation of the turbine shaft causes the oil to pick up air which will cause the hot oil to foam, the drain pipe must be of much larger bore than the oil feed pipe. The minimum inside diameter of the pipe, or any connections, should not be less than ½-in inside diameter on the smallest turbochargers and preferably 9/16-in on units such as the AiResearch and Rotomaster T04B.

As the oil return is by gravity, the pipe must slope downwards throughout its length, even if only at a slight angle, and have no kinks or loops to act as a trap for the oil. Oil drains should preferably be manufactured substantially in steel tube, with a short flexible section to allow for expansion and alignment of the pipe. Flexible pipes can be satisfactory provided they have a steel outer protective covering or are routed well clear of the turbine and exhaust, or insulated in some way to prevent scorching and eventual failure. The oil drain outlet from the bearing housing should be angled from vertical by not more than 35°.

Normally, the oil is returned to the sump, and must enter above the oil level in the sump, allowing for oil surge. It is also possible to return the oil via the timing cover or a crankcase breather on some engines, providing sufficient breather capacity is maintained.

It is sometimes satisfactory to return the oil via the camshaft or rocker cover if the mounting position of the turbocharger allows this and if the oil return to the sump cannot build up inside the cover. Another drain location can be the place where the mechanical fuel pump would be fitted. If the mechanical pump is replaced by an electric pump, the oil drain can be routed via the mechanical pump attachment point. On vee engines, oil can also be returned via the valve lifter gallery. On engines with a dry sump lubrication system, the oil is best returned to the main oil tank.

When space or other design considerations dictate that the turbo oil outlet is at or below the level of the oil in the engine sump, a separate scavenge pump will be necessary to extract the oil from a collection tank below the turbocharger oil outlet and then return it to the sump.

The oil, as it passes around the bearing housing bearings and turbine shaft, will be at a very high temperature. A particularly critical time is when the engine is switched off and the oil supply is stopped. These high oil temperatures tend to make the oil carbonise and build up as deposits, which in turn make the oil start to lose its lubrication properties. For this reason it is essential that the engine oil and filter are changed regularly in line with manufacturer's requirements; on after market converted vehicles, oil should be changed every 3,000 miles, unless high quality synthetic oils are used. There is a section devoted to these oils in the following pages, as the importance of lubrication for both turbcharger and engine cannot be stressed too much.

Because of the high temperature of the oil as it passes through the turbo and round the engine, ash deposits tend to build up more quickly than with a normally-aspirated engine. Dirty oil can shorten the life of the turbocharger bearings, so more frequent oil changes are recommended. A heavy duty oil such as Rotella TX 20/40 or Series 3 diesel engine oil will combat the build-up of deposits and reduce the chance of premature bearing or shaft wear.

When fitting a new turbocharger, or refitting a reconditioned unit, the oil and oil filter should always be changed. Most large trucks are now turbocharged and the turbocharger manufacturers have in the past had problems with insufficient oil reaching the turbo

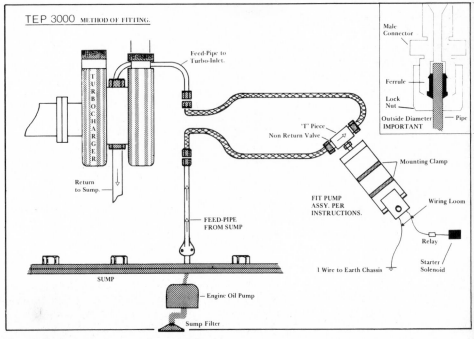

Fig 70: *Typical turbocharger primary lubrication pump.*

bearings when starting from cold and revving up the engine immediately. Another problem was caused when switching off the engine after a period of heavy duty usage, when the turbine acts as a heat sink. The heat spreads to the shaft and bearings, now without an oil supply, and in extreme cases the oil is burnt off and a veneer or carbon deposit left on the bearing surface, which can lead to scoring of the shaft, rapid wear and oil leaks. Although this occurrence is less likely on most car turbocharging systems, it is nevertheless good practice *not* to rev the engine immediately when starting up and to let the engine idle for a minute or so before switching of after hard usage.

Synthetic oils
Synthetic oils are 'synthetic' because they are man-amde by synthesizing dissimilar materials in a chemical reaction to form a new compound. They are not found in nature, unlike the basis of conventional lubricants, although some of the raw materials used to manufacture synthetic lubricants include components found in petroleum-based lubricants. For this reason they can be formulated to provide superior performance in resistance to heat and degradation, under the most extreme conditions.

These lubricants are produced in four classifications which account for over 90 per cent of synthetic usage. Of these the organicesters are the ones which are applicable to most automobiles. These are either diester or polyol types. The polyol esters are used principally in aviation and industrial turbine lubrication.

The diester synthetic oils have a number of signficant advantages over normal petroleum-based mineral oil lubricants:

1. Increased wear protection, resulting from very stable viscosity over a far wider range of operating temperatures.

2. Reduced deposit formation, resulting from the fact that these lubricants do not start to oxidize until about 200°F above conventional lubricants.

3. High film strength, which means less contact between moving engine components and a reduction in wear and friction. This in turn can give substantial improvements in both fuel consumption and power output and allow the engine to run cooler.

4. Improved cold weather starting. Synthetics retain their fluidity right down to −60°F. This can be demonstrated by the fact that to crank a normal engine at 250 rpm with a temperature of −40°F requires about 22 amps with synthetic oil and 270 amps with conventional oils.

5. Increased service life—from three to five times longer than conventional oils. Instead of changing oils every 6,000 miles (3,000 miles with after market turbo systems) oil drains can be extended to 25,000 miles (10,000 miles).

Mazda RX7 fitted with Rotomaster TO4B turbocharger. Carburettor is HIF6 SU (Autocar).

Synthetics can provide better lubrication at extremes of temperatures without degrading and forming resins and acids. They are able to disperse acids and hold insoluble particles in suspension.

Para-synthetic oils are also available. These are a blend of carefully selected synthetic and natural base stocks. By this method, most of the benefits of synthetic oil is retained, together with the lower price of conventional oil. All in all, synthetic lubricants appear to have many factors in their favour and we are likely to see them more widely used for turbocharged engines in the future. There are, however, one or two factors against synthetic oils at present. For a start they are expensive, so engines with oil leaks or with high oil consumption are not recommended. Because of the very slippery nature of the lubricant and its ability to reduce friction to a minimum, it is not advisable to use synthetic oil in a new engine, so wait until the rings have bedded in, say after 5,000-6,000 miles.

Turbocharger primary lubrication pump (TEP 3000—page 126)

The turbocharger primary lubrication system, as developed by Trans Europe sales and service, consists of a two-stage pump which is connected into the oil feed line to the turbocharger. The functions of the pump are to provide 15 psi oil pressure immediately on engine start-up at the turbocharger bearings. During normal running the pump is recharged by engine oil pressure and then immediately the engine is switched off, the pump piston is released from engine oil pressure and a spring pushes the piston forward to deliver oil at 20 psi to the turbocharger bearings for up to two minutes after the engine is switched off. As this is the most critical time for the turbocharger bearings, this ingenious device can considerably extend turbocharger bearing life.

Shorrock vane-type supercharger lubrication

As with the turbo-supercharger, correct lubrication is important for optimum supercharger functioning.

The oil is obtained in the same way as for the turbocharging system and routed to the lubricator at the centre of the supercharger rear casing. There is a drilling inside either the lubricator body or casing. An oil metering restrictor pin is fitted inside the oil drilling. The fitment of the pin in the oil way determines the amount of oil which can pass between the pin and the oil way. A small spring is fitted behind the pin to ease removal for inspection and cleaning and to prevent sediment building up and clogging the oil way. Pins are usually marked 'A' or 'B'. The 'B' pin is .0005-in smaller in diameter than the 'A' pin, so allowing more oil into the supercharger. If the plug in the lubricator or the lubricator body is removed, a screwdriver slot will be revealed in the end of the pin. With the aid of the spring and a few turns of a screwdriver, the pin can be easily removed.

The amount of oil required to lubricate the front and rear bearings and the eight vane bearings is quite small: approximately half a pint for 500 miles' motoring.

New superchargers are normally fitted with a 'B' pin, but if over-oiling was experienced, which would show as excessive exhaust smoke on starting up, then the .0005-in larger 'A' pin would be fitted. Occasionally an 'A'-plus pin would be needed if the engine had a very high oil pressure.

Every 5-10,000 miles the metering pin should be cleaned. On special sprint engines, it is satisfactory to arrange a gravity oil feed system—obviously with a much larger pin-to-oil way clearance.

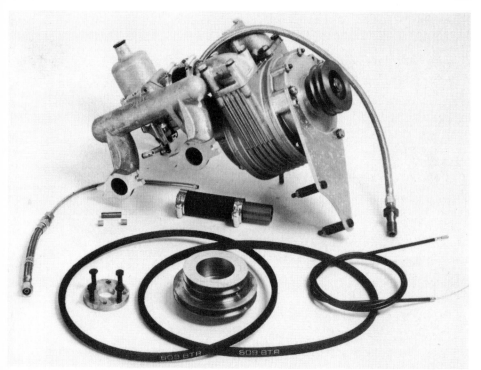

Above *Typical Shorrock supercharger kit, this one for 'A' Series engine (no longer produced) with twin 'V' belt drive.*

Below Fig 71: *Typical total loss vane type supercharger lubrication system with pressure feed from engine and restrictor metering pin fitted inside rear housing. The fine clearance between pin and the oil way controls the flow of oil to the bearings.*

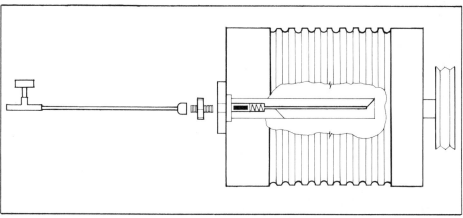

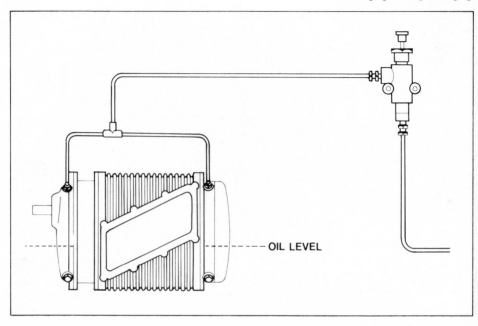

OIL LEVEL

The oil system therefore is a total loss system with the oil mixing with fuel/air mixture and not returning to the engine lubrication system.

Roots-type supercharger lubrication

Lubrication is required for the rotor phasing gears and front and rear bearings. No oil pressure feed is required and therefore the oil can be separate from the normal engine oiling system, being self contained within the front and rear housings of the supercharger. Seals between bearing and rotors ensure that the air chest remains substantially oil-free.

It is possible to arrange an oiling system as shown in Fig 72, but as oil consumption should not be more than a quarter of a pint for 2,000 miles, the usual practice is to top up the oil when putting in engine oil. Normally, engine oil is used but EP80 or 90 will reduce oil consumption and gear noise.

Wade-type superchargers should only be filled to approximately a quarter of the total chamber capacity, or oil may be drawn into the air chest. For competition applications where the blower will most likely be used for a very short duration, minimal lubrication is required.

Effects of altitude

A naturally-aspirated internal combustion engine will lose power as altitude increases due to a reduction in air density. The reduced air density lowers the volumetric efficiency of the engine and its ability to breathe in sufficient air to maintain sea level power output. As an engine will produce power in proportion to the density or mass flow of air breathed in, supercharging to increase air density can be used to maintain sea level power output as altitude increases.

At an altitude of 5,000 ft (1,650 m), a normally-aspirated engine will have lost approximately 14 per cent of its sea-level power output. So an engine which produced 100 bhp at sea level will produce only 86 bhp at 5,000 ft and at 10,000 ft the corresponding figure will be 74 bhp.

For land vehicles, the requirement may be to maintain power with a vehicle operating continuously at high altitude, in which case the turbocharger must be matched to suit these conditions. In most cases, however, an engine will be supercharged at or near sea level and as little loss as possible will be required as it is taken to higher altitudes.

Fig 73 shows comparative power outputs for a turbocharged and normally-aspirated engine at various altitudes and the additional boost pressure which would be required to maintain sea level power with increasing altitude. It can be seen that when an engine is turbocharged, it will also lose power with an increase in altitude, but the loss will be considerably less than for a normally-aspirated engine. This is accounted for by the fact that the turbine speed of a free-floating turbocharger increases in direct relation to the pressure differential existing across the turbine. As altitude increases, the pressure in the turbine discharge pipe drops due to a drop in ambient air pressure, but the pressure existing in the exhaust manifold (expansion ratio) remains substantially the same. It is worth noting therefore, that if the maximum boost gauge reading is 7.0 psi at sea level, then it will still show 7.0 psi as altitude increases since it is only the ambient air pressure which has been reduced.

A small A/R ratio turbine can be used with a wastegate to maintain maximum boost at the required level up to an altitude at which the wastegate remains closed. At higher altitude the engine will lose power in the same manner as a free-floating turbocharged engine.

Above left Fig 72: *A lubrication system for a 'roots' type supercharger with a manually operated valve in the oil supply pipe. Oil consumption with this type of supercharger is very low, so only occasional topping up would be necessary.*

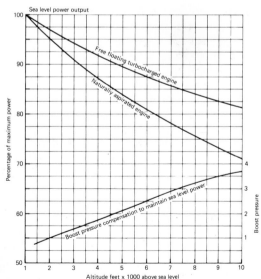

Right Fig 73: *Altitude effect on engine power.*

Chapter 7

Turbocharging small diesels

In the last ten years there has been a large increase in the number of turbocharged diesel-powered vehicles. Initially most turbocharged diesel engines were, in automobile terms, relatively large, but the last few years with ready availability of smaller, lighter and cheaper turbochargers, have seen the increasing use of turbochargers on some smaller diesel engines too.

In view of the substantial benefits of turbocharging diesel engines of all sizes, it is perhaps suprising that they have not been more widely used on the smaller diesel engines to date. These benefits include substantially improved specific fuel consumption over the engine's whole operating range, coupled with a large increase in power and torque from a given cylinder displacement.

There are other benefits too since, unlike a petrol engine, a diesel is not sensitive to detonation; in other words, it is not knock-limited. It is, however, smoke-limited, the smoke being the excess of fuel not fully burned during the combustion process.

The power output of a diesel engine is dependent upon the weight of fuel burnt and the maximum rating at any speed is determined by the mass of air available to burn the fuel efficiently. The air mass flow into a normally-aspirated engine is limited by engine piston displacement and an increase in engine power output has to be achieved by increasing engine rated speed and/or engine cubic capacity.

With the aid of a turbocharger, a very substantial increase in air mass flow and density can be achieved. When additional fuel is added to the increased mass air flow, the resultant power increase is limited only by the mechanical and thermal capabilities of the engine. The matching of a turbocharger to a small diesel engine must follow closely the requirements for a petrol engine since it has to operate over a relatively wide speed range and give similar performance to a naturally-aspirated petrol engine of the same displacement.

The turbocharger should be matched to provide boost from as low an engine speed as possible, preferably from 1,200 rpm, without causing excessive back pressure in the exhaust manifold. High back pressures will reflect back to the engine causing high cylinder pressures and a fall in specific fuel consumption. Increased pump fueling will, however, control the percentage power increase, and also to a certain extent the boost rpm curve at the higher engine speeds.

As far as turbocharger conversions are concerned, the relatively wide engine speed range of high speed diesels makes the job of adjusting the fuel injection pump to provide the correct fueling curve very difficult. Inevitably a compromise will have to be made and some over-fueling and therefore smoke may be evident at idle, low cruising speeds and on initial acceleration.

If the fuel pump is one which has a fuel delivery which is boost-controlled, this problem is eliminated since extra fuel will not be injected until the boost is sufficient to permit

Above *Land Rover diesel turbocharger by Allard Turbochargers gives similar performance to the petrol-engined Land Rover, but with far better economy.*

Right *Allard Turbocharging System on Massey Ferguson 590 tractor boosts power by over 20 per cent.*

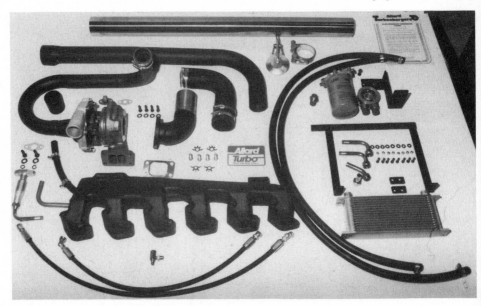

Above *John Deere Tractor 3140/3040 turbocharger kit.*

Below *Toyota Landcruiser Diesel. Although this engine produces plenty of power in naturally aspirated form—up to 30% increase in torque after turbocharging transforms its hillclimbing and pulling ability.*

Above *Turbocharger system fitted to Toyota Hi-Lux diesel. This engine responds well to turbocharging and there is ample room for easy installation.*

Below *Land Rover 2.5-litre diesel with IHI turbocharger and integral wastegate turns the Land Rover into a good workhorse and makes fifth gear a working gear rather than just for cruising.*

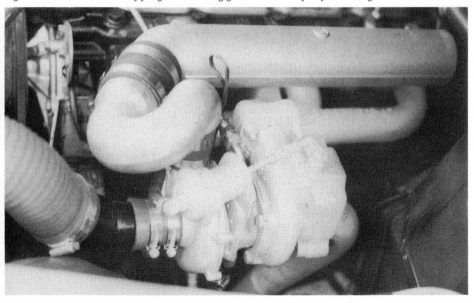

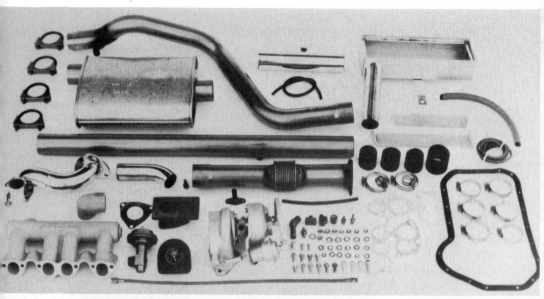

Above *Complete kit laid out for VW Golf/Rabbit diesel. The turbocharger is an IHI RHB5 with integral wastegate.*

Left *VW Golf/Rabbit diesel utilising Callaway turbocharger system; many of these systems, which can improve upon the already good economy of this engine, have been sold, particularly in America.*

smoke-free combustion.

As a rule of thumb, fueling should be increased by 10-15 per cent for a power increase of 20-30 per cent and a peak torque increase of 35-45 per cent with a 20 per cent improvement at 50 per cent of rated speed. The large power and torque increase in proportion to the increase in fuelling is brought about by the improved mechanical efficiency, specific performance and scavenging of the cylinder allowing more complete combustion.

A reasonable boost/rpm curve can be obtained with a turbocharger matched to give a maximum boost of 9-10 psi at engine rated speed, accompanied by a slight restriction in

Above *Shorrock supercharged Land Rover diesel. This was one of the first supercharger conversions carried out by the Allard Motor Company back in 1959. Vehicle went to Kenya for high altitude work.*

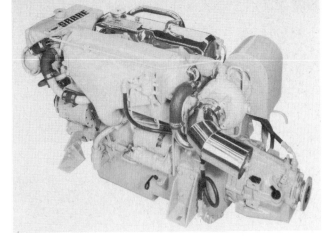

Right *The Sabre 140 marine diesel engine is a turbocharged and intercooled 4-cylinder unit intended for small high speed work boats. It develops 140 hp and weighs 1,060 lb.*

the exhaust downstream of the turbine. However, to obtain the best torque curve at low rpm, a turbocharger must be matched in such a way that it will inevitably give a dangerously high boost at engine rated speed. Such a low match turbocharger will need a wastegate to control maximum boost to safe levels, just as is the case with a petrol engine.

Many small naturally-aspirated diesels have compression ratios in the range 20-23:1. Such a high ratio does put strict limits on the power increase which can be extracted without running into reliability problems, unless measures are taken to reduce peak cylinder pressures. A compression ratio nearer 17.0:1 would be more suitable.

Exhaust gas temperatures are normally several hundred degrees lower than would be experienced with a petrol engine, so no problems arise through excessive exhaust temperature. An exhaust manifold with a small volume assists low speed boost by making better use of the exhaust pulse energy. The smaller the exhaust manifold volume, the more rapidly it is filled when each exhaust valve opens, resulting in a smaller pressure drop during the exhaust cycle, allowing an increase in energy at the turbine. To aid this process the turbocharger should be mounted centrally on the exhaust manifold. The present trend in smaller diesels is towards higher speed direct-injection engines with the probability that most of them will be turbocharged within the next few years. The Comprex pressure wave supercharger may also be an answer to low speed performance.

Larger diesels are moving towards a wider use of pressure ratios exceeding 3.0:1 with intercooling, variable geometry turbochargers and possibly hyperbar and other high pressure ratio systems.

Chapter 8

Turbocharging and supercharging for maximum power

It is intended that the information in this chapter should be of practical use and interest to the majority of those people interested in motor sporting activities, or just high performance. For this reason the majority of the information is related to turbocharging vehicles within the categories which readers are most likely to drive, and not specifically to Formula One or exotic sports racing machinery which is out of the reach of all but a handful of individuals.

Ever since the very early days of motor sport, it has been realised that the use of a pump to provide pressurised induction could produce substantially more torque and maximum power output from an engine than could be obtained from a similar capacity normally-aspirated engine. Supercharging in various forms has been used as a method of obtaining maximum power output from a given cylinder displacement.

After a gap of over 20 years Renault, with their turbocharged V6 1.5-litre engine, were the first to explore the power potential of turbocharged Formula One engines in 1975, power output at that time being over 500 bhp. To achieve this sort of power output with relatively good reliability under the most extreme conditions possible was no mean achievement. Indeed, only a couple of years previously, most so-called informed opinion would have said that this was impossible. At that time no other racing engine had come anywhere near this figure on petrol and the only engines to exceed this figure were those using alcohol or special blends of fuel. By the 1984 season all the leading contenders were using turbocharged engines producing in race trim a minimum of 700 bhp and figures of over 1,000 bhp are now being talked about for qualifying engines. This equates to over 650 bhp per litre which is a truly staggering figure.

In 1950-51 the introduction of the 1½-litre supercharged or 4½-litre unsupercharged Formula in Grand Prix racing saw the demise of the supercharged engine, as the handicap was too great and therefore unfavourable to supercharged engines. The use of 100 octane fuel did not help either. Since that time until the appearance of the Renault Formula One in 1975, no Grand Prix or single-seater racing car had been supercharged except for a handful of hillclimb cars with almost bolt-on superchargers and, of course, dragsters.

A turbo-supercharger employs a centrifugal supercharger of inherently high pumping efficiency (adiabatic efficiency) and is capable of producing over 4.0 atms with single-stage compression; with two or even three stages and intercooling, manifold pressures of well over 100 psi (6.8 atms) have been observed in tractor pulling contests, for example.

In this chapter, since we are dealing with the use of forced induction to obtain

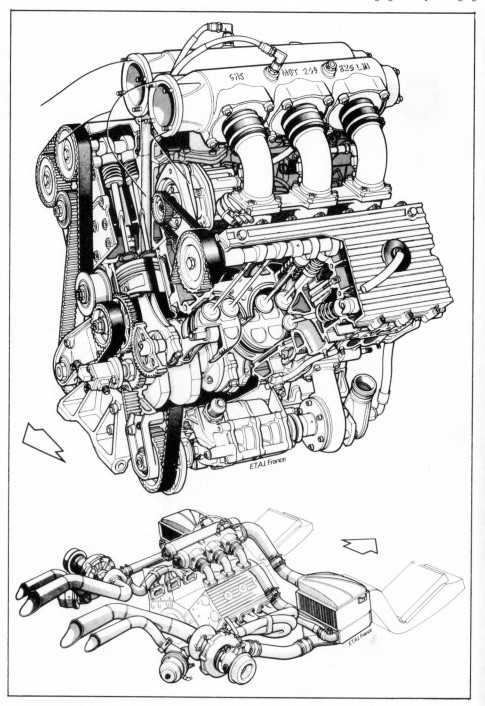

Left Fig 74: *Formula 1 Renault Gordini V6 1,500 cc engine with twin turbochargers.*

Right *Renault F1. Louis Renault having patented the idea of turbocharging way back in 1909, Renault led the way in turbocharging for F1, proving that over 500 bhp from only 1,500 cc was obtainable even when using normal pump fuel.*

Below *Ferrari Formula 1 1.5-litre V6 engine, developed to produce over 750 bhp with twin KKK turbochargers and single, separately mounted, wastegate. In this photo it is activated by pre-turbine pressure. Note also the complicated exhaust manifolding.*

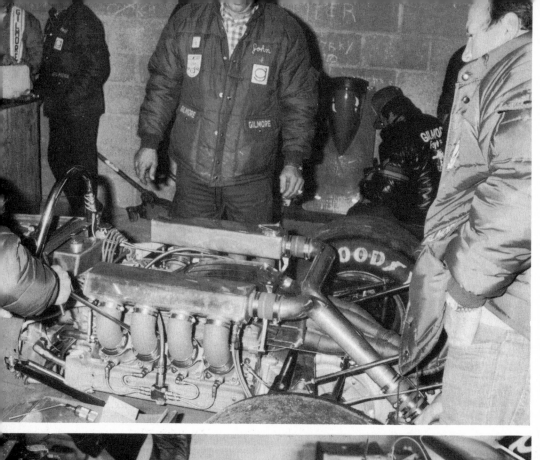

Left *Offenhauser Turbo—these 160CID (2.5-litre) 4-cylinder engines, designed exclusively for events like the Indianapolis 500, can produce over 900 bhp when running boosts of over 50 psi for qualifying.*

Below left *BMW F1 750 bhp 4-cylinder engine. The single KKK turbocharger delivers air to the inter-cooler which is mounted close to the engine inlet ports.*

Right *Hart-Toleman Formula 1 engine— developed by Brian Hart and his team. A very compact and light 4-cylinder unit with a considerable amount of further development.*

Below *Turbocharged Cosworth DFX four-cam V8 designed primarily for Indianapolis and similar races. The massive turbo sits astride the trans-axle. Has proved very successful.*

maximum power output, it is necessary to discuss the use of superchargers in sport as this has a bearing either directly or indirectly on the adoption or otherwise of forced induction by manufacturers and engineering companies. Also, because the rules governing motor sport have had such an influence on the development of supercharged engines, they must be mentioned in broad terms to give a background to a possible reason why it has taken so long for automobile engineers to look at forced induction more favourably.

In motor sport since the mid-1930s, supercharged engines have generally had some handicap factor set against them in an effort to equate them with unsupercharged engines. If the supercharged engine still remained superior then a heavier handicapping factor was introduced until the supercharged engine became uncompetitive, with the result that there was no further development of the supercharged engine for competition use. It is true in motor sport generally, and at the higher levels in particular, that the regulations have not favoured supercharged engines: not the least of these being the use of 100 octane pump fuel as opposed to methanol.

When the regulations have been less restrictive, such as in drag racing, hillclimb and sprint events, then the results obtained with supercharged engines have been much more in evidence, even though the available superchargers have often been units designed way

Left *Porsche 917 flat-12 1,100 bhp engine with twin KKK turbochargers.*

Below left *Jaguar XJ6 injection 4.2-litre turbo installation (a one-off using a Freon intercooler).*

Below *Ford 1600 BDA turbo rally engine developed and rallied by Alan Allard in 1971. Holset 3LD turbo, pressurised twin 40 DCOE carburettors, modified fuel pump to control fuel pressure; additional throttle butterfly fitted so that engine could run naturally aspirated when off boost.*

Left *Rover V8 SDI Twin Turbo system from Janspeed. As can be seen, the system is well laid out, but makes plug changing something one would not wish to do too often.*

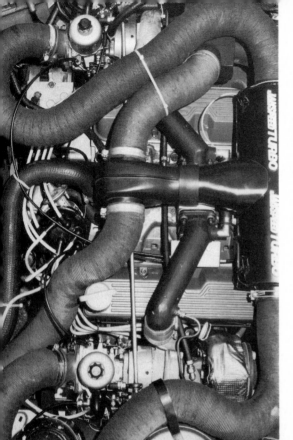

Below *Allard Turbochargers have developed a twin turbo system for the Rover V8 engine using IHI turbos. This one is designed to run on petrol at part throttle, but has a methanol injection system which comes into operation at full throttle. Power output is over 350 bhp with only 12.0 psi boost and the engine has a very wide torque band.*

Below right *Saab 16-valve 175 bhp turbocharged engine—latest development by Saab—has yet to be further boosted for competition use.*

back in the 1930s and have been bolted to engines with minimal engine development.

It is not generally realised how strong an influence the motor manufacturers have had in many classes of motor sport, particularly over the last 15 years. As an example, international rallying is now completely dominated by manufacturers' teams.

It was not until automobile manufacturers started producing supercharged or turbocharged models in sufficient numbers to be FIA approved (homologated) for a particular class, that supercharged cars were seen in international competition. Generally, many automobile engineers have been, at least until recent years, unsure of the effectiveness or suitability of forced induction for most classes of motor sport, particularly rallying. The situation has now changed dramatically since Saab made such a success with their turbocharged rally car and turned what was basically an uncompetitive engine and chassis combination into a successful competition vehicle, due entirely to the turbocharged engine. Now with others such as Audi, Porsche, Renault, Lancia, Peugeot and Colt. Turbo-supercharging has become common practice for international rallying.

With the introduction of the Group B category in international rallying, the sky appears to be the limit and costs and technical sophistication are soaring, but there is still considerable scope for further development.

Generally, many automobile engineers have been sceptical of the effectiveness of forced induction and this has no doubt been partly responsible for its delayed development. Had the rules been more favourable, thereby making it worthwhile for a company to develop a supercharged engine and prove to the world its effectiveness, we could have had turbocharged engines to the present state of development some ten years ago since the basic components were available then. The fact that Saab made such a success with their turbo production cars and turned what was basically an uncompetitive engine and chassis combination into a successful competition vehicle due entirely to the turbocharged engine, has now together with Porsche, Renault, Audi and BMW made turbocharging

Left *Allard-Wade 'roots' blower set-up on Leyland 'A' series competition engine gave tremendous torque, would pull away from almost a standstill in top gear, and also had top end power of around 155 bhp.*

Below right *AiResearch T3 turbocharged Mini with separate Rotomaster wastegate, and free flow exhaust manifold by Janspeed.*

respectable and has shown what can be done when engineers devote some of their time to forced induction. Yet there is still a great deal of potential scope for development.

From a theoretical point of view a mechanically-driven blower should be used when it is necessary to achieve maximum acceleration from a standing start, such as in drag racing or sprints, but this may not be true much longer. At the other end of the scale, when maximum full throttle power is required for more than a few seconds, then the turbo-supercharger should have a distinct advantage. For all the areas in between, the theoretical advantages and disadvantages between each type are not so distinct, at least not in road performance as opposed to thermodynamic performance. But the practical considerations are the most important in regard to the actual choice of supercharging equipment.

The question of the throttle lag is inevitably at the heart of any discussion on turbocharging. I am probably in a good position to understand this characteristic from practical experience, as well as the theory, having actually designed, built, fitted, rallied and raced many both mechanically-driven and turbocharged cars, including dragsters.

All competition vehicles, whether supercharged or not, require different driving requirements to achieve optimum results and the driver has to learn the characteristics and adapt his or her technique to achieve the best performance.

A production normally-aspirated engine has different on-the-road characteristics from those of a highly 'tuned' competition version of the same engine, and driving techniques will need to be altered to obtain optimum performance. When supercharged, the characteristics will change again and yet again when the engine is turbocharged. In each case driving technique will need to be adapted to suit.

The throttle lag effect of a turbocharged engine is best divided into two categories, which if combined can ruin the performance ability of the vehicle. The first category covers lag occasioned by poor turbo system design, including such items as incorrect match of turbo to engine, carburation, ignition timing, inlet and exhaust tract and valve timing. With correct engineering development each of these causes can be eliminated.

The second category covers the inherent lag occasioned as the turbine increases in speed from its cruising speed of say 30,000 rpm with throttle partly closed to 90,000 rpm-plus at full throttle, full boost.

The first category throttle lag, on the road, will be experienced in its worst form, as if the throttle is connected to the engine by an elastic band, so that when the throttle is depressed nothing happens for one or two seconds, then the power comes in with a surge. On closing the throttle there is a similar action in reverse. This can make the vehicle not only difficult to drive, but dangerous. As already stated, this effect can be engineered out of the system.

The second type of throttle lag need not be detrimental to performance, with the correct throttle technique, requiring a slightly earlier throttle opening when acceleration is

required and earlier lift-off when slowing for a bend to counter the slight over-run effect.

It will also be noticeable under rally conditions that, due to the lower compression pressures when the engine is running on over-run and the inertia effect, there will be less braking effect from the engine.

With a correctly-engineered production-based competition turbocharged engine, boost should show on the gauge by 2,000-2,500 rpm, although it may be at somewhat higher rpm in first and second gears, as there is insufficient load available or sufficient time for the turbine to reach the necessary speed. If we take a rpm vs boost curve with the waste-gate operating at 4,250 rpm and 12 psi boost, if the engine is running on light load at 4,250 with a vacuum reading of say 10 in hg and the throttle is then opened wide, the gauge should flick to zero and the car start to accelerate immediately and then from 0-12 psi boost should need 1.5-2.5 seconds only.

This delay before maximum power can be obtained can be largely overcome by opening the throttle sooner when accelerating out of a bend than would be the case with a normally aspirated engine. Another important factor is the fact that the turbo-supercharged engine will have a wider torque band than an unsupercharged engine of similar capacity and maximum power output, and even at half maximum boost will have at least as much torque. It is torque which gives acceleration. The increased torque also means that less gear changing is necessary. Such a smooth delivery of power can also make

Left *Turbocharged 'dragster' sand racer, based on Ford 2000 SOHC motor* (Photo courtesy David Vizard).

Right *Experimental 350 bhp Ford 2000 SOHC (Pinto) engine made the working life of the con-rods rather shorter than the manufacturer originally intended* (Photo courtesy David Vizard).

driving control easier by limiting wheel spin, particularly in slippery conditions.

When turbocharging production cars for maximum performance it is essential that the engine is treated as a supercharged engine and not as an engine with a bolt-on turbocharger or supercharger.

It should be borne in mind that the most efficient supercharged engine is one which employs the lowest maximum boost pressure to obtain the necessary power. In other words, the engine should be built to the optimum technical specification as would be the case with a naturally-aspirated high-performance engine, without resorting to the use of an excessively high boost pressure in an attempt to overcome the shortcomings of the basic engine.

With a modest boost of only 7.0 psi (1.5 pressure ratio), it is possible to obtain 140-150 bhp from most standard production single-camshaft 2.0-litre engines with a compression ratio of 7.5-8.5:1, then by using normal tuning methods such as fitting a camshaft with modest increase in lift and overlap, fitting a free flow exhaust system and increasing valve and port sizes, power outputs in the region of 185 bhp can be obtained.

The next stage is to increase boost to 12 psi and install an intercooler. In my view, every supercharging system delivering more than 10.0 psi boost should include an air-to-air intercooler. Apart from reducing the charge temperature and thereby reducing the thermal loading and any chance of detonation, the cooler charge means a denser and heavier charge and therefore more power per psi boost. With this set-up, over 220 bhp is

readily available and with excellent torque characteristics.

It is not always fully realised that, except possibly for high-speed circuit racing, torque is as important if not more important than maximum power. It is torque which gives acceleration.

From this point onwards, to obtain more power with reliability means no cutting of corners. Not only do the increased thermal stresses have to be handled, but cylinder pressures and inertia loads also. With an increase in boost to 18-20 psi and with a fully-prepared competition engine, power output could increase to 450 bhp from 2,000 cc.

Based on current techniques and using pump fuel, over 750 bhp should be attainable with a fully-developed 2.0-litre race engine employing a pressure ratio of up to 3.5.

We have seen over 125 bhp at the wheels from a supercharged 1,293 cc Leyland 'A' series engine and 175 bhp at the flywheel with a turbocharged version. The Rover 3.5-litre V8 with twin-turbo arrangement is capable of producing up to 375 bhp on pump fuel and around 450 bhp on methanol and in this form could provide a relatively cheap competition motor.

Producing a competitive engine these days is not cheap whichever route you choose to take, but turbocharging or supercharging looks increasingly attractive in terms of bhp gained for money spent.

There are several key areas which need careful attention when supercharging for maximum performance. Special attention is primarily required directly as a result of the increased thermal loading which is an inevitable result of applying air under pressure to the cylinders. Supercharging in whatever form means increased running temperature/pressure of various components. Principally these concern valves, cylinder head and pistons. There is a critical point governed by the temperature/pressure within the cylinder which will vary from engine to engine at which pre-ignition or detonation will commence and, if sustained for more than a few seconds at full engine load, failure of one or more components will result due to a rapid and uncontrollable temperature increase, unless measures are taken to stabilise the maximum sustained cylinder temperature.

The final cylinder temperature can be maintained at a safe level by a combination of various means, commencing with the temperature of the air inlet to compressor. Thereafter the higher the (adiabatic) pumping efficiency of the compressor, the lower will be the charge air temperature for a given boost. Charge air cooling is by means of an intercooler. In addition to these methods of cooling, there are the less orthodox ways such as injecting water, alcohol or a water/alcohol mixture, or the use of alcohol fuels.

Once the charge has entered the cylinder, the temperature can be kept to within tolerable limits by reducing the compression ratio and thereby the compression pressures for a given boost. Ignition timing and valve timing can also influence cylinder temperature, together with sodium-cooled valves and oil-cooled pistons. In addition, extra oil cooling and improved cooling water circulation through the cylinder head and block are important.

Steps should be taken to maintain mechanical reliability of the engine by using reinforced cylinder head gaskets, with strengthened or stepped sealing rings, or with a solid steel core. The cylinder head face and/or block face can be machined with a circular groove round each bore to accept a gas-filled or solid wire ring, usually of copper.

When supercharging with a roots-type supercharger, the pumping efficiency rapidly falls when pumping against manifold pressures above 1.7 pressure ratio (10 psi). With the vane-type supercharger it is somewhat higher, in the range 14-16 psi.

Engine cooling

Since for every pound of boost used there will be an increase in heat generated within the engine proportional to the overall efficiency of the supercharging system, it can be seen that cooling, both of the inlet charge and the engine internals, plays a very important part in the effectiveness of any supercharging system.

The cooling requirements will vary considerably according to the pressure ratio or boost used.

It has long been demonstrated that the introduction of fuel into the inlet charge has a valuable cooling effect through the latent heat of evaporation of the fuel. As an example, if we take a blower of 50 per cent adiabatic efficiency producing 7.0 psi boost with an ambient air inlet temperature of 20°C, the air after being compressed will have increased in temperature to 90°C at the supercharger outlet port, but with the addition of petrol the delivery temperature will drop by up to 25°C. If alcohol fuel is used the charge temperature drop will be considerably more, possibly to ambient or lower. The benefits of the cooler charge are twofold. Firstly, the cooler air is denser and therefore a heavier weight or mass of charge will be induced by the engine, so providing a greater quantity of fuel for combustion; and secondly, a cooler inlet charge means that the combustion chamber will be working at cooler and therefore safer and more efficient temperatures.

Often it will be found of little value to introduce the cost and complication of an intercooler when using pressures of up to 6.0 psi, since even the most efficient intercoolers cause some pressure drop through the core. However, when dealing with

Below Fig 75: *Pressurised carburettor system with intercooler and bypass pipe.*

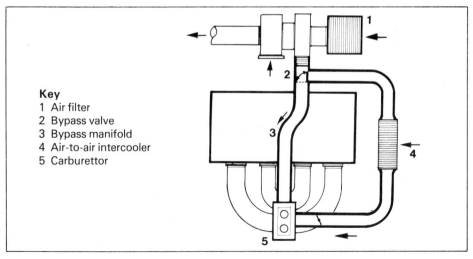

Key
1 Air filter
2 Bypass valve
3 Bypass manifold
4 Air-to-air intercooler
5 Carburettor

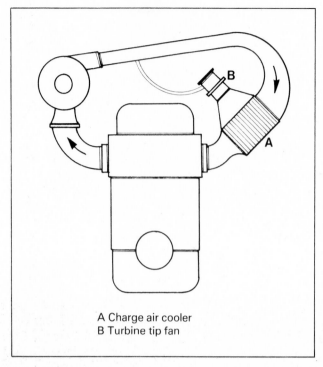

A Charge air cooler
B Turbine tip fan

Right *Even Land Rovers can fly when turbocharged and driven by Warrant Officer Les Dalton of the Army rally team.*

pressures over 6.0 psi (when using petrol), there is an increasing benefit from the use of an intercooler, even with the most efficient compressors currently available.

Generally, on current production vehicles no increase in water radiator capacity will be necessary for normal road low boost applications; however, an oil cooler with thermostat is recommended for most systems, for cooling both the oil flowing through the turbocharger and the vital components of the engine.

It is also beneficial to keep the under-bonnet temperature as low as possible by insulating the turbine housing and by ducting additional cool air through the engine bay. It is often worthwhile having a cool air pick-up for the air filter from an area outside the hot engine bay, remembering of course that a hot air pickup may be required in winter for easy starting. This can be drawn from an area above the turbine housing by adapting a heat shield to accept a trunking which feeds hot air to the carburettor.

Increased water circulation through the cylinder head may also be helpful in reducing local hotspots and the use of sodium-cooled exhaust valves will substantially reduce peak cylinder temperatures by transferring heat away from the valve head more rapidly.

Camshafts

This is a subject which has considerable potential for experimentation and development and one can only give a generalisation as to the effects an alteration in valve timing may have on a supercharged engine. All supercharged engines can perform well with what might be termed 'mild' camshafts. A camshaft which gives peak torque at the lowest engine rpm is particularly suited to a turbocharged engine, as it is easy to achieve maximum power targets, but not so easy to achieve low speed torque backup.

Generally, a 'modified' camshaft, if fitted to a supercharged engine, will have a similar effect on performance as it would if fitted to naturally-aspirated engine. Camshafts with more than 50-60° overlap will result in some blow-through of unburnt or partially burnt fuel/air mixture, causing an increase in specific fuel consumption; at the same time, however, it will contribute to a reduction in cylinder, piston and exhaust valve temperatures.

Blow-through during the valve overlap period can drop the indicated boost pressure; and with a turbocharger the cooler exhaust may slow the turbine down and so cause a loss of boost. Excessive overlap, particularly if used with nitro fuel blends, can cause the fuel to re-ignite or continue to burn in the turbine housing, with probable damage to the turbine due to the extreme heat.

As already pointed out, the power output of a supercharged/turbocharged engine can be increased by fitting a modified camshaft. Earlier opening of the inlet valve will result in an improvement in power output, by improving volumetric efficiency, which can be enhanced by increasing the duration. Theoretically, earlier opening of the exhaust valve should show a benefit throughout the rpm range by increasing the exhaust pulse energy

available to the turbine. Against this has to be balanced the fact that it may produce sufficient overlap to allow blow-through to cause a reduction in exhaust gas temperature and pressure with a corresponding diminution of the heat energy available to the turbine.

Two-stage supercharging

Two-stage supercharging involves the use of two superchargers in series. One supercharger raises the manifold pressure from ambient to, say 15 psi, which then pumps into another supercharger to raise the pressure still more and thereby improves the overall pumping efficiency above that which could be obtained by using one supercharger to obtain a similar boost.

Mercedes Benz were the first to develop two-stage supercharging for racing with their 3-litre Grand Prix cars of 1939. This engine produced 483 bhp at 2.6 atms boost, with the use of methanol fuel which was used for its effective cooling properties: without it the heating of the inlet charge would have been excessive. The methanol was in effect used as an intercooler to keep temperatures within the cylinder down to safe levels. Even with two stages of compression, roots blowers cannot be used effectively above approximately 2.6 atms, the reason being that the power consumed in driving the supercharger and the heating of the charge offsets any power gain from a further increase in boost. With the

Below left Fig 77: *Two-stage turbocharged, with intercoolers between each stage of compression. Such a system could produce a pressure ratio of over 5.0:1 (85 psi boost) with 60 per cent compressor efficiency.*

Below right Fig 78: *Two-stage supercharged, with first stage by supercharger for low and mid-range power and second stage with a turbocharger matched for maximum top end power. An intercooler is fitted between each stage. A further refinement of the system would be to include an electromagnetic clutch to disengage the supercharger at high rpm and use a bypass pipe.*

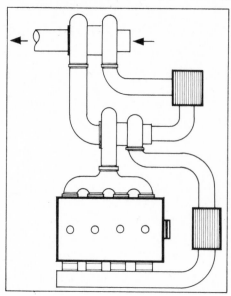
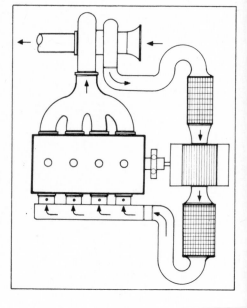

most efficient vane types it is possible to employ up to 35 psi, with a single-stage supercharger using methanol blends of fuel, and theoretically up to 50 psi (3.4 atms) with two vane-type compressors in series.

Some current turbochargers are capable of providing 4.0:1 pressure ratio in a single stage of compression with reasonable efficiency. This is equivalent to a boost pressure of 60 psi. In special events such as tractor pulling, two- or even three-stage turbo-supercharging is employed to provide boosts of over 100 psi.

Use of special fuels and additives

Water injection/steam injection—methanol (methyl alcohol CH_3OH)—Nitro—nitrous oxide. To convert a substance from a liquid to a gas by evaporation requires an input of energy. The latent heat of evaporation of a liquid is the amount of heat required to change it from a liquid to a gas at its boiling point. This figure is normally expressed in BTUs (British Thermal Units).

Water injection

The use of water injection has been practised for many years as a method of suppressing detonation. This is achieved primarily by the cooling effect brought about by the water vapourising and turning to steam. Injection of steam or water vapour has also been used with the same idea in mind. The use of water injection, therefore, can allow the use of a higher compression ratio, or the use of a lower octane fuel, or a higher boost pressure before the onset of detonation.

Fig 79: *Fuel enrichment with a solenoid valve fitted upstream of the turbocharger. The solenoid is operated by a pressure-sensitive switch fitted in the inlet manifold and is connected into the fuel line.*

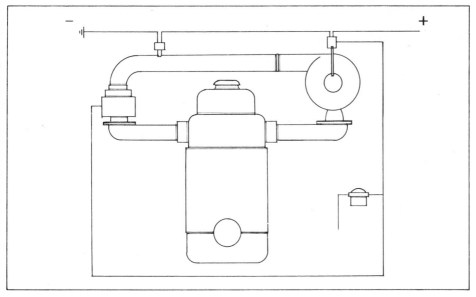

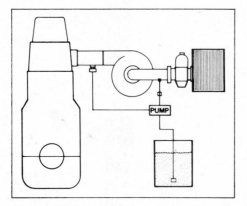 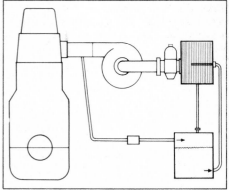

Above left Fig 80: *Water injection system with a pressure switch in the inlet manifold, which triggers an electric pump to inject water when a predetermined boost pressure is reached. A jet is fitted to the carburettor manifold. The size of the jet will depend on the engine but one in the region of .035-05-in is usually adequate.*

Above right Fig 81: *In this water injection system boost pressure is used to pressurise the water tank, from where the water is fed into the mouth of the carburettor. A one-way valve in the line between tank and inlet manifold prevents water being drawn from the tank when a vacuum exists in the inlet manifold.*

As methanol is hygroscopic and completely miscible with water, methanol is often added to water to increase the volatility of the mixture and its cooling capacity. It is also useful as an anti-freeze.

It has been found that adding greater than 50 per cent methanol to water gives no further power increase. Although the injection of water and water/alcohol mixtures have been demonstrated to work on many applications, the system must be tailored to match the requirements of each engine to obtain satisfactory results. There are various ways in which the water injection system can be operated and there are several American kits on the market. The most sophisticated incorporate an electronic monitoring system to measure engine rpm and load and calculate the exact amount of fluid injection required for optimum performance and economy. I have included diagrams of some simple systems.

There are sometimes additional benefits. It is possible to obtain some improvement in fuel consumption by allowing a slightly leaner mixture, particularly under load and if the use of water injection makes it safe to use a higher basic compression ratio; this in itself will improve the thermal efficiency of the engine with a corresponding fuel consumption improvement. Also, engines running with water injection will be purged of any carbon deposits in the combustion chamber.

So what are the drawbacks?

Well, the water tank will need frequent topping up, as average consumption will be from half to one gallon for every 250 miles.

Anti-freeze additives, such as methylated spirits, are required and too much water injection (which results in a residue being left in the cylinder after the engine is turned off) can cause internal corrosion.

Right *Volvo Rallycross car engine bay. Won the 1980 European Rallycross championship driven by Per Inge Walfridsson. Note massive intercooler across front of engine bay* (Volvo).

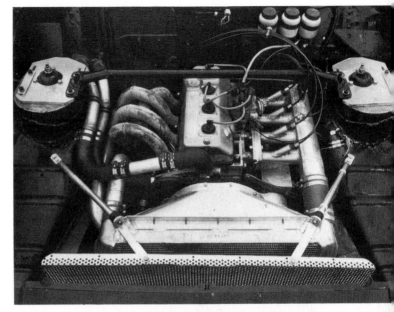

Below *An experimental turbocharged Chevette 2.3-litre twin cam 16-valve engine by Bill Blydenstein, now fitted to a drag racer, competition altered.*

The water can be injected before or after the supercharger or turbocharger. Injecting before the supercharger inlet port is the easiest method as a high pressure pump is not required. However, although tests with superchargers appear to show that it is best to inject water—or, indeed, fuel—before the supercharger, with turbochargers the injection of water or other additives *after* the compressor (where it cannot be subjected to any centrifugal effect and where the temperature of the ingoing charge is at its highest point) may be the optimum position.

Tests with water injection into diesels have also shown some benefits with a useful improvement in fuel consumption.

Methanol (Methyl alcohol, CH_3OH)

The great advantage of using methanol as fuel, particularly in a supercharged engine with its inherently higher cylinder temperatures, lies in its high latent heat of evaporation and

Above right *An historic photo. 3,000-plus bhp unleashed in an epic duel between Tommy Ivo and Don Garlits. One of the first appearances of American supercharged dragsters this side of the Atlantic, at the first drag festival in 1964.*

Right *Allard Dragster, showing front-mounted GMC supercharger with Hilborn twin port fuel injection. Dragsters nowadays mount blower and fuel injection on top of engine, as this gives more power with heavy fuel loads.*

Below *The second Allard Dragster which held the official standing quarter mile world record in 1967, with a two-way average of 9.3 seconds, driven by Alan Allard. At that time the fastest dragsters in the USA were down to times of around 7.8 seconds, but they had not attempted to establish an officially observed record. This machine was subsequently driven by Clive Skilton and fitted with top mounted 'roots' blower as shown in this photo.*

the fact that a much richer mixture and thus a greater mass can be burnt in the cylinder than with petrol. A gallon of methanol has less than half the energy contained in a gallon of petrol, so it is necessary for the engine to use more than twice the amount when running on methanol. For maximum power output the air/fuel ratio should be around 6.5:1 and even richer mixtures can be tolerated under full throttle supercharged conditions (the excess unburnt fuel being used as a cooling agent).

When rejetting from petrol settings to run on straight methanol, approximately double the fuel flow is required. To double the flow the jet area will have to be increased by 40 per cent, but settings should err on the rich side, as lean mixtures with methanol can lead to pre-ignition. This can happen because a lean mixture means that the fuel burns more slowly, allowing the valves and cylinder to be overheated, so that when the next fresh charge enters the cylinder, it is pre-ignited by the hot residual gases and valves, thereby starting a chain reaction with possible engine damage.

As alcohol burns more slowly than petrol, more ignition advance will be required: up to

15° in some cases. Because of the increased advance, the rich mixture and the over-cooling effect which can be experienced before the engine has had time to warm up, the ignition system must be in top condition, or starting may be a problem—particularly on a cool day. Under these conditions a simple system to inject a small quantity of petrol could be arranged to aid starting or additives, such as benzine and acetone, can be mixed in small percentages with methanol.

It is possible to run the same engine with a compression ratio of two, or possibly as much as four, ratios higher when using straight methanol as opposed to petrol. Normally in a supercharged engine, higher boost pressures would be employed to achieve a similar effect. As much as 30 per cent increase in power can be gained on the least efficient engines, when compared with the power output, when running on petrol, but an average figure should be from 10-15 per cent. It is not necessary to use castor-based oils; normal engine oil is quite satisfactory, but frequent oil changes are necessary as some of the fuel tends to find its way past the rings to mix with the sump oil, particularly in an engine with racing piston to bore clearances.

A mixture of methanol and nitro methane, sometimes with other additive(s) to aid starting, is regularly used by all the fastest dragsters and drag bike boys. Nitromethane, when ignited, produces a large quantity of oxygen and can increase power output roughly in proportion to the percentage of nitro used, but it must be used with great care as it causes a big increase in cylinder temperatures and a little too much 'tipping of the can' can turn an engine into a load of scrap iron.

Nitrous oxide (N_2O)

The use of nitrous oxide for an engine power boost dates back to the Second World War when it was used in many British and German aircraft as a means of maintaining power output with an increase in altitude. However, it was not until drag racing had become highly competitive in the USA that N_2O injection systems began to be experimented with by a few competitors hoping to gain an edge over the opposition. In the last few years N_2O systems have been widely used in the States, but very little in Europe.

Nitrous oxide is strictly not a 'fuel', as an engine will not actually run on nitrous oxide alone, since it will not burn on its own without the additional 'real' fuel. Nitrous oxide separates into its components of oxygen and nitrogen when heated to approximately 572°F, and the liberated oxygen will then burn with the 'real' fuel to produce more power. At the same time (because of the high latent heat of evaporation of the liquid N_2O), the charge temperature is lowered, thus providing a substantial intercooling effect.

Top left *Rear-engined dragster fueler competing at Santa Pod. Engine is a Chrysler Hemi supercharged and fuel injected. With full nitro load, 1,500 plus bhp can be expected to hurl this machine to over 200 mph in around 6.5 seconds* (Roger Gorringe).

Above left *Competition altered Panic: the familiar 6-71 blower on top of the big V8 provides instant get up and go* (Roger Gorringe).

Left *Funny Car, really a dragster fitted with a fully enveloping glass fibre body. The injector scoop mounted on top of the GMC 6-71 supercharger can be seen protruding through the bodywork* (Roger Gorringe).

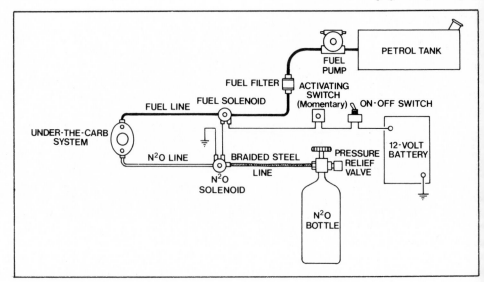

Fig 82: *Nitrous-Oxide injection system.*

An important point from the cooling aspect is that, whilst this process is in progress, the temperature of the substance remains the same, -129°F in this case. So it can be seen that the intercooling effect of N_2O injection is considerable.

N_2O can be injected as a gas to combine with fuel as an oxygen-enrichening agent, but it loses its cooling effect by so doing, in contrast to its injection as a liquid. It should be remembered, too, that because of its low boiling point at -129°F, in addition to its latent heat vapourisation cooling effect, heat will be absorbed as it mixes with the inlet charge at a much higher temperature in the cylinder.

N_2O can be injected either before the carburettor or after but, if it is allowed to vaporise before entering the cylinder, although it will considerably lower the inlet charge temperature, the increased quantity of oxygen thus released will cause a very lean air/fuel ratio with the strong possibility of overheating. This is why all current N_2O injection systems add a carefully metered amount of additional fuel with the N_2O to avoid a lean air-to-fuel situation. With exhaustive testing, it has been determined that between 4.5-5.0 lb/min of pressurised N_2O for 100 bhp increase is the optimum figure and correspondingly 2.2-2.5 lb/min will give a 50 bhp increase, the percentage power increase being almost linear, and being limited largely by the mechanical strength of the engine.

Other tests have demonstrated that N_2O increases the knock (or detonation) limit of an engine and that spark timing can be retarded as the percentage of N_2O injected is increased.

A typical nitrous oxide injection system includes the following components: a high pressure bottle for N_2O liquid with mounting brackets; carburettor adaptor plate; solenoid valve; high pressure hoses; steel feed pipes with nozzles; electric switches and fittings.

Intercooling

Intercooling, aftercooling or charge air cooling are all terms used to describe the method of cooling the air inlet charge to an engine by installing a heat exchanger in the inlet manifolding between the compressor discharge and the engine.

Readers who have progressed this far through the book will, I am sure, have noted how temperature plays such an important part in any supercharged engine, whether it be air inlet temperature, cylinder temperature or exhaust gas temperatures.

The use of an intercooler is important for two reasons. In the first place an intercooler, by cooling the charge air, increases the density of the charge and therefore its mass flow into the engine. The greater mass flow of air allows a greater quantity of fuel/air mixture to be converted to power.

Secondly, and by no means of lesser importance, it reduces the thermal loading on an engine for given boost and power output. The reason for this is that, for every degree drop in temperature of the inlet charge, there is a roughly similar drop on the exhaust side, which contributes to a reduction in thermal loading on valves and pistons and reduces the amount of heat which has to be dissipated by the engine.

An intercooler is a heat exchanger very similar to a car radiator in principle, but construction is somewhat different in that the core through which the charge air flows must offer as little restriction as possible. At the same time it must present the maximum

Below left *Renault 18 Turbo. The intercooler incorporates an air temperature-controlled valve so that the intercooler can be bypassed when the temperature is low. It is also very light, weighing less than 6 lb.*

Below right *Porsche Turbo 3.3-litre engine with KKK turbocharger and massive wastegate with separate exhaust pipe to silencer. Air-to-air intercooler is mounted above engine cooling fan* (Photo courtesy Porsche).

Left *Rover V8 twin IHI turbo charged using pressurised SU car burettors.*

Right *IHI RHB51 915 cc turbo charged Imp of Ian Fidoe.*

surface contact area with the cooling medium.

Intercoolers are usually of the air-to-charge air, or water-to-air variety, the cooling medium being ambient air or engine jacket water, or sea water in the case of marine applications.

Generally there is a greater difference in temperature between the ambient air and charge air than there is between engine jacket coolant and charge air. A greater difference in temperature between the air in the intercooler and the cooling medium allows the intercooler to be more thermally effective and for this reason the air-to-air type is normally adopted for high performance petrol engine applications, although it will be more bulky than an air-to-water system.

It is perfectly possible to use alcohol, iced water, or various other liquids as the cooling medium and, indeed, this has often been the practice for short duration racing and record attempts. For certain classes of motor racing this might prove attractive although, where the rules allow, the use of alcohol as the fuel is generally an easier alternative than installing an intercooler for short duration events such as drag racing, sprints and hillclimbs.

If we take as an example an engine with a maximum boost of 12.0 psi (1.8 pressure ratio), compressor efficiency of 65 per cent and an ambient air temperature of 20°C, the compressed air discharge temperature will be approximately 130°C after passing through the turbocharger.

If we then fit a 70 per cent efficient intercooler, the temperature of the air entering the engine will have been reduced to 53°C.

This is calculated as follows: discharge temperature minus ambient air temperature

times intercooler efficiency equals temperature drop. So, if 130°C - 20°C × .70 = 77°C, then the temperature of the air entering the engine is 130°C - 77°C = 53°C.

The 77°C reduction in charge temperature can be calculated to give an increase in density ratio of 1.09, but allowance has to be made for the loss of some boost pressure through the restricting effect of the narrow passages of the intercooler core. In this case it will probably be about 1.0 psi, which equates to a loss in density ratio of 0.05. The actual effective density ratio increase is therefore only 0.004, which would give an additional four per cent power increase at the flywheel.

This serves to illustrate the point made earlier that approximately 1.5 pressure ratio is the lower limit of boost that would make the fitting of an intercooler worthwhile, although it must be realised that, even though the power increase may not be substantial, there is still an additional benefit from the reduction in thermal loading on the engine due to the lower inlet charge temperature. At the other end of the scale, where pressure ratios of over 2.5 are used, an intercooler is essential and power increases are considerable. Some figures show a gain of as much as 1 bhp increase for 1.0°C temperature drop.

Usually, intercooler efficiency will be in the range of 60-70 per cent and it will also cause some restriction to the flow of air, resulting in a small but significant pressure drop across the core which will vary with the size and design of the system. This loss in pressure has to be balanced against the benefits of an increase in air density due to a decrease in charge air temperature. The pressure drop and the degree of effectiveness, combined with the complication of an intercooling system, is sufficient to make the installation of such a system impractical with boost pressure ratios of less than approximately 1.5.

The fuel octane requirement of a supercharged engine is crucial to peak engine performance. The use of an intercooler, by reducing cylinder temperatures, allows the use of fuel with a lower octane rating, or a higher compression ratio, with fuel of the same octane number. It also allows the use of a higher compression ratio and increased ignition advance, which can improve thermal efficiency and specific fuel consumption.

As far as competition engines are concerned, intercooling allows an increase in super-charge pressure ratio without exceeding the thermal design limits of the engine. It is possible to link two or even three turbochargers in series to give two or three stages of compression respectively and reach manifold pressures in excess of 100 psig. But to do so, heat exchangers are required between each stage of compression and between compressor and engine.

It is normally considered impractical and possibly hazardous to employ a wet compressor arrangement, which would mean pumping an air/fuel mixture through an intercooler. The cooling process clearly presents wet fuel handling problems, particularly at low engine speeds, and a backfire could cause an explosion in the intercooler. However, with some form of intercooler bypass at low engine speeds, when the intercooler can be more of a liability than an asset, it might be possible to largely eliminate these problems.

'Y' Table

For calculation of air temperature rise through a compressor for a given pressure ratio.
   r = pressure ratio, $Y = r.283 - 1$

r	Y						
		1.6	.142	2.1	.234	2.6	.311
1.2	.053	1.7	.162	2.2	.250	2.7	.325
1.3	.077	1.8	.181	2.3	.266	2.8	.338
1.4	.100	1.9	.199	2.4	.281	2.9	.352
1.5	.121	2.0	.217	2.5	.296	3.0	.365

Intercooler calculations:
   The formula to calculate the temperature rise at 100 per cent efficiency is:

$$T2 = T1 \times \left(\frac{P2}{P1}\right) \times .283$$

where T1 = inlet temperature (°R); T2 = outlet temperature (°R); P1 = inlet pressure absolute (ABS); P2 = outlet pressure absolute (ABS); °R = °F + 460.

The actual temperature rise determined from this formula would need to be divided by the actual adiabatic efficiency of the compressor as actual temperature rise

$$= \frac{\text{ideal temperature rise}}{\text{adiabatic efficiency}}$$

However, by using the 'Y' table shown above the calculations are much simplified.

Example

To determine temperature rise with air inlet at a temperature of 65°F, pressure ratio 2.0 and compressor efficiency (N_C) 65 per cent:

From 'Y' table r = 2.0 and Y = .217.
Ideal temperature rise (100 per cent efficiency) =

$$\Delta \text{T ideal} = (\text{inlet temperature } °R) \times Y$$
$$= (460° + 65°) \times .217$$
$$= 113.9°$$

Actual temperature rise =

$$\Delta \text{T actual} = \frac{\text{ideal temperature rise}}{\text{compressor efficiency}}$$
$$= \frac{113.9}{.65}$$
$$= 175.3°F$$

Compressor discharge temperature =
Inlet temperature + actual temperature rise

$$= 65° + 175.3°F$$
$$= 240.3°F$$

If a 70 per cent effective air-to-air intercooler (heat exchanger) is installed between the compressor and engine it will lower the charge temperature.
Reduction in charge air temperature =

$$\text{Outlet temperature - inlet temperature} \times .70 =$$
$$(240°F - 65°F) \times .70 = 175 \times .7 = 122°F$$

Temperature now entering engine will be 240°F – 122°F = 118°F

Therefore, with an engine turbocharged at a maximum of 15.0 psi (2.0 PR), 30 in Hg gauge and 30 in Hg barometer, ambient inlet air at 65°F, compressor efficiency 65 per cent and compressor discharge temperature of 240.3°F: to calculate increase in air density and therefore increase in power output with intercooler:

$$= \frac{\text{Compressor outlet absolute pressure}}{\text{Compressor inlet absolute pressure}}$$

There will usually be some loss of boost (pressure drop) through an intercooler. In this case the drop is assumed to be 2 in Hg.
The increase in air density will be as follows:

$$\frac{240 + 460}{118 + 460} \times \frac{30 + 28}{30 + 30} = \frac{700}{578} \times \frac{58}{60} = 1.10$$

It can be seen, therefore, that the increase in air density due to fitting an intercooler can increase engine power output by ten per cent for a temperature reduction of 122°F.

Motor cycles

The fitting of a turbocharger or supercharger to a motor cycle must be considered as seeking maximum performance from a small capacity engine and therefore I have included it in this particular chapter, although if space permitted, a full chapter could have been allocated to this subject alone.

The supercharging of motor cycles has (at least in Europe) been largely confined to the use of positive-displacement types and the Shorrock vane-type in particular, but recently some of the larger machines have been turbocharged.

The Shorrock supercharger has been fitted to many sprinting machines with great success. The Shorrock C75B is suitable for fitting to machines with engine capacities ranging from 500-850 cc and the larger C142B unit for 750-1200 cc engines.

Although the adiabatic pumping efficiency of the vane-type supercharger with eccentric rotor can be comparatively high, in the range of 65-70 per cent with boost pressures of over 1 atm, due to the internal compression within the supercharger, the effect of the characteristic eccentricity of the rotor is to impart an oscillating motion and an out balance force to the rotating assembly, which increases at the square of the speed of rotation. As a consequence the maximum rpm of the Shorrock C75B and C142B should not exceed 7,500 and 6,500 respectively, if reasonable life is to be maintained. Some tuners have, however, managed to exceed these figures substantially with reasonable reliability in between careful rebuilds.

Left *Turbocharged Kawasaki 1000 by Blake Enterprises. This well-engineered system turns a fast machine into one with rocket-like performance with a power-to-weight ratio equivalent to current Formula 1 Grand Prix cars.*

Right *Another turbocharged bike —this Suzuki by Blake Enterprises uses a Rajay turbocharger with Blake wastegate and carburation system.*

The smaller roots-type blowers can be used equally successfully and although their overall pumping efficiency is less than for the vane type, this can be partly compensated for as the roots blower has the advantages of being in balance and having comparatively low mechanical friction. In consequence, very high rpm can be used at the expense of high charge outlet temperatures.

Lubrication of the roots types should present no problem, the oil being contained in chambers at either end of the supercharger casing and requiring to be topped up from time to time to approximately the quarter full level in each chamber. For motor cycle applications, the Shorrock can be adapted to use a gravity-fed total loss drip feed system, with a consumption rate of half a pint for 500-750 miles.

The best type of drive system for either type of supercharger is by means of a Powergrip rubber-toothed belt with dural-toothed pulleys mounted on steel adaptor hubs. The Shorrock unit in particular is rather susceptible to drive shock loadings which can cause the rotor drive shaft to shear off. Therefore, some form of shock-absorbing device should be incorporated in the system, such as an outrigger drive shaft, resilient coupling or spring-loaded belt tensioner. This is very beneficial in reducing drive shaft failure. In case of backfires in the inlet manifold causing damage to the supercharger, a simple backfire gas release valve or valves should be incorporated in the inlet tract as close to the inlet ports as feasible.

Inlet manifold design needs careful attention when supercharging small-capacity

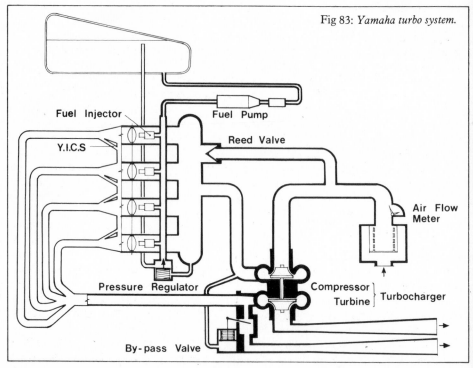

Fig 83: *Yamaha turbo system.*

Fuel Injector

Fuel Pump

Y.I.C.S

Reed Valve

Air Flow Meter

Pressure Regulator

Compressor ⎤
Turbine ⎦ Turbocharger

By-pass Valve

engines, particularly single- and twin-cylinder types, which have uneven valve opening periods. The resultant pulsation effect in the inlet tract can, if not smoothed out, have a choking effect and limit the maximum power potential of the engine. In order to avoid this, the capacity of the inlet tract should be between two and three times the volume of one cylinder. The object of this is to smooth out the inlet charge pulsation. Turbochargers and vane-type superchargers have an air delivery which is almost constant. Roots types have a pulsating-type delivery and therefore the inlet tract volume can be even more critical.

A large valve overlap can cause a considerable drop in maximum boost and power by allowing a substantial percentage of unburnt charge to be blown right through the cylinder. Fuel consumption will suffer too. However, if the effect is to lower the overall cylinder temperature, the power loss can be offset, so that it is possible to have a lower boost with lower and safer cylinder temperatures, but still achieve the same peak power output. Therefore, for maximum power, valve timing which allows a good boost together with enough overlap to reduce cylinder temperature will give the best results.

A similar approach can be applied to turbo-superchargers, but since turbine speed is governed (together with other factors) by exhaust gas temperature, the reduction in this temperature is much more critical and will not only reduce turbine speed and therefore maximum boost for a given rpm, but also increase throttle lag.

In addition, it is possible to have raw fuel burning inside the turbine housing, which can cause excessive temperatures and damage the turbine blades. Fuel laced with a large percentage of 'nitro' can have this effect too.

The usual way to overcome loss of boost at a given rpm would be to fit a turbine housing with a small A/R ratio to increase turbine speed for a given mass exhaust flow. This may not always be possible as generally the motor cycle engine, with a capacity of between 500-1,000 cc, will already be using the smallest A/R ratio housing available.

Lubrication for the mechanically-driven supercharger should present no problem and full details are given earlier. The turbocharger, on the other hand, can present some problems. Although the actual oil consumption of a turbo is insignificant, the volume required to cool and lubricate the bearing is quite substantial—sufficient in some cases to reduce oil pressure to a critical level. Oil pressure and temperature gauges should, therefore, be installed. A minimum of 25 psi oil pressure under load is essential.

To cure the oil pressure problem, the oil pump and sump capacities may need to be increased, or a separate oil tank and scavenge pump fitted. This facility is *essential* when turbocharging a two-stroke engine.

Two-stroke engines have been successfully supercharged, but supercharging as opposed to scavenging to clear out residual exhaust gases is only possible on the Uniflow two-stroke. Two-strokes of the loop or crank scavenger type have symmetrical timing, which means that the exhaust port opens before and closes after the inlet, so that no supercharger pressure can be held in the cylinder. Two-stroke engines of the Uniflow design can be supercharged as the port opening can be arranged so that the inlet port stays open for a short period after the exhaust port closes, so allowing the supercharger pressure to be induced and held in the cylinder.

It should be noted that, because a two-stroke has one power stroke for every revolution, it requires approximately twice as much air as an equivalent-capacity four-stroke engine.

Another important factor to remember when supercharging a two-stroke is the necessity of having a percentage of oil mixed with the fuel. As oil when mixed with fuel has the effect of lowering the fuel octane rating, it can be seen that this can lead to detonation problems.

Although two-stroke engines have been supercharged only to a limited extent in comparison with four-strokes, their potential power output should be similar to that of the four-stroke engine.

Having given some rather dry technical information, I am sure readers would be interested in details of one or two examples of turbocharged and supercharged bikes.

It seems as if several of the Japanese motor cycle manufacturers will shortly be competing with turbocharged machines, at least on the road, if not on the track. Yamaha have released details of their new turbo system which is designed specifically to give both high performance and low fuel consumption. An interesting feature of the system is the reed valve which is fitted in a bypass between air filter and compressor inlet. This is fitted to overcome the effect of any turbo lag when suddenly opening the throttle. The reed valve opens at any time the pressure is lower on the inlet manifold side of the valve than it is on the air filter side and in doing so bypasses the compressor. The system also includes a wastegate valve, actuated by inlet manifold pressure, and electronic fuel injection with fuel pressure controlled by boost pressure.

The Dealer: *Wade-supercharged 1,200 cc Kawasaki drag racing bike.*

There have been many spectacular and technically interesting supercharged drag bikes, from the days of George Brown with *Super Nero* and Maurice Brierley with *Methamon* to John Hobbs with his twin 1,200 cc Weslake-engined Shorrock supercharged *Hobbit*, who achieved a best elapsed time for the standing start quarter mile of 8.27 seconds with a terminal speed of 187 mph.

Of more recent time, the Wade 4RO20 supercharged 1,200 cc Kawasaki of Pat O'Neal is a classic example of a drag race bike and I have therefore included a technical specification of this machine.

The Dealer—built and ridden by Pat O'Neal. Supercharged Kawasaki 1,200 DOHC 4-cylinder.

The motor is bored to 1,198 cc and fitted with 6:1 forged pistons in an MTC super block. Head ported by Phil Manzano. Valves stainless steel. 37 mm inlets, 34 mm exhausts. Camshafts by Kenny Harman with lift of .470 in. Timing 35°-65° 60°-35°. Exhausts are 1¾-in bore, stainless steel, 22-in long angled up at 50° to give about 20 lb down thrust at 11,000 rpm.

The crankshaft has a splined output shaft which drives an 11-in Crowerglide clutch set to engage at 4,000 rpm. Primary drive is via 3½-in wide toothed belt as used on supercharged dragsters. The clutch drives a two-speed Cadillac overdrive in a special housing. The box is charged by nitrogen at 170 psi with a handlebar lever. Gear ratios work out at 158 and 187 mph. The front wheel uses a 325 x 18 Goodyear slick. The back wheel is of three-piece magnesium design and 10 in wide. Rear tyre is a 12.50 x 15 Goodyear slick.

Supercharger installation: Wade 4RO20 with deep notch ball bearings on drive side. It is driven at engine speed through a 30 mm x 8 mm toothed belt. The steel-shafted rotors are solid and double pinned. Clearances, rotor to case (radial), .018 in; rotor to end cover,

.004 in; rotor to rotor mesh clearance, .004 in. The rotors have PTFE sealing inserts. These raise boost from 17-20 psi at 11,000 rpm.

Carburettor is an early design of SU which has been reworked to give a bore of 2½ in and set up to handle 60 per cent nitro, 5 per cent polypropolene, 35 per cent methanol mixture. Bike uses three gallons for one mile. Needle lifts right out of .140-in jet at full throttle. A Hilborn gear pump provides up to 60 psi fuel pressure at 11,000 rpm. 20 per cent of the fuel is injected directly into the inlet ports to cure mixture bias.

To date Pat has covered the standing quarter mile in a time of 8.75 seconds with a terminal speed of 168 mph. I believe the fastest recorded bike time by anyone is around 8.0 seconds, so this target may well be within reach.

Marine applications

Matching of a turbocharger to a marine engine is somewhat different to the matching requirements for a road-going car. Usually a marine engine requires maximum power to coincide with maximum compressor efficiency, rather than matching to obtain peak torque at relatively low rpm and allowing some fall in compressor efficiency as maximum engine speed is reached. The marine engine-matching requirement is similar, in fact, to the requirements for a racing car engine, so a compressor and turbine of higher flow capacity will be necessary, unless the turbocharger is required to enable the boat to reach the hull planing speed. In this case a lower match turbocharger may be required and a wastegate fitted. Boost in a marine turbo system is often controlled by an internal drilling in the turbine housing which bypasses some exhaust gas all the time that the engine is running.

Most systems employ raw water-to-air heat exchangers, and obtain engine cooling through water jacketing of exhaust manifolds and turbine housing.

Gale Banks is one of the leading marine turbocharging exponents in the USA and produces some very professionally engineered turbocharged engine packages, mostly based on the Chevrolet V8 petrol engine assembly.

Sabre Marine can perhaps be described as the UK equivalent, although their turbocharging systems are based on the Ford 360 and 140 diesel engines. Sabre Engines kindly sent detailed information and photographs and so I have included a technical specification in addition to photographs of their turbocharged marine diesel engines.

Offshore powerboat racing provides the conditions where no horsepower rating is too extreme and where much experience is gained by operating engines beyond normal limits. The rules governing powerboat racing allow diesel engines to have twice the displacement of petrol engines. One might therefore have imagined that, bearing in mind the gruelling nature of this sport, diesel engines with their superior reliability would be able to overcome their weight and power disadvantage. However, this was not possible until Sabre Marine developed their two-stage turbocharged 420 diesel engine based on the Ford Dorset cylinder assembly. This engine in its latest form produces 420 HP at 2,400 rpm with a BMEP of over 400 psi at maximum torque.

The turbocharger system and engine specification is as follows: displacement 6.22 litres. Piston temperature is controlled by directing a jet of oil at the underside of the piston crown. At full speed each piston receives about 1.5 GPM of oil. The standard camshaft with minimal overlap is retained. Fuel injection is by CAV HD Minimex

Left *The highly developed Sabre 420 diesel engine uses two-stage turbocharging, intercooling and aftercooling to give an output of 420 hp from 6 litres displacement* (Photo provided by Sabre Marine).

Right *View of* Romans Sabre *with engine hatches removed.*

Below Romans Sabre *at 60 knots. This 33-ft aluminium catamaran is fitted with twin Sabre 420 engines.*

injection pump.

To reach the new level of power output a compressor pressure ratio as high as 5:1 was found to be necessary. Two-stage turbocharging was adopted, as a single-stage turbocharger capable of producing such a high pressure was not readily available. A Holset 4LGK turbocharger supplies the first stage of compression, raising the pressure to 2:1 pressure ratio, and a smaller 3FJ Holset unit provides the second stage of compression. By employing two stages of compression each turbocharger is able to operate at peak efficiency. Both an intercooler mounted between the compressors and an aftercooler are necessary to reduce air temperature as much as possible. At full boost the air temperature is kept as low as 24°C by using raw water at a temperature of 12°C. Both the exhaust manifold and the duct connecting the turbine housings are water cooled.

To bring the cylinder firing pressure down to a level at which the bearings and cylinder head gasket will survive, the compression ratio has been reduced to 11:1. Such a low ratio in a compression ignition engine is bound to affect cold starting adversely, so a small hand pump is used to inject a spray of air and ignition fluid to start the engine. Another problem aggravated by the very high pitched propellers and fixed gear ratio combined with extreme hull design, was the inability to generate enough power at very low engine

Marinised Gale Banks motor, beautifully turned out, with twin turbochargers, intercooler and single Holley carburettor, cranks out 850 bhp.

speed to drive the boat 'over the hump' and up to planing speeds.

Earlier engines had used additional oxygen injection for a very short period to produce the extra low speed torque required. However, with this more powerful version a less potentially engine-damaging method was deemed necessary. So Sabre chose a steel powder coupling system. In this design the powder partly fills a chamber in the flywheel, together with a wavy-edged rotor which transmits the drive through to the propeller. At low rotational speeds the rotor is able to slip, but at higher speeds the centrifugal force acting on the powder locks the rotor to the flywheel, thereby transmitting the drive. It was also found necessary to be able to lock the drive at low speed in order to allow the engine to reach working temperature. This was achieved by incorporating a lock-up clutch in the drive line.

The photographs accompanying this section show the Sabre 420 engines installed in *Romans Sabre*, an aluminium catamaran designed by James Beard of Cougar Marine and built by S.P. Metal Hulls. It is 33 ft long and 11 ft 8 in wide. In the 1980 season, *Romans Sabre* won the European Class 2 Championship and the British Championship for Classes 1 and 2.

Chapter 9

Rally and Competition cars 1969-1986

As outlined in the beginnings of supercharging in Chapter 1 of this book, there have been many and varied examples of supercharged and turbo-supercharged competition cars since the early part of this century. This chapter, however, deals with some of the most interesting examples in the years between 1969 and 1986.

BMW

The BMW 2002 TI Turbo first appeared in 1969 and could be said to be the first of the new generation of supercharged (turbo-supercharged) vehicles to be produced by manufacturers or manufacturer-supported teams since 1950, with the demise of the supercharged Grand Prix cars. The BMW 2002 Turbo was designed to win the European Saloon Car Racing Championship which it did for BMW in 1970.

Porsche 917

Porsche developed this machine for the Can-Am Sports Car Championship in the USA. The 917, with 2.1 litres and 510 bhp, first raced in 1973 and convincingly won all the Championship races, hitherto the preserve of the big V8 engines. Ultimately the Can-Am Porsches were fitted with 1,100 bhp turbocharged flat-12 engines which completely eliminated all opposition, until a change in the regulations banished these exotic machines.

These potent cars could accelerate from 0-100 mph in about 3.0 seconds and reach 200 mph in under 12 seconds, and probably had about the same power-to-weight ratio as the most highly boosted, qualifying engines in the 1986 Formula 1 Grand Prix cars.

Renault

With the start of the 1975 season, Renault unveiled their then-revolutionary turbocharged 1,500 cc V6 Formula 1 engine into the world of the all-conquering Ford Cosworth 3.0-litre V8. At the time most so-called expert opinion thought Renault were wasting their time trying to beat the unturbocharged 3-litre V8 engines with their tiny 1.5-litre turbo V6. Turbocharging or supercharging using pump fuels was considered impractical, as it was thought that turbocharged engines of this capacity would require such high boost pressures in order to produce a competitive power output of around 450-500 bhp that they would result in intolerably high internal engine temperatures. The so-called turbo lag problem would at the same time mean that turbo engines in F1 would require even more power to overcome lack of acceleration in response to initial throttle opening. In practice this was not

Above *The most powerful circuit racing car ever, the Porsche 917/30, with 1,100 bhp from its turbocharged 12-cylinder 5.4-litre engine.*

Above right *Renault 5 Maxi Turbo—shown here winning the Tour De Corse (Corsica) International Rally on its first outing in the hands of Jean Ragnotti. Possibly the last win on an International Champion-ship Rally by a two-wheel-drive car.*

Right *The engine of the 2.0-litre Saab rally car. Fuel injected engine with AiResearch turbocharger supplying boost at 17.0 psi delivers 250 bhp, coupled with tremendous mid-range torque.*

so evident since the torque spread of the turbocharged engine is relatively wide compared with an equivalent non-turbocharged engine and driving techniques can be altered to match a particular engine's characteristics to some extent.

Saab

In 1975 Saab became one of the trend-setters with the announcement of their turbocharged 2.0-litre single overhead camshaft engine to be used in their rally cars. Saab later used some of the lessons learnt in competition to produce successful turbocharged production vehicles.

Initially the rally engine produced around 170 bhp, but ultimately was developed to produce over 260 bhp. Despite the lack of a suitable transmission and four-wheel drive to handle this sort of power, the turbocharged engine allowed Saab to make their mark in International rallying and to turn the Saab 99 into a highly competitive rally car, but soon to be superseded by the next generation of more complex and powerful four-wheel drive turbo cars of the 1980s.

Porsche Carrera RSR Turbo prototype and 935 Turbo

With the exclusion of the turbocharged Porsche 917 from competition due to a change in the regulations, Porsche decided to develop a turbocharged Carrera RSR and run it in the Group

6 prototype category to gain experience for future production-derived Group 5 Sports Car Championships.

The regulations limited a turbocharged engine to 2,142 cc. The engine produced 500 bhp at 7,400 rpm and maximum torque of 408 lb/ft at 5,400 rpm. Despite considerable weight and drag penalties compared to the other 3-litre racing prototypes, Porsche were able to come in second at Le Mans and at the Watkins Glen 6 hour race. In all, four turbo-Carreras were built. They were able to reach 186 mph on the Mulsanne straight and accelerate from 0 to 124 mph in 8.8 seconds.

New Group 5 regulations in 1976 allowed Porsche to race the new 935 Turbo based on the experience gained with the RSR prototypes and from the outset the 935 was successful and dominated the racing scene in 1976 and 1977.

The air-cooled six-cylinder twin turbocharged engine produced over 590 bhp at 7,900 rpm and 438 lb/ft torque at 5,400 rpm from 2,856 cc. Maximum boost was normally 22 psi, but could be adjusted by the driver from the cockpit, and because of regulations which limited where the intercooler cooler could be mounted, twin water-to-air intercoolers were incorporated in the system.

Audi Quattro

The competition version of the Audi Quattro first appeared in 1980 and took the international rally scene by storm. The then unique (to rallying) four-wheel drive system, coupled with a potent turbocharged engine, more than compensated for its comparative lack

Audi Quattro A2—seen on the 1985 Swedish Rally.

1985 Audi Sport Quattro (2nd Evolution revised engine bay layout).

of controllability due to its heavy front-mounted 5-cylinder engine and long wheelbase. Since then there have been many evolution models, all based around the 5-cylinder front-mounted turbocharged engine and relatively simple 4 × 4 drive system with its fixed percentage torque split between the drive to the front and rear wheels.

Initially the engines produced 300 bhp which has risen as reliability and development of components and systems improved to over 450, with the introduction of an all-aluminium engine and 16-valve twin overhead camshaft cylinder head.

The Audi Sport appeared in 1985, this being basically a 450 bhp lighter and shorter wheel-based machine, built with a similar mechanical specification. Such innovations as water injection and water-cooled brakes have also been tried with varying degrees of success.

Zakspeed Turbo Racing Capri

Two versions of the turbocharged 16-valve overhead camshaft aluminium engine were developed. These are the 1,426 cc engine for use in the up to 2.0-litre racing class and a larger 1,745 cc engine which was used in the over 2.0-litre division.

Comparative engine performance figures are, for the 1,426 cc engine, 540 bhp at 10,000 rpm and maximum torque of 410 lb/ft at 7,200 rpm, with a compression ratio of 7.0:1; and for the 1,745 cc engine, 620 bhp at 9,000 rpm and maximum torque of 482 lb/ft at 6,800 rpm, with a compression ratio of 7.0:1. With a weight of only 135 kg, this engine was one of the most powerful units ever raced, pound for pound, with specific output of over 308 bhp/litre.

Peugeot 205 16 Turbo

Launched on the international rally scene in 1984 with three outright wins out of five starts, this machine became the one to beat. The last three or four years have seen power outputs rise rapidly from the then seemingly tremendous 260 bhp of the 1,400 cc Renault 5 Turbo, to the 300-plus bhp of the supercharged Lancia rally car, then 350 bhp for the Quattro in 1983, rising to over 450 bhp for the Quattro Sport in 1985.

The 1,775 cc twin overhead camshaft 16-valve Peugeot was launched with around 350 bhp—further boosted to more than 420 bhp in 1985. In common with other leading contenders, the Peugeot 205 16 Turbo is a four-wheel drive machine with variable torque split front to rear to get the best grip to make the most use of the tremendous power available under constantly varying track conditions. The engine is positioned transversely at the rear with a Garrett turbocharger mounted over the bell housing area and with large remotely mounted wastegate arrangement. A relatively compact water-to-air intercooler is used with cooling water fed from the radiator system.

Lancia Delta S4 (038) Group 'B' Rally car

This machine, which rapidly proved itself to be a leading contender for the International Group 'B' Rally Championship, contested its first competitive event in August 1985 with

Peugeot 205 Turbo 16 (E2), Group B, four-wheel-drive rally car. Winner of the Manufacturers World Rally Championship in 1985.

Peugeot 205 Turbo 16 (2nd Evolution engine bay). In this Group B rally specification, the rear mounted engine produced up to 425 bhp.

the 1000 Lakes Rally in Finland, followed by the RAC and 1986 Monte Carlo Rally—both of which it won in convincing style.

The engine specification is particularly revolutionary in the way that it is both super-charged with a mechanically driven supercharger for maximum low speed power and turbocharged for high rpm performance. Such an idea would have been considered too complicated and probably unworkable only a few years ago, but such is the advance of tech-nology, and even more because of the acceptance of forced induction, that a large manufacturer has seen fit to produce such a machine.

It may be appropriate to mention here that, like most things, the idea of linking a supercharger and a turbocharger is not entirely new, as it has been tried briefly by several experimentors, but without the sustained and detailed development work as put into it by Lancia.

The Lancia Delta S4 engine is an all-new twin OHC 16-valve unit with aluminium cylin-der head and block. Compression ratio is 7.0:1 and a sophisticated electronic Marelli-Weber ignition/injection system handles ignition and fuel feed. The most interesting and ingenious feature of the engine is its compound supercharger and turbocharger, supercharging system. The basic thinking behind this arrangement is to combine the low speed pumping efficiency and instant response of a mechanically driven supercharger, with the higher speed range

Above left *The Supercharged Lancia 037 seen here on one of its last competitive events, the 1985 Monte Carlo Rally, in the hands of Henri Toivonen—it was the best two-wheel-drive car.*

Left *Lancia 037 Supercharged Group B engine. The 'roots' type supercharger with twin lobed rotors is gear-driven from the crankshaft. The engine power output in its final specification with fuel injection was approximately 330 bhp.*

Above *Lancia Delta S4 (038)—1st Overall Henri Toivonen/Sergio Cresto in the Monte Carlo Rally 1986.*

Right *Lancia Delta S4 showing highly cramped and complicated engine bay layout with massive twin intercoolers. A power output of up to 450 bhp is claimed for the 1986 specification engine.*

thermodynamic efficiency of a turbocharger. Above approximately 3,500 rpm the turbo-charger provides the forced charge, the air flow through the mechanically driven super-charger being throttled and bypassed according to engine speed and load. Large intercoolers are used in the inlet tract between supercharger and turbocharger and after the turbocharger.

This four-wheel-drive car with continually variable torque split being supplied to front and rear wheels to suit varying road conditions, already had a power output of up to 420 bhp by early 1986.

Citroen BX4TC

This group 'B' 4 × 4 rally car is probably one of the cars least changed from the original road going version, the turbocharged four-cylinder 2,141 cc engine being mounted well forward in line in the chassis.

Ten prototypes were built for development and testing and a total of 200 must be built to comply with Group 'B' International Rally regulations. Road cars weigh up to 1,280 kg, but the so-called works evolution car may get down towards the class minimum of 960 kg with extensive use of kevlar and carbon fibre components.

The use of the unique Citroen Hydro-Pneumatic Suspension allows the driver to alter ride height according to conditions, by moving a lever in the cockpit which changes the pressure in hydraulic assemblies at each corner of the vehicle.

Citroen BX4 TC—photo showing road specification and Group B rally evolution model.

Citroen BX4 TC engine bay, showing front-mounted 4-cylinder 2.0-litre turbocharged engine.

The rally engine is equipped with a KKK K26 turbocharger, providing 19.0 psi boost pressure. The engine produced around 380-400 bhp at 7,000 rpm during the first few outings and this is expected to be increased to 450 bhp as the engine is further developed.

Ford RS200 High Performance 'Production' Competition Car

It was Ford's intention to produce a run of 200 identical cars to comply with Group 'B' homologation requirements, but at the same time to produce a vehicle of such a highly developed specification that little or no modifications will need to be made to make it an outright contender for the International Rally Championship. This was a different approach to that of other contenders such as Peugeot, Lancia and Audi who built 200 examples of their Group 'B' rally cars to comply with the regulations, but thereafter carried out permissible additional modifications to their own rally team cars to greatly increase the performance potential from the original homologated specifications. Only time will tell whether this commendable idea on Ford's part is capable of being put into practice.

The RS200's engine is basically the Brian Hart-developed RS1700T, in road specification giving 230 bhp and over 380 bhp in the rally car from its 1,803 cc four-cylinder twin OHC fuel-injected unit. There is a massive air-to-air intercooler mounted in the roof panel to the rear of the driver's head. The turbocharger is a Garrett-AiResearch T04 with large F1-type wastegate mounted separately, but close to the turbine housing. A special Bosch fuel

Above *Ford RS200 Group B four-wheel-drive turbocharged rally car, shown here in its world championship debut on the 1986 Swedish Rally, when it finished 3rd overall in the hands of Kalle Grundel.*

Right *Ford RS200. Garrett-AiResearch turbocharged fuel-injected twin cam engine with large roof-mounted air-to-air intercooler.*

Below *Debut of the Mitsubishi Starion four-wheel-drive Group B rally car on the 1984 1,000 Pistes Rally. Driver Lasse Lampi.*

injection system is used with twin injectors per cylinder in conjunction with Ford's EEC IV electronic engine management system. Due to the volumetric efficiency of the engine and its high rev capability in naturally aspirated form, comparatively low boost pressures in the region of 15 psi are used to obtain 380 bhp, but something over 22.0 psi (1.5 bar) may be required to match the competition.

Ford turbocharged Formula 1 120° V6 engine announced February 1986

The engine has very compact dimensions, particularly along the line of the crankshaft, which eases the job of fitting it to the new breed of Formula 1 cars. It is a 120° V6 with a Garrett turbocharger mounted at the end of a short fabricated exhaust manifold on éach cylinder bank. Each turbocharger has its own separate wastegate valve assembly mounted close to the turbine inlet port, with its own separate exhaust pipe. Cast aluminium plenums, one for each bank of four cylinders, collect the cooled air from the side pod-mounted intercoolers.

With fuel efficiency in Formula 1 becoming all-important in 1986, Ford have employed their EEC IV electronic engine management system, which, in addition to monitoring ignition, fuel injection and turbocharging systems, is also capable of diagnosing a fault within the system and reprogramming the system to optimise its functions.

Chapter 10

Turbocharged and supercharged production cars

I started compiling information for a book on turbocharging and supercharging way back in 1975, at which time, apart from one or two specialised machines, turbocharged production cars were virtually unheard of. In 1977 there were still only three turbocharged cars in production, yet in the space of four years, by the end of 1980, this had increased to approximately 18 models and now there are over 80 petrol and diesel turbo models available to the public, with a further large number of new turbo models either to be announced shortly or under development. It is because of this continuing trend by the car manufacturers that this section has been considerably expanded and updated in this new edition of *Turbocharging and Supercharging*.

By 1986 it looks as if every major motor manufacturer will have at least one turbocharged model in its range.

Turbocharged (supercharged) production cars up to January 1986 (petrol-engined) in order of acceleration performance:

Made and model	0-60 mph (0-100 km/h)	Max speed mph/km/h
Ferrari 308 GTO V8	4.9	190/306
Porsche 911 Turbo 3.3	5.1	162/261
Audi Quattro Sport	5.1	150/241
Peugeot 205 Turbo 16	5.9	128/206
Porsche 944T	6.0	152/245
Renault 5 Turbo	6.0	124/199
Lotus Esprit Turbo	6.2	148/238
Nissan 300 ZX Turbo	6.6	136/219
Maserati Bi-Turbo	6.7	136/219
Ford Sierra RS Turbo	6.8	137/220
Bristol Brigand	6.8	142/228
Nissan Skyline DDOHC Turbo	6.8	134/215
BMW 745i	7.2	140/225
Bentley Mulsanne Turbo	7.2	135/217
MG Montego Turbo	7.3	126/203
Audi Quattro	7.4	135/217

Turbocharged (supercharged) production cars up to January 1986 (petrol-engined) in order of acceleration performance:

Mitsubishi Starion EX	7.6	133/214
Ford Escort RS	7.8	121/195
Porsche 924 Turbo	7.8	142/228
Citroen CX GT1 Turbo	7.9	136/219
Mitsubishi Lancer 2000	8.0	127/204
Saab 16 Valve Turbo	8.0	130/209
Pontiac Sunbird 2000	8.2	122/196
Mitsubishi Galant	8.4	127/204
Saab 900 Turbo	8.4	125/201
Audi 200 Turbo	8.4	142/228
Volvo 760 GLE	8.5	125/201
Toyota Carina Turbo	8.5	125/201
Nissan Silvia Turbo	8.6	125/201
Fiat Uno Turbo	8.6	120/193
Mazda Luce	8.7	124/199
Pontiac Trans Am Turbo	8.7	120/193
Volvo 240 Turbo	8.7	117/188
Honda City Turbo	8.7	111/179
Fiat Uno Turbo	8.8	112/180
Renault 11 Turbo	8.9	114/183
Lancia Delta HF	8.9	122/196
Renault 5 (Alpine) Turbo	9.1	114/183
Renault Fuego Turbo	9.3	118/190
Mitsubishi Cordia	9.3	118/190
Lancia Volumex Coupé	9.3	122/196
Subaro 1.8 XT	9.5	120/193
Mitsubishi Tredia	9.5	114/183
Nissan Sunny Turbo	9.5	112/180
Fiat Argenta Volumex	9.5	118/190
MG Metro Turbo	9.5	110/177
Lancia Y10	9.5	108/174
Peugeot 505 Injection	9.6	125/201
Mitsubishi Mirage 1400	9.8	112/180
Nissan Micra	9.8	110/177
Ford Mustang 2.3 Turbo	10.2	110/177
Buick Riviera	10.4	112/180
Ford Mercury Capri 2.3 Turbo	10.4	112/180
Nissan Fairlady	10.6	110/177
Renault 18 Turbo	10.8	112/180
Toyota Cressida	10.9	110/177
Daihatsu Charade	11.3	100/161

Turbocharged diesel cars

Most turbocharged vehicles, right from the early days of turbocharging, have been diesels and in the production car market there is therefore a wide range. Listed below are most of the better known models—photos and text on many of these appear in this chapter.

Alfa Romeo 90	Peugeot 505 GRD
Alfa Romeo 6	Peugeot 604 GTD
Alfa Guilietta	Renault 11 GTD
Audi 80 TD	Renault 18 TD
Audi 100 TD	Renault 20 TD
BMW 524 TD	Rover 2400 SD
Citroen CX25 DTR	Talbot Tagora 2.3
Colt Shogun	Toyota Cressida
Colt Galant 1800 TD	Toyota Crown
Fiat Argenta 2.4	Toyota Camry
Mercedes 300 TD	Volkswagen Golf
Nissan Bluebird TD	Volvo 760 GLE
Opel Rekord 2.3	

Lotus Esprit Turbo 910

Lotus were particularly helpful in supplying technical information, together with excellent photographs, one of which is used on the front cover. I am indebted to Martin Cliffe who showed me around the factory and took me for a demonstration in the turbo-charged Esprit on the Hethel circuit.

In February 1980, Lotus announced the new Essex Commemorative Lotus Esprit Turbo after a development period of two years. It is evident from the lengthy development that a great deal of re-design and testing had been carried out on the car and

The striking lines of the Lotus Esprit demand turbo power (Photo courtesy Lotus Cars).

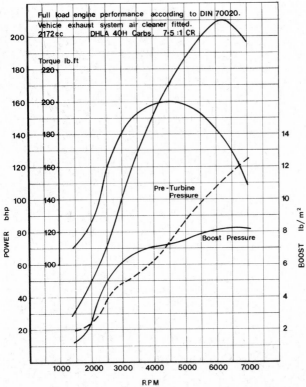

Full load engine performance according to DIN 70020.
Vehicle exhaust system air cleaner fitted.
2172cc   DHLA 40H Carbs.   7.5 :1 CR

Pre-Turbine Pressure

Boost Pressure

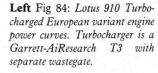

Left Fig 84: *Lotus 910 Turbocharged European variant engine power curves. Turbocharger is a Garrett-AiResearch T3 with separate wastegate.*

Below right *Lotus Esprit turbocharged twin-cam 2.2-litre engine. Photo clearly shows specially designed exhaust manifold and wastegate* (Lotus).

this applied not only to the turbocharged engine, designated the 910 2.2-litre turbo, but also to the bodywork, chassis, suspension and interior styling. From the outset it was the intention of the Lotus engineers to develop a turbocharged engine with good low speed performance, as well as top end power, coupled with immediate throttle response throughout the rpm range. The peak power and torque output targets are 200 bhp and 190 lb ft respectively (both of which are bettered by production engines).

A turbocharged engine will respond to carburettor choke size and camshaft timing in a similar way to a normally-aspirated engine and for a given target engine performance, many different parameters can be chosen, such as turbocharger match, compression ratio, boost pressure and engine displacement. Obviously, the best combination is the one which achieves the target performance with the lowest possible boost pressure. It was considered that a turbocharging system employing a blow-through pressurised carburation system would provide the best results, as opposed to a suck-through system, which Lotus considered might suffer from wet fuel handling problems on cold start-up, inferior mixture distribution and throttle response.

Lotus would have liked to use fuel injection, but because of the additional development time involved, this was ruled out, at least for the time being. During the development programme many different configurations of plenum chamber and diffuser manifolding between compressor outlet and inlet manifold were experimented with, and optimising the layout included reducing the plenum volume and shaping the compressor delivery, or diffuser, pipe in such a way as to gradually increase its inside diameter until it connected with the plenum chamber. It was found that, for improved throttle response, a small plenum chamber was necessary. However, if the chamber is too small, cylinder-to-cylinder air transfer becomes critical, as does carburettor ram pipe entry shape. It was also found that, by varying the position of the wastegate sensor pipe take-off point, the shape of the boost vs rpm curve could be varied. Variations such as these accounted for an increase in peak power output by as much as 25 bhp and a similar amount in peak torque.

Interestingly, continuing the same line of thought, to ensure instant throttle response from low rpm, carburettor throttle butterflies were moved as close to the inlet valves as possible by installing very short inlet manifolds, the carburettors almost being bolted direct to the cylinder head, together with relatively small carburettor venturis.

The turbocharged engine

To further improve low-speed punch, the engine capacity was increased from 2.0 to 2.2 litres by means of a longer-stroke crankshaft. New camshafts with higher lift and longer overlap helped in raising peak performance also. To cope with the increased thermal loads, there are a number of improvements incorporated in the 910 turbo engine. These include sodium-filled exhaust valves which run in hidurel guides and employ Stellite valve seats and re-designed valve springs. Tests indicate that this arrangement reduces peak

temperature at the valve by a useful 100°C. The cylinder head has improved coolant circulation which is assisted by a higher-capacity water pump.

As the compression ratio is a critical factor in any turbocharged engine, Lotus paid particular attention to the design of the new pistons, which have an enlarged dish with reduced crown height, the combination serving to reduce the compression ratio to 7.5:1 and eliminating the possibility of detonation under maximum load conditions. The effective ratio under full boost is the same as the normally-aspirated engine. The pistons also have lower ring packs and re-designed skirts to combat the higher cylinder temperatures and working loads. Similarly, to maintain optimum lubrication and temperature distribution under extremely high acceleration, braking and cornering conditions, the engine has a sophisticated dry sump lubrication system. By a simple but effective modification to the con rod, additional oil is able to reach the underside of the pistons to provide extra cooling in this sensitive area. The main bearing panel is also re-designed for increased strength.

The turbocharging system
The Garrett AiResearch T3 turbocharger delivers a maximum boost of 8.0 psi at 5,500 rpm, corresponding to a peak turbine speed of 110,000 rpm, well within the capabilities of the turbine. The boost vs engine rpm curve is controlled by a wastegate exhaust gas bypass system which limits turbine speed. The wastegate commences opening at 2,500 rpm and is actuated by inlet manifold pressure sensed from the compressor housing volute.

This photo shows the carburation and induction system with twin Dellorto carburettors and fuel pressure regulating valve (Lotus).

Extensive testing indicated that the wastegate should have a separate outlet of $1\frac{5}{8}$-in diameter not entering the main exhaust discharge pipe until it meets the large-capacity silencer box. High-speed testing also indicated that all the exhaust piping from the turbine exducer discharge to the rear of the car should be manufactured from stainless steel and incorporate a stainless steel double-skinned bellows-type expansion joint to relieve the turbine housing of any unnecessary piping loads.

The exhaust manifold is cast in high-silicon molybdenum iron with a four into two tract configuration which extends up to the turbine inlet flange. The turbine housing at present used, in fact, has a single-port entry, but a twin entry type may be used when one of suitable manufacture becomes available. The turbocharger is mounted on an extension to the main manifold, together with the wastegate which is manufactured by Boostguard. Maximum pre-turbine temperatures and pressures of up to 1,000°C and 12.5 psi respectively have been indicated.

The method of carburation adopted by Lotus is unusual in that the specially-developed twin Dellorto carburettors are fed air under pressure, the whole inlet system being designed for this method of carburation. Fuel pressure within the carburettors is supplied by a Lucas 4 FP pump and is maintained at a constant 4.5 psi above boost pressure by means of a regulator valve sensing the plenum pressure and returning excess fuel to the tank.

Manufacturer:	Lotus
Model:	Esprit Turbo 910
Performance:	0-60 mph: 5.55 seconds
	0-100 mph: 14.65 seconds
	Maximum speed: 152 mph

Engine

Type:	All aluminium DOHC 4-cylinder in-line.
Capacity:	2,174 cc
Compression ratio:	7.5:1
Carburation:	Twin Dellorto 40 DHLA(H) pressurised
Maximum power:	210 bhp (DIN) at 6,250 rpm
Maximum torque:	200 lb/ft (DIN) at 4,500 rpm

Turbocharging system

Turbocharger:	Garrett-AiResearch T3
Maximum boost pressure:	8.0 psi
Boost control:	Wastegate

Porsche

In 1972 Porsche produced the 917 Turbo for the Can-Am series of races and clearly demonstrated the tremendous power outputs which can be obtained by turbocharging. For example, in 5.0-litre form, the flat 12-cylinder engine produced a healthy 1,000 bhp, but when the capacity was increased to 5.4 litres in 1973, the power output was a staggering 1,100 bhp at 7,800 rpm with a colossal 820 lb ft of torque. Total weight of the engine, complete with twin KKK turbochargers, was 628 lb. Fuel consumption was 2.8-

Left Porsche 911 3.0-litre turbo
flat-six air-cooled engine produces
260 bhp in roadgoing form.
Turbocharger is a KKK unit.

Below Fig 85: *Porsche 935/936
turbo system.*

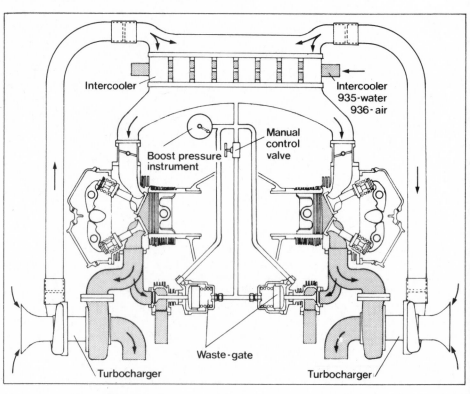

Intercooler

Intercooler
935-water
936-air

Boost pressure
instrument

Manual
control
valve

Waste-gate

Turbocharger   Turbocharger

Right *Porsche 911 Turbo engine showing turbocharging system with KKK turbocharger and air-to-air intercooler mounted above engine cooling fan.*

3.7 mpg and acceleration from 0-100 mph in under 5.0 seconds. Maximum timed speed was 241 mph.

Although this engine was originally designed as a naturally-aspirated engine producing 630 bhp in 5.0-litre form, Porsche found that only a few changes were necessary for the turbocharged version, principally an increase in cooling fan drive speed. The valve lift and duration were reduced by using the original exhaust camshaft profile for both intake and exhaust. Chrome plating of the valve stems, together with an improved oil supply, overcame the heat dissipation problems in this area. Porsche also discovered at this time that, unlike a naturally-aspirated engine, the turbocharged engine could not be matched for optimum track performance on a test bed, but required a great deal of road testing.

In 1973 the turbocharged 917 Porsches won all the races in the Can-Am Championship. Up to this time it had generally been thought that turbocharged engines were only suitable for high-speed races such as Indianapolis. Porsche had proved otherwise. In 1973, with a change in the regulations, Porsche developed a turbocharged version of their 6-cylinder 911 engine. In 2.1-litre racing form it developed 470 hp and with the addition of an intercooler this was raised to 510 hp.

In 1976 the turbocharged Porsche 936 became the first turbocharged car to win the 24-hour Le Mans race, just about the toughest race test for any engine, showing that turbocharged engines could be made durable as well as powerful. Porsche won Le Mans again in 1977 with the 936 turbo and also the World Championship of Makes with the type 935. It was also found, contrary to most opinion at that time, that the specific fuel consumption of their turbocharged race engines was superior to the naturally-aspirated engines.

Encouraged by the performances of their turbocharged competition vehicles, and learning a great deal about turbocharging through their racing programme, Porsche produced the road-going 911 Turbo in 1975. From a displacement of 2,994 cc, this engine produced 260 bhp at 5,500 rpm with 253 lb ft of torque, a compression ratio of

Left *Porsche 924 Turbo.*

Right *Renault 5 turbocharged engine. Produces 160 bhp in road trim with 12.0 psi boost and over 260 bhp when used in rally form* (Photo courtesy Renault).

Far right *Renault 5 Turbo. Homologation special, built for competition, but still makes an exhilarating everyday road car if you can afford one* (Photo courtesy Renault).

6.5:1 and maximum boost of 11.4 psi. Extensive changes to the 911 engine in turbocharged form were not necessary, although sodium-filled exhaust valves are fitted, to improve heat dissipation from the valve area. The performance of the fan was increased, new pistons reduced the compression ratio to 6.5:1 and the valve timing was changed to suit the characteristics of the turbocharged engine. Due to the low mounting position of the turbocharger, oil drained from the turbocharger has to be returned to the engine by a scavenge pump.

In 1978 the 3.3-litre turbocharged engine was introduced. Power output increased to 300 hp at 5,500 rpm and torque to 304 lb ft. Compression ratio was raised to 7:1, but boost remained at 0.8 bar (11.4 psi). The use of an intercooler accounted for a five per cent increase in specific performance, leading to improved fuel economy. This engine, in common with the earlier 3-litre unit, is also able to meet the severe Californian emission standards.

Manufacturer:	Porsche
Model:	930 Turbo (production model)
Performance:	0-60 mph: 5.5 seconds
	0-100 mph: 11.8 seconds
	Maximum speed: 160 mph

Engine

Type:	Flat 6-cylinder air-cooled 930/50
Capacity:	3.3 litres
Compression ratio:	7.0:1
Injection:	Bosch K-Jetronic
Maximum power:	300 bhp (DIN) at 5,500 rpm
Maximum torque:	307 lb/ft (DIN)

Turbocharging system

Turbocharger:	KKK
Maximum boost pressure:	12.0 psi
Boost control:	Wastegate and inlet charge recirculation air-to-air intercooler fitted

924 Turbo

The 924 Turbo was announced in 1979. The turbocharged engine is based on the Audi 100 2.0-litre push-rod block assembly and fitted with a SOHC cylinder head to give a compression ratio initially of 7.5:1, more recently increased to 8.5:1 to obtain improvement in low-speed throttle response and specific performance from the engine. Power output is 180 bhp at 5,500 rpm and maximum rpm is limited to 6,600 by a mechanical rev-limiter. Fuel injection is Bosch K-Jetronic.

Manufacturer: Porsche
Model: 924 Turbo
Performance: 0-60 mph: 7.5 seconds
0-100 mph: 18.7 seconds
Maximum speed: 145 mph

Engine
Type: 4-cylinder single overhead camshaft
Capacity: 2.0 litres
Compression ratio: 7.5:1
Injection: Bosch K-Jetronic
Maximum power: 170 bhp at 5,500 rpm
Maximum torque: 180 lb/ft at 3,500 rpm

Turbocharging system
Turbocharger: KKK
Maximum boost pressure: 10.0 psi
Boost control: Wastegate

(System also includes an inlet manifold 'blow-off' valve to reduce back pressure in system when the throttle is closed.)

Turbo 944

Announced in July 1984, the new Porsche 944 Turbo replaced the 924 model. The engine is a 2,479 cc aluminium SOHC 4-cylinder, twin balancer shaft, water-cooled unit mounted conventionally at the front, producing 220 bhp at 5,800 rpm and 242 lb/ft torque at 3,500 rpm. A 0-60 mph time of under 6.0 seconds and maximum speed of 152 mph is claimed. A 4-valve per cylinder, cylinder head is under development.

The KKK K26 turbocharger with remotely mounted wastegate incorporates a water cooled bearing housing to provide extended turbocharger bearing life.

A Bosch Motronic engine management system linked to a sophisticated anti-knock, piezo-ceramic sensor and throttle butterfly potentiometer, control precisely fuel injection, ignition and boost, even allowing individual cylinders to be advanced or retarded if detonation is sensed. This arrangement allows the use of up to 11.0 psi boost with 10 per cent overboost permissible for brief periods, even with an 8.0:1 compression ratio.

Renault

Such is the commitment of Renault to turbocharging that by mid-1984 they had some nine turbocharged models in production—five petrol- and four diesel-engined—probably the widest range of any manufacturer with an output of around 300 turbocharged cars per day. These include the latest addition, the Renault 11 Turbo with its low inertia Garrett T2 turbo. Yet despite this wide range, more turbo models are being produced.

R5 Turbo

Renault were quick to point out that the R5 Turbo was designed first and foremost as a competition car. However, in order for Renault to be able to use it in international rallies, it had to be built in sufficient numbers to qualify for homologation into Group Two. Subsequently, it has been developed into an extremely potent road car with the superb handling and traction that one might expect from a small mid-engined car with rear wheel drive. The normal road version has 160 bhp (DIN) at 6,000 rpm and maximum torque of 155 lb ft at 3,250 rpm. In competition Group Two form the power output is increased to around 260 bhp. As the 0-60 mph time of the road version is quoted as 6.0 seconds approximately, with another 100-odd bhp, the competition car must have rocket-like acceleration.

Manufacturer:	Renault
Model:	5 Turbo
Performance:	0-60 mph: 6.0 seconds
	0-100 mph: 17.0 seconds
	Maximum speed: 124 mph

Engine

Type:	4-cylinder in-line OHV water-cooled
Capacity:	1,397 cc
Compression ratio:	7.0:1
Injection:	Bosch K-Jetronic
Maximum power:	160 bhp at 6,000 rpm
Maximum torque:	155 lb/ft at 3,250 rpm

Turbocharging system

Turbocharger:	Garrett-AiResearch T3
Maximum boost pressure:	10.0 psi
Boost control:	Wastegate with double acting diaphragm; intercooler incorporated in turbocharging system

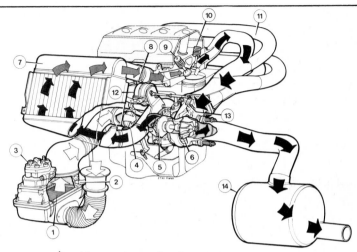

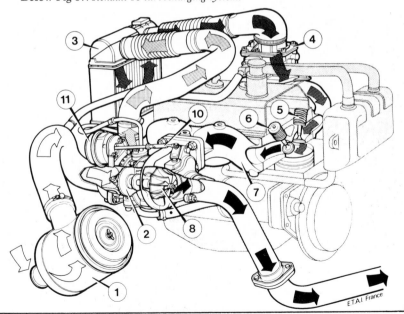

⇨ Air at atmospheric pressure
▶ Pressurised charge air
▶ Pressurised and recooled charge air
▶ Exhaust gases

Above Fig 86: *Renault 5 turbocharging system, based on Gordini 1,397 cc engine.*
Below Fig 87: *Renault 18 turbocharging system.*

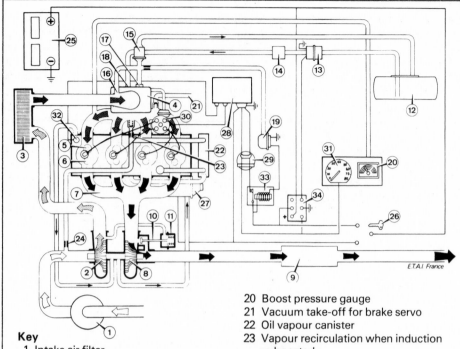

Key

1 Intake air filter
2 Centrifugal-impeller supercharger
3 Charge air intercooler
4 Pressurised carburettor
5 Inlet valve
6 Exhaust valve
7 Exhaust manifold
8 Exhaust gas-driven radial-flow turbine
9 Exhaust expansion and resonance chamber
10 Exhaust turbine bypass valve
11 Boost pressure-sensing capsule
12 Fuel tank
13 Fuel pump
14 Fuel filter
15 Fuel pressure regulator
16 Boost pressure-sensing lead to fuel pressure regulator
17 Pressure balancer for fuel return
18 Fuel supply
19 Pressure-sensitive switch (in case of excess boost pressure)
20 Boost pressure gauge
21 Vacuum take-off for brake servo
22 Oil vapour canister
23 Vapour recirculation when induction unboosted
24 Vapour recirculation when induction supercharged
25 Battery
26 Ignition switch
27 Starter
28 Electronic ignition control box
29 Ignition coil
30 Ignition distributor
31 Tachometer
32 Knock-detector (if knock occurs, the detector retards the ignition by 4°, with reversion to normal after 15 seconds)
33 Ignition cut-out relay (controlled by the pressure switch 19, it interrupts the ignition circuit if the boost pressure exceeds permitted limit)
34 Engine-speed relay (cuts off supply to fuel pump if the ignition is left switched on while the engine remains stationary)

Fig 88: *Schematic diagram showing the operation of the Renault 18 Turbo.*

Renault 18 Turbo

With the Renault 18 Turbo Renault were the first major manufacturer to turbocharge the petrol engine of a mass-production family saloon as opposed to a top of the range prestige model. This shows how much Renault believe in the suitability of turbocharging for almost all classes of vehicle, whether it be for Formula One, international rallying, or the family saloon. With the introduction of this car, Renault may have begun a new chapter in the evolution of supercharging mass-production engines. The turbocharging system itself is unusual in that a pressurised single-choke Solex carburettor is employed, as opposed to the more usual fuel injection system. An intercooler is fitted and an interesting feature of this system is that a thermostatically-controlled flap valve allows the intercooler to be bypassed if the temperature of the air passing through it is less than 43°C. This means that the air flow to the engine is not slowed down by the intercooler at times of light load, or at low rpm when there may be little or no boost to heat up the inlet charge. This feature could eliminate one of the possible drawbacks of an intercooler at low speeds and so enhance low-speed performance. A 'knock detector' fitted to the cylinder head retards the ignition by 4° if it senses detonation and as an additional safety device, if over-boost occurs for any reason, an ignition cut-out cuts ignition to the engine.

Manufacturer:	Renault
Model:	18 Turbo
Performance:	0-60 mph: 9.5 seconds
	0-100 mph: 25.2 seconds
	Maximum speed: 115 mph

Engine

Type:	4-cylinder OHV aluminium cylinder head
Capacity:	1,565 cc
Compression ratio:	8.6:1
Carburation:	Pressurised carburettor
Maximum power:	110 bhp (DIN) at 5,000 rpm
Maximum torque:	133.8 lb/ft (DIN) at 2,250 rpm

Turbocharging system

Turbocharger:	Garrett-AiResearch T3
Maximum boost pressure:	8.0 psi
Boost control:	Wastegate integral with turbine

(System features computerised electronic ignition, incorporating detonation sensor and an air-to-air charge cooler.)

Changes incorporated in 1983 models raised the bhp from 110 to 125 at 5,500 rpm. This pushes the top speed up from 115 to 121 mph.

11 Turbo

Launched in April 1984, this is the latest in the growing line of turbocharged models available from Renault. The turbo system incorporates the recently introduced Garrett T2 unit which is basically a 15 per cent smaller and 40 per cent lighter T3 turbo and a far better match for this 1,397 cc engine, thereby producing a very flat torque curve with improved bottom end performance and throttle response.

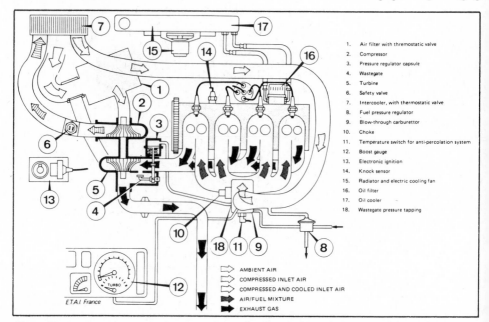

1. Air filter with thremostatic valve
2. Compressor
3. Pressure regulator capsule
4. Wastegate
5. Turbine
6. Safety valve
7. Intercooler, with thermostatic valve
8. Fuel pressure regulator
9. Blow-through carburettor
10. Choke
11. Temperature switch for anti-percolation system
12. Boost gauge
13. Electronic ignition
14. Knock sensor
15. Radiator and electric cooling fan
16. Oil filter
17. Oil cooler
18. Wastegate pressure tapping

⇨ AMBIENT AIR
⇨ COMPRESSED INLET AIR
⇨ COMPRESSED AND COOLED INLET AIR
⇨ AIR/FUEL MIXTURE
⇨ EXHAUST GAS

E.T.A.I. France

Above Fig 89: *Renault 11 turbocharging system, using Garrett T2 turbocharger with integral wastegate.*

Below *Renault 11 Turbo. 1985 addition to the range of turbo models available from Renault.*

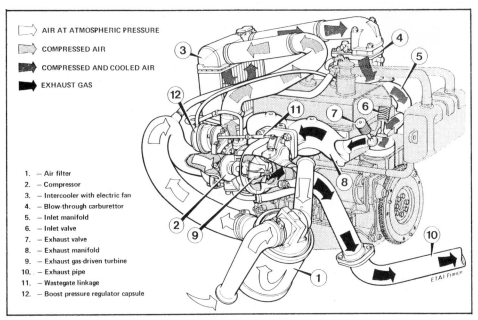

Key:

⇨ AIR AT ATMOSPHERIC PRESSURE

⇨ COMPRESSED AIR

⇨ COMPRESSED AND COOLED AIR

⇨ EXHAUST GAS

1. — Air filter
2. — Compressor
3. — Intercooler with electric fan
4. — Blow-through carburettor
5. — Inlet manifold
6. — Inlet valve
7. — Exhaust valve
8. — Exhaust manifold
9. — Exhaust gas-driven turbine
10. — Exhaust pipe
11. — Wastegate linkage
12. — Boost pressure regulator capsule

Above Fig 90: *Renault Fuego Turbo System.*

Below *Renault Fuego Turbo.*

Maximum bhp is 105 at 5,500 rpm. The engine is a 4-cylinder OHV design with aluminium cylinder head. The turbo intake air is fed from a thermostatically controlled valve to an air-to-air intercooler. It then blows through a special Solex carburettor cast in magnesium for improved rigidity and to save weight. Maximum boost is 1.62 atm (9.0 psi). Safety controls include a detonation sensor and an overboost valve which cuts the ignition should the boost rise above 11.0 psi. In contrast to the similar capacity Gordini turbo, maximum torque is developed at a very low 2,500 rpm with 90 per cent of peak available from 2,000-5,000 rpm.

Fuego Turbo
Capitalising on the success of the 5 and 18 turbo models, Renault have added the Fuego Turbo to their range, giving it the right sort of performance to match its styling. The 1,515 cc engine is derived from the 18 Turbo, but with the accent more on performance. The boost pressure is increased to a maximum of 11.0 psi with the compression ratio being lowered to 8:1. Power output is up to 132 bhp and maximum torque 147.5 lb/ft at 3,000 rpm, compared with the 125 bhp and 134 lb/ft at 2,500 rpm for the R18 Turbo.

The system also includes an electronic detonation (knock) sensor and employs a pressurised carburettor arrangement with an air-to-air intercooler with an integral cooling fan which switches on after turning off the engine to prevent heat soak causing carburettor fuel vaporisation and consequent hot start problems.

Volvo
Volvo have introduced the B21.E turbo based on their tried and tested B21.E 2-litre engine. Power output is increased from 120 hp to 155 hp at the slightly lower rpm of 5,500. Torque is increased over the whole range from 1,000-5,500 rpm with maximum increase of 47 per cent at 3,500 rpm. The engine differs from the naturally-aspirated version in the following way. The compression ratio is reduced from 9.3 to 7.5:1 with new pistons having concave piston crowns. Piston-to-bore clearance is increased by 0.01 mm. The camshaft has a modified profile and lift of 9.94 mm. Exhaust valves are sodium-cooled with Stellite seats, and the flow capacity of the fuel injectors and pump is increased. In other respects the engine, including the cylinder head, block and crankshaft assembly, are unaltered. A competition version of this engine has already shown great promise, and may well point the way to go in the rally and rallycross world.

Manufacturer:	Volvo
Model:	B21.E turbo
Performance:	0-60 mph: 8.6 seconds
	0-100 mph: 20.8 seconds
	Maximum speed: 124 mph

Engine

Capacity:	2,127 cc
Compression ratio:	7.5:1
Injection:	Bosch K-Jetronic
Maximum power:	155 bhp (DIN) at 5,500 rpm
Maximum torque:	155 lb/ft (DIN) at 3,500 rpm

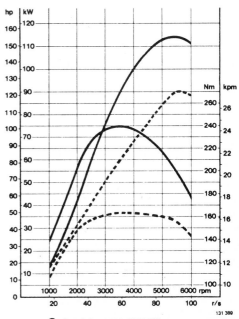

Above *Volvo B21.E turbocharged 2.1-litre engine.*

Right Fig 91: *Power and torque curves for the Volvo B21.E turbocharged and unturbocharged engine.*

Output-torque curves

——— = B 21 E-Turbo
- - - - - - = B 21 E

Below *Volvo 760 Turbo.*

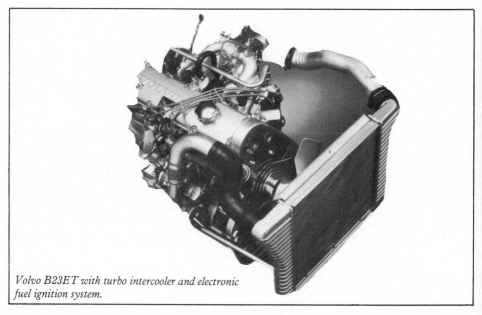

Volvo B23ET with turbo intercooler and electronic fuel ignition system.

Turbocharging system

Turbocharger:	Garrett-AiResearch T3
Maximum boost pressure:	9.0 psi
Boost control:	Integral wastegate

With the announcement of the turbocharged 760 series in 1983, Volvo created a range of technically advanced high performance vehicles which considerably enhance their somewhat conservative image.

760 Turbo (2.3-litre in-line 6-cylinder)

The Volvo 760 Turbo's fuel and ignition systems are both controlled by a micro computer which is programmed to give optimum fuel and ignition setting for every situation. This enables a relatively high 9.0:1 compression ratio to be used when linked to a large and efficient intercooler. This in turn produces a very flat torque curve and excellent low speed performance.

This optimisation of fuel supply and ignition setting has the advantage that the Volvo 760 Turbo does not require an exhaust emission control system. The micro computer ensures exhaust gases that are as clean as possible without the need of emission control equipment, and in addition, optimum fuel efficiency and the best possible performance. The Volvo 760 Turbo is therefore an economical car. Furthermore, the ignition system has few moving parts, being contactless, this implying excellent reliability and low wear. Only the spark plugs need replacing at recommended intervals. The ignition timing is also more exact since it monitors the position of the actual crankshaft and therefore remains unaffected by possible distributor wear. These factors produce consistently low fuel consumption and a low exhaust emission level.

The engine, which provides good acceleration of 0-60 mph in 8.5 seconds, is of 2,383 cc capacity giving 109 bhp at 4,850 rpm and 151 lb/ft of torque at 2,400 rpm.

Saab

In response to the tremendous interest shown, particularly by their American dealers, in the Saab 99 Turbo, Saab introduced this new model in 1977 somewhat earlier than they had at first envisaged. The aim of the Saab engineers from the outset was to obtain the performance of a 6-cylinder engine from their existing 4-cylinder 99 EMS unit. By developing a turbocharged version of the 99 Series engine, Saab were able to eliminate the substantial cost of tooling up for a new 6-cylinder engine, or of having to purchase someone else's engine. In addition, they could obtain better fuel consumption and lower exhaust emissions with the smaller turbocharged 4-cylinder unit. To achieve their objectives, Garrett AiResearch were asked to supply a suitable turbocharger, the aim being to achieve maximum torque back-up at low rpm, as closely related as possible to the figures which could be expected from a 6-cylinder engine.

AiResearch designed the T3 turbocharger, incorporating an integral wastegate, as the first of a new generation of small turbochargers. On the 99 Series models, the wastegate is

Underbonnet engine bay layout of the 99 Turbo—looks impressive.

operated by sensing exhaust manifold pressure as opposed to inlet manifold boost, pressure. By this method boost reaches a maximum pressure at only 3,000 rpm and falls gradually thereafter. As a boost pressure curve corresponds closely to an engine's torque curve, excellent low-speed torque backup is achieved.

At the Geneva Motor Show in March 1980, Saab unveiled the 900 Turbo with the new 'H' series engine. This is based on the original 2-litre engine, but is ten per cent lighter and gives better fuel economy. Saab considered that 145 bhp was sufficient for most of their customers, so maximum power output remained the same. Saab also reverted to the more usual practice of activating the wastegate by sensing inlet manifold pressure. But by utilising a smaller turbine and housing, low-speed throttle response is improved. The turbocharged engines supplied to some markets were fitted with an APC system (automatic performance control). This system uses an electronic sensing unit which picks up signals from three sources: a detonation sensor on the engine block, a pressure sensor in the inlet manifold, and from the distributor to sense engine rpm. The 'black box' processes this information and passes a signal to a solenoid valve which opens or closes the controlling pressurised air supply to the wastegate so that boost pressure can be controlled very precisely according to operating conditions. This system allows the use of 91-97 octane fuel without the need to reset the ignition timing and produces a further improvement in fuel consumption.

AiResearch T3 turbocharger on Saab's 'H' engine (Saab).

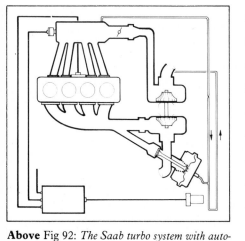

Above Fig 92: *The Saab turbo system with auto-matic performance control.*

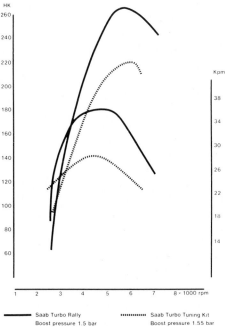

Right Fig 93: *Saab produce two tuning kits; one raises the power output from 145 to 220 bhp and the rally version to 260 bhp at 5,750 rpm.*

—— Saab Turbo Rally   ·········· Saab Turbo Tuning Kit
Boost pressure 1.5 bar   Boost pressure 1.55 bar
Compression ratio 6.5:1   Compression ratio 6.5:1

Manufacturer:	Saab
Model:	99 Turbo (and 900 turbo)
Performance:	0-60 mph: 8.2 seconds
	0-100 mph: 21.4 seconds
	Maximum speed: 125 mph

Engine

Type:	4-cylinder in-line SOHC
Capacity:	1,985 cc
Compression ratio:	7.5:1
Injection:	Bosch K-Jetronic
Maximum power:	145 bhp (DIN) at 5,000 rpm
Maximum torque:	148 lb/ft at 2,800 rpm

Turbocharging system

Turbocharger:	Garrett-AiResearch T3
Maximum boost pressure:	9.5 psi
Boost control:	Wastegate, mounted integrally with turbine

In 1983 Saab launched their third generation 2.0-litre 175 bhp turbocharged engine—the turbo 16-valve with four valves per cylinder, light alloy, twin overhead camshaft cylinder head, incorporating sodium-cooled exhaust valves, hydraulic cam followers and hemi-spherical combustion chambers—thus demonstrating their ability to keep at the forefront in turbocharged engine development for production cars.

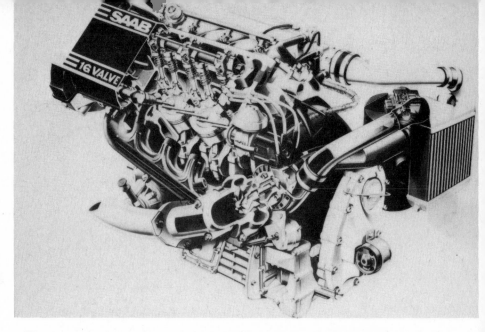

The new turbocharging system with its APC (Automatic Performance Control) allows the engine to use a relatively high 9.0:1 compression ratio and can automatically adjust ignition requirements for fuel with as low an octane rating as 92 (RON). This is achieved by reducing the boost pressure as previously described, but in addition the new engine employs the Bosch LH fuel injection system with its mass air flow sensor, as opposed to the purely volume control sensor. By sensing the density or weight of the incoming air, fuel flow is more accurately metered according to ambient conditions.

The new system also includes an air-to-air intercooler with bypass valve and latest 'mini-sized' Garrett AiResearch T2 turbocharger with integral wastegate.

Audi Quattro and 200 Turbo

The Audi 200, 2,144 cc 5-cylinder turbocharged engine is available in two forms, one for the Audi 2000 Saloon and the four-wheel-drive Quattro Coupé. When originally introduced, the four-wheel-drive turbocharged Audi Quattro caused quite a stir in the motoring world, being a forerunner of turbocharging coupled to a four-wheel-drive system.

The turbocharged engine was based on the 5-cylinder Audi 100 2.1-litre engine which needed only comparatively little internal modification, apart from new pistons with bowl in crown to reduce the compression ratio to 7.0:1, with additional oil cooling jets directed to the underside of the pistons and sodium-cooled exhaust valves, which contribute to a reduction in cylinder temperatures.

The exhaust manifold developed by Audi is cast in nodular iron with 20 per cent chromium and has some unusual features. Exhaust flows from each cylinder are kept separate for as long as possible to utilise the pulse created in the manifold during the engine's exhaust stroke, for increased turbine speed. Before entering the turbine the exhaust flows are merged into an outlet from the exhaust manifold which is divided into three parts, two large and one small. Flows from cylinders two and three and four and five discharge through the two larger ports and cylinder one from the small port.

Above left *Saab 16 valve turbocharged engine, displaying many advanced design features.*

Above *Audi 200 Turbo.*

Below *Audi 200 Turbo cutaway view of engine, transmission and suspension system layout.*

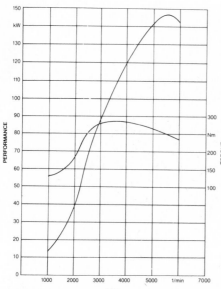

Left Fig 94: *2.2-litre, five-cylinder fuel-injected engine with turbocharging, air cooling, and fully electronic ignition.*

Below *Turbocharged Audi 200.5E 5-cylinder engine produces 170 bhp without intercooler* (Audi-VW).

Right Fig 95: *Sectional view of the internals of the turbocharged Audi-Quattro engine. Note special pistons with modified skirt and oil jet directed to cool the underside of the piston crown.*

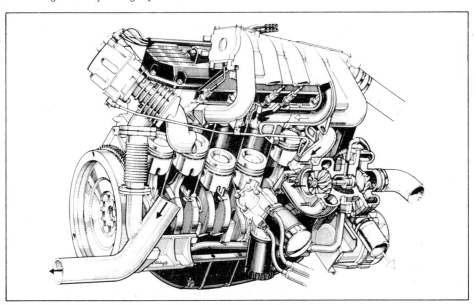

Even with air to air intercooling, a sophisticated computerised ignition system with ignition retard is still required to cater for conditions of heavy load and limited speed, when insufficient cooling air may pass through the intercooler to cool the inlet charge and thereby increase the tendency to detonate.

This engine is also used in the Audi 200 Turbo, in somewhat less powerful specification.

Over the last few years considerable development of the rally Quattro has taken place. This has culminated in the new shorter wheelbase Quattro Sport with 300 bhp in standard road-going trim and well over 400 bhp in a rally specification, with a staggering 354 lb/ft of torque (480 Nm) for a 2.2-litre engine at only 5,000 rpm.

The main features of the new engine are an aluminium shorter stroke block with thin walled cast iron liners and aluminium 16-valve cylinder head with a relatively high compression ratio of 8.0:1 with a maximum boost of up to 20 psi.

The turbocharger system employs a very large intercooler which can drop the charge temperature by as much as 75°C and an ingenious charge air recycling system which serves to maintain compressor rpm during off-boost conditions, so that boost is more instantly available on demand. Latest versions of the KKK turbocharger fitted to the Audi Quattro incorporate a water-cooled bearing housing to improve turbocharger bearing life.

Manufacturer:	Audi
Model:	Quattro
Performance:	0-60 mph: 6.8 seconds
	0-100 mph: Figures unavailable
	Maximum speed: 137 mph

Engine

Type:	5-cylinder in-line SOHC aluminium cylinder head

Mercedes 3.0-litre turbodiesel with AiResearch T3 turbocharger (Photo courtesy Mercedes-Benz).

Capacity:	2,144 cc
Compression ratio:	7.0:1
Injection:	Bosch K-Jetronic
Maximum power:	200 bhp (DIN) at 5,500 rpm
Maximum torque:	210 lb/ft (DIN) at 3,500 rpm

Turbocharging system

Turbocharger:	KKK
Maximum boost pressure:	12.0 psi
Boost control:	By separately mounted wastegate

Mercedes-Benz

Encouraged by initial tests which indicated the suitability of the Mercedes diesel pre-combustion chamber design for turbocharging, together with success of the world record runs in their C.III diesel-powered car, which also demonstrated the mechanical reliability of the engine, Mercedes announced their 5-cylinder turbodiesel in 1978 (engine designation O.M. 617A). By turbocharging Mercedes were able to increase torque by 42 per cent at the same engine speed of 2,400 rpm as the naturally-aspirated engine for a total engine weight increase of only seven per cent. By using a Garrett AiResearch turbo-charger employing a compressor with backward curve blade design, very high compressor efficiencies are achieved over a wide rpm range, so that it is possible to reach maximum boost pressure by only 2,000 rpm.

A capsule which senses charge pressure is linked to the injection pump governor and precisely controls the amount of fuel injected to maintain the optimum fuel/air ratio and lowest smoke emissions under all conditions of load and speed. Under conditions of medium and high load it is possible with this turbo system to use a leaner air/fuel ratio than is possible with a naturally-aspirated engine, allowing improved specific fuel consumption. Engine improvements include a nitrided crankshaft, oil jets to cool the pistons via a drilling in the piston, a re-machined combustion chamber and sodium-cooled exhaust valves.

Manufacturer:	Mercedes Benz
Model:	300 TD (Turbodiesel)
Performance:	0-60 mph: 14.6 seconds
	0-100 mph: Figures unavailable
	Maximum speed: 102 mph

Engine

Type:	5-cylinder diesel
Capacity:	2,998 cc
Maximum power:	125 bhp at 4,350 rpm
Maximum torque:	175 lb/ft at 2,400 rpm

Turbocharging system

Turbocharger:	Garrett-AiResearch T3 with integral wastegate
Maximum boost pressure:	Figures unavailable
Boost control:	By integral wastegate

(The Bosch diesel injection pump is specially adapted to suit the requirements of the turbocharged engine.)

BMW

BMW were the first major car manufacturer to experiment with turbocharging in Europe back in 1969, when they developed the KKK-turbocharged 2002, mainly as a publicity exercise and to provide the bhp to win the European Saloon Car Championship. This 2-litre engine produced 270 bhp in racing trim and led to the limited production version which appeared in 1973.

By 1984 BMW had two listed turbo models, these being the 2.4-litre turbo-diesel and the top-of-the-range 745i producing 252 bhp from its 3,430 cc.

745i Turbo

The 745i turbocharged BMW has had the engine capacity increased from 3,210 to 3,430 cc. Major changes incorporated into this engine in 1983 include higher compression ratio, up from 7.5 to 8.0:1, digital engine electronics (DEE), charging pressure and knock control, redesigned pistons with bowl in crown, nimonic exhaust valves, oil spray jet to cool piston crowns and larger water pump. The flow resistance of the intercooler has been improved and the air bypass valve is no longer fitted.

With the increase in capacity, maximum power remains the same, but is achieved at lower rpm (4,900 as opposed to 5,500) and low speed torque is considerably improved with 280 lb/ft at 2,200 as opposed to 270 lb/ft at 2,500 rpm.

The incorporation of a solenoid linked to the wastegate and a potentiometer on the throttle linkage has made it possible to have the wastegate open under conditions of low power demand, thereby reducing the charge air temperature and enabling the engine to run cooler, even with leaner mixtures. The end result is a cooler-running and more economical engine.

Manufacturer:	BMW
Model:	745.i
Performance:	0-60 mph: 7.1 seconds
	0-100 mph: 18.7 seconds
	Maximum speed: 140 mph

Engine

Type:	346E in-line 6-cylinder with SOHC aluminium cylinder head
Capacity:	3,430 cc
Compression ratio:	8.0:1
Injection:	Digital engine electronics
Maximum power:	252 bhp (DIN) at 5,500 rpm
Maximum torque:	280 lb/ft (DIN) at 2,200 rpm

Turbocharging system

Turbocharger:	KKK
Maximum boost pressure:	7.5 psi
Boost control:	By separately mounted wastegate

(System features digital motor electronics and an air-to-air intercooler.)

Turbocharged Diesel

This power unit is based on the 6-cylinder M20 engine with a longer stroke which increases the displacement to 2,443 cc. In common with many current turbocharged engines, oil spray jets are incorporated to spray cooling oil on to the undersides of the piston crowns. The compression ratio is 22:1 and the cylinder head incorporates a separate turbulence chamber, in which the initial ignition takes place before progressing to the main chamber formed in the piston crown. In this way more complete and accurate combustion is obtained, resulting in improved engine performance. The turbocharger boost is controlled to a maximum pressure

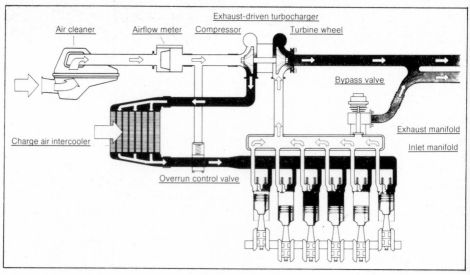

Right *BMW 745i turbo is tucked down well out of sight, but design of inlet manifold is interesting* (Photo provided by BMW).

Below left Fig 98: *How the BMW exhaust-driven turbocharger works. The wastegate or overrun control valve ensures that the compressor unit continues to run at high speed on the overrun, and is ready to boost the combustion airflow as soon as the throttle is reopened. The bypass valve diverts part of the exhaust gas into the exhaust pipe, depending on the maximum boost pressure; this avoids possibly harmful pressure peaks.*

of 0.8 bar (12.0 psi) and there is an additional over-boost safety valve mounted on the air collector. Maximum power is 115 bhp at 4,800 rpm and torque 208 lb/ft at 2,400 rpm.

Nissan-Nissan

At the time of writing, Nissan produced some seven different turbocharged engines, several only available in Japan.

The latest in the long line of ZX models dating back to 1969 is the 300ZX, which features a 2,960 cc 60° V6 turbocharged engine producing 228 bhp at 5,200 rpm, with a single overhead camshaft per bank, operating two valves per cylinder with rocker arms and hydraulic lifters. Electronic fuel injection incorporating Nissan's ECCS engine management system is employed. There is a 2.0-litre version of this engine producing 170 bhp at 6,000 rpm. .

The Skyline RS Turbo and RS-X Turbo now have the new FJ20E-T engine. This is an intercooled twin overhead camshaft engine with four valves per cylinder, producing a maximum power output of 205 bhp at 6,400 rpm and maximum torque of 240 lb/ft at 4,400

Above *Nissan 300 ZX Turbo. Latest model in the long established ZX line.*

Below *View of engine bay layout Nissan V6 300 ZX turbo.*

Above *Nissan Cherry Turbo—high performance small car—joins the hot hatch-back league.*

Below *Nissan Cherry transversely mounted turbocharged engine.*

Above *Nissan Silvia 2.0 litre turbo.*

Below *Nissan Silvia turbo engine bay.*

rpm. This engine is also available for the Silvia model. The Silvia/Gazelle and Bluebird models can be supplied with an 1,809 cc 4-cylinder single overhead camshaft engine (designated the CA18E.T.) producing 135 bhp at 6,000 rpm. This is a fuel-injected engine with two plugs per cylinder and swirl-inducing intake ports which contribute to the high power output with maximum economy. A knock sensor is also incorporated, which allows the engine to use an 8.0:1 compression ratio.

The Nissan Cherry Turbo was introduced in 1984 with a fuel-injected Garrett T2-turbocharged 1,488 cc engine with aluminium SOHC head and 7.4:1 compression ratio, which produces 114 bhp (DIN) at 5,600 rpm. With this power output, performance is one of the best in its class, as can be seen with a standing start 1/4-mile time of 16.3 seconds and 0-90 mph in 17.8 seconds.

Silvia ZX Turbo
The 1,809 cc SOHC 4-cylinder fuel-injected turbocharged engine produces 135 bhp at 6,000 rpm and 42 lb/ft at 4,000 rpm, sufficient to produce 0-60 mph acceleration of 8.6 seconds and top speed of 125 mph.

This model is the first under 2.0-litre turbocharged sports saloon from Nissan to be widely sold in Europe and could be said to represent a new generation of high performance sporting saloons.

Safari Patrol Turbo Diesel
Completing the line-up of turbocharged engines is the SD33T 6-cylinder turbo diesel engine. In common with many turbocharged engines, oil cooling jets are directed to the undersides of the piston crowns. Pistons are strengthened around the piston pin and wide rings are used to increase heat dissipation to the cooling medium.

Ford Escort RS Turbo
The Ford Escort RS Turbo was developed by Ford Special Vehicle Engineering and is expected to contest the Group A saloon car racing championship amongst other competitions with bhp increased to well over 200 bhp. The engine is a further development of the turbocharged Escort XR3i 1600.

In standard road going specification, the 1,596 cc CVH engine puts out an impressive 132 bhp—26 per cent more than the standard XR3i. To achieve this comparatively little has been done to the basic engine internally. The aluminium cylinder head has improved inlet and exhaust porting and is fitted with Nimonic exhaust valves. The hydraulic tappets are retained. New stronger pistons with a lower dome-shaped crown reduce the compression ratio to 8.3:1 and are fitted on to stronger gudgeon pins, but the con-rods and complete bottom end remain as original except that heavy duty copper-lead big end shells are fitted in place of the aluminium-tin used in the unturbocharged engine.

The now widely used Garrett-AiResearch T3 turbocharger is mounted on a heavy, but flowed exhaust manifold cast in high nickel-content iron to withstand exhaust gas temperatures of up to 900°C. A large bore free flow stainless steel exhaust system handles the waste exhaust gases from the turbine discharge port.

The compressed air from the turbocharger at a maximum pressure of 7.0 psi, controlled by an integral wastegate valve, passes through an air-to-air intercooler mounted alongside the radiator.

Bosch electronically controlled KE-Jetronic fuel injection is used. There is an ingenious

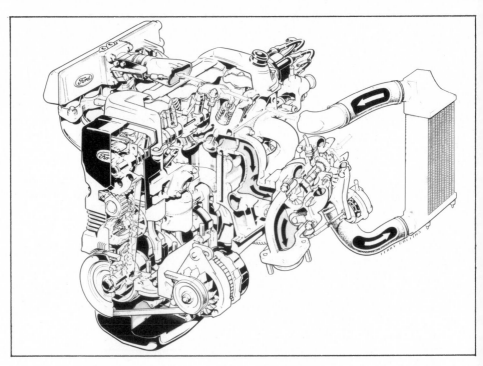

Above left *Ford Escort RS Turbo.*

Left Fig 97: *Cutaway view of Escort RS Turbo engine.*

Above *Turbocharged Ford Sierra RS Cosworth.*

electronic engine management system which controls both ignition and boost pressure. When the intake temperature rises to a previously determined maximum value, a microprocessor signals to a solenoid valve connected to the wastegate that the boost pressure should be lowered to avoid detonation, so the wastegate is opened to reduce the pressure. The ignition timing is fully programmed to adopt the optimum timing under a given set of conditions.

By using revised valve timing and careful matching of turbo to engine, maximum boost is reached by 2,500 rpm. Peak torque is 180 Nm at 3,000 rpm and the resultant torque curve is commendably flat.

Sierra RS Cosworth

Aimed ultimately at Group A production saloon car racing, the Ford Sierra RS (Cosworth) is being built in the Ford factory in Belgium. Five thousand examples will have to be manufactured to enable it to be homologated into Group 'A'. Its turbocharged 2.0-litre engine is based on the Ford Pinto 2.0-litre block assembly, on which is mounted a Cosworth-developed 16-valve twin OHC aluminium head. Weber electronic fuel injection is used, together with Marelli transistorised ignition. The turbocharger is a Garrett T3 unit. The road-going version produces 200 bhp, but at least 400 bhp is expected from the full race version.

Leyland MG Metro Turbo

This is the most powerful production version of the somewhat 'long in the tooth' 'A' Series engine to date, with 93 bhp at 6,150 rpm, which is 21 per cent more than the 1275 S Mini Cooper, and gives 85 lb/ft torque at a remarkably low 2,650 rpm at which point 2.0 psi boost is already available. Good low speed performance is partly achieved by retaining a 9.4:1 compression ratio. However, in order to avoid engine-damaging detonation under full load conditions, an electronically controlled air bleed connected to the wastegate pressure control pipe is used to open the wastegate under these conditions and limit boost to a maximum of 4.0 psi. When this control is not operating, maximum boost rises to 4.8 at 5,000 rpm, 7.3 at 6,000 and 7.7 at 6,300 rpm.

Modifications to the original unturbocharged engine specification include stronger pistons and big end caps, together with forged and nitrided crankshaft. Exhaust valves are sodium-filled, water passages in the cylinder head are enlarged and the oil pump has increased capacity. Ignition is Ducellier electronic. The clutch has a solid centre plate instead of the normal spring-loaded type.

MG Montego Turbo

Claimed to be the fastest production MG ever and certainly the fastest accelerating production car in terms of cost, the Garrett T3 turbocharged 1,994 cc O-Series produces 150 bhp at 5,100 rpm and maximum torque of 169 lb/ft at 3,500 rpm. Carburation is by a variable choke ARG modified SU-based pressurised carburettor. Fuel is supplied by a high pressure Bosch fuel pump coupled to a fuel pressure regulator which maintains fuel pressure at 5.0 psi above boost pressure. A conventional wastegate bypass valve controls maximum boost to 10 psi. Compression ratio is 8.5:1 and as is common practice with turbocharged engines, sodium-cooled exhaust valves are fitted. A knock sensor, which can retard the ignition timing for individual cylinders, is programmed with the ignition system.

Fiat Argenta VX

Introduced in 1984, this was the first mass production Fiat to be available with a supercharged engine. The supercharger system follows very closely that of the Lancia Volumex with twin lobed 'roots'-type supercharger, with a displacement of 1,130 cc, driven from the crankshaft by a rubber toothed belt at 1.32:1 drive ratio to engine speed and drawing through a twin choke downdraught Weber carburettor.

To eliminate excessive loading of the engine when cold, a pneumatic governor cuts out the carburettor second choke, until the engine is at working temperature. There is also a pneumatic water temperature regulator to cut off hot water circulation to the water-heated inlet manifold when the engine is being used in the boosted condition.

Uno Turbo

The Fiat Uno Turbo combines big engine performance and technology and, although based on the Uno 70, has a completely reworked engine which only retains the cast iron cylinder block. This is probably unique at this time. There is a new SOHC aluminium cylinder head with sodium-cooled exhaust valves, with bronze guides, sintered alloy seats, high temperature (NI-Resist) exhaust port inserts and special stainless steel reinforced head gasket. Other features designed for heat dissipation include oil jets to spray the underside of the special pistons and increased water circulation around the cylinder liners.

Fig 98: *Volumex supercharged Fiat Argenta VX engine.*

The turbocharger is a new IHI RHB52(W), the 'W' denoting water cooled bearing housing, with integral wastegate limiting maximum boost to 9.5 psi (0.65 bar). Maximum turbine speed is 130,000 rpm. Bosch LE fuel injection and Marelli microplex electronic ignition control, linked to a cylinder head-mounted detonation sensor, are used. The mapped ignition advance settings are controlled via two electro-magnetic sensors which measure top dead centre and flywheel speed—similar to the system used on the HF Delta turbo. The system also includes an air-to-air intercooler and an air bypass which is designed to maintain turbine speed under light throttle conditions, so improving subsequent throttle response.

105 bhp at 5,750 rpm is produced by this 1,300 cc engine, resulting in a power to weight ratio of 126 bhp per ton. An impressive 108 lb/ft of torque at only 3,200 rpm, combined with less than 20% variation over the 2,500-5,000 rpm range, produces very brisk performance for a 1,300 cc machine—0-60 mph in 8.6 seconds and a top speed of 120 mph.

Daihatsu Charade Turbo
Launched in April 1984 as the first production turbocharged car of under 1,000 cc with

Above left *Turbocharged Daihatsu Charade.*

Left *1.8 Litre Turbocharged Pontiac Sunbird.*

Above *GM Pontiac Sunbird turbocharged engine.*

Right Fig 99: *Pontiac Sunbird engine performance curves.*

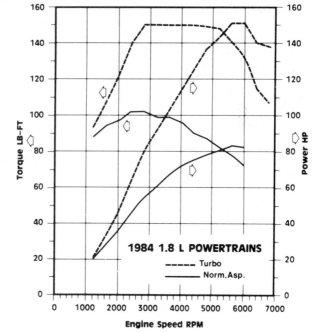

1984 1.8 L POWERTRAINS

- - - - - Turbo
———— Norm. Asp.

Torque LB-FT

Power HP

Engine Speed RPM

power output of 68 bhp at 5,500 rpm, the Charade Turbo has brisk performance for its size with 100 mph top speed.

Pontiac 2000 Sunbird

Launched in September 1983, the Sunbird has a 1.8-litre 4-cylinder SOHC port fuel-injected engine, producing 150 bhp at 5,600 rpm and 150 lb/ft torque at 2,800 rpm.

The Garrett AiResearch T2 turbo with integral wastegate produces a maximum boost of 9.4 psi. Long ram tuned runners feed the cylinders from a large plenum chamber, which fattens the power curve before the boost comes in. Spark timing and boost are fully electronically controlled. The exhaust manifold is unusual in that it is fabricated in stainless steel as opposed to the usual high nickel cast iron manifold.

Bentley Mulsanne Turbo

The Bentley Mulsanne Turbo is the world's fastest accelerating prestige limousine, considering its huge weight at nearly 5,000 lb, as can be seen in the chart at the beginning of this section. Its all-alloy 6,750 cc 90° V8 engine is as used in the naturally aspirated Rolls-Royce Silver Spirit, apart from modifications to accommodate the turbocharging system. These include a reduction in compression ratio to 8.0:1 and the fitment of a pressurised four-barrel, two-stage Solex carburettor.

The single Garrett T04B turbocharger is positioned at the end of the left-hand exhaust bank looking at the front of the engine. There is no intercooler in the system, but the compressed air from the turbo can be recirculated back to the air inlet side to maintain compressor speed as much as possible, and to reduce possible turbine lag to a minimum. The wastegate boost control system is activated by vacuum from the throttle cruise control pump.

As an additional safety device, in case of overspeed or wastegate malfunction, vacuum from the throttle cruise control pump can be used to open a valve in the plenum chamber to restrict boost to a maximum of 8.0 psi.

Toyota

Although Toyota had only one turbocharged model on sale in the UK in 1984, this being the Camry GL Turbo diesel launched in april 1984, they offer a much wider range of turbo models for the Japanese market. These include the 1,770 cc Corina, Celica and Corona—all using basically the same power unit which incorporates a Toyota-designed and manu-factured turbocharger and control system, although some earlier engines employed Garrett turbochargers as fitted to the 2.0-litre Crown and Cressida models. Another turbo model not available in Europe is the Toyota Crown 2.4-litre turbo diesel.

Peugeot

In line with their intended image boost, Peugeot have introduced their limited production 205 Turbo 16-valve, together with improvements to the 505 Turbo injection, and are planning to offer a 200 bhp high-performance version. Together with the turbo diesel models available, this brings the number of turbo models available to three.

205 Turbo 16

For a cool £26,000 (1984 price) you can buy one of these and join the super car league.

Above *Bentley Mulsanne Turbo.*

Below *Bentley Mulsanne Turbo engine bay layout*

Above *Toyota Camry 1.8 litre turbo-diesel.*
Below *Peugeot 505 turbocharged and fuel injected.*

Peugeot's 205 Turbo 16-valve, four-wheel-drive, mid-engined projectile has been developed for the prime purpose of winning the world rally championship and thereby obtaining the worldwide publicity and prestige that goes with winning this title.

The 1,775 cc engine of the road-going version has a compression ratio of 6.5:1 which produces 200 bhp at 6,500 rpm and maximum torque of 188 lb/ft at 4,000 rpm. It has a KKK turbocharger and employs an air-to-air intercooler. It accelerates from 0-60 mph in 5.9 seconds.

With an increase in boost pressure from the normal 0.7 to around 1.4 BAR, the competition versions will have power output expected to be well in excess of 300 bhp on tap and drastic lightening will reduce the weight from a relatively heavy 2,500 lb.

The transmission of all this power to the road is handled by a Ferguson-type epicycloidal differential, mounted centrally which splits the power 34/66 per cent front to rear. The percentage split can be varied to suit different rally conditions and it is said to take rally mechanics only nine minutes to do this.

505 Turbo Injection

Introduced in 1983, the Garrett T3-turbocharged Peugeot 505, fitted with the Bosch fuel-injected Talbot Tagora engine of 2,165 cc, received improvements for 1984 by incorporating an air-to-air intercooler, plus other detail changes including a higher compression ratio which serves to increase power output from 150 to 160 bhp and improve fuel consumption.

Peugeot 604D turbocharged diesel engine.

604 (Diesel) GTD Turbo

The old SRD-turbo introduced in 1980 is now the GTD turbo. The engine capacity is increased from 2,304 to 2,498 cc and power output rises from 80 bhp (DIN) to 94 bhp.

Ford (North America)

By 1984, Ford in North America had ten models equipped with turbocharged engines of two types: either the 1600 EFI (electric fuel injection) CVH engine or the 2,300 cc EFI single overhead camshaft turbo engine in two specifications, producing 145 and 175 bhp respectively.

The Escort, Lynx and EXP use the 1.6L EFI CVH engine; the Thunderbird, Cougar XR7, Mustang and Capri the 2.3L EFI SOHC.

Available in two specifications, the higher 175 bhp version has an air-to-air intercooler and maximum boost raised from 10.5 to 14.0 psi. This engine also employs an EEC-IV computer, an oil-to-water oil cooler and a dash-mounted switch which allows the driver to adjust the ignition timing for opeeration on high or low octane fuel.

Since the latter half of 1984 the Sierra XR4i has also been produced in 2.3-litre turbocharged form for the American market.

Citroen

Citroen's CX GTI turbo with a top speed of 136 mph and acceleration from 0-60 mph of 7.9 seconds, makes it the fastest production Citroen ever produced with the possible exception of the 1970's Citroen Maserati.

The 2.5-litre 4-cylinder engine is fitted with a Garrett AiResearch T3 turbocharger, which boosts power output to 168 bhp and maximum torque to 217 lb/ft at a relatively low 3,250

Below left *Turbocharged 2.3-litre Ford Cougar.*

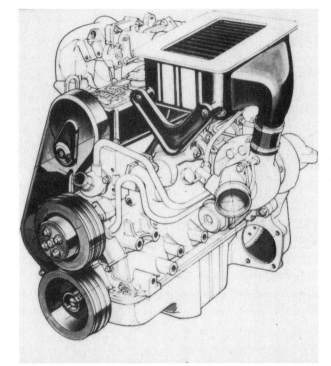

Right *Ford turbocharged 2.3-litre 4-cylinder SOHC.*

Below *Ford Cougar, cutaway view.*

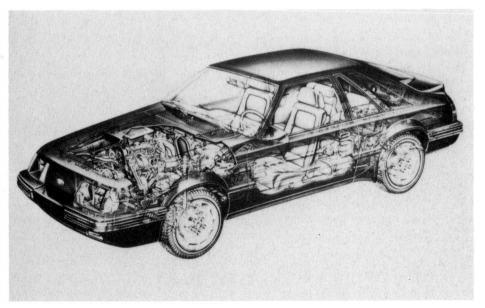

rpm. The boost pressure versus rpm curve gives a maximum pressure of 0.57 BAR (8.0 psi boost) at only 3,250 rpm, corresponding to the torque peak. Peak power is at 5,000 rpm, but at this point boost is engineered to drop to 6.0 psi. Fully mapped electronic ignition, incorporating a knock sensor, retards ignition timing at the onset of detonation. Fuel injection is Bosch L-Jetronic.

Mitsubishi Colt, Cordia and Tredia Turbo

Each of these models, introduced in 1982, is fitted with the same 4-cylinder OHC 1,597 cc turbocharged engine—power output being only some 8 bhp up on the smaller 1,410 cc unit at 113 bhp at 5,500 rpm. However, as might be expected, there is a far larger increase in torque with 125.3 lb/ft as opposed to 78.1 lb/ft at 3,500 rpm. Compression ratio is slightly lower at 8.5:1.

The Mitsubishi TC-04 turbocharger is one of the most compact units in production, with a compressor wheel of only 1.9-in in diameter and, unlike most turbo carburation systems, the single twin-choke downdraught carburettor is fitted upstream of the turbocharger and is therefore not pressurised. Maximum boost is 8.0 psi with a turbine speed of 90,000 rpm.

Colt Starion Turbo EX

The top of the performance range Starion is fitted with the same 1,997 cc 4-cylinder turbocharged engine as the Lancer 2000 Turbo, with ultrasonic electronic fuel injection. The turbocharging system is also similar to that of the Galant and Sapporo models with a maximum power output of 168 bhp at 5,500 rpm, and maximum boost of 0.91 BAR is provided by the Mitsubishi turbocharger at 3,500 rpm.

Performance too is impressive for a 2.0-litre mass-production car, with maximum speed of 137 mph and acceleration from 0-60 mph in 7.6 seconds.

Colt Starion

The new 1985 model now has a water-cooled Mitsubishi turbocharger and an air-to-air intercooler, which together with other detail improvements, increases power output to 177 bhp at 6,000 rpm and torque from 180 to 214 lb/ft. Top speed is increased to 143 mph.

Colt Galant/Sapporo Turbo

Both these models are fitted with a 2.0-litre 4-cylinder in-line engine, with fuel injection producing an impressive 168 bhp at 5,500 rpm and maximum torque of 181 lb/ft, at 3,500 rpm. Compression ratio is 7.6:1.

The turbocharger is a very compact Mitsubishi-designed unit with integral wastegate. The turbocharger system is an extremely well-engineered package, with a computer-controlled electronic (ECI) fuel injection system with sensors for ultrasonic airflow, air temperature, throttle position, throttle movement boost, engine speed and temperature, water temperature and battery voltage. Two injectors are used to provide the best swirl pattern which aids combustion efficiency. Again the injection pulses are computer-controlled to provide maximum performance for a minimum of fuel consumed, together with good driveability and low speed performance.

Above *Colt Cordia 1600 Turbo.*

Below *Colt Starion Turbo.*

Colt Shogun Turbo Diesel 4 wheel drive.

Colt Mirage Turbo

Introduced in 1982, this is the smallest-engined turbocharged model available in UK, with an OHC 4-cylinder in-line 1,410 cc engine producing 105 bhp at 5,500 rpm and 78.1 lb/ft torque at 3,500 rpm Carburation is by a single twin-choke unit. Compression ratio is 8.7:1. The engine is mounted transversely and drives the front wheels.

Ferrari

Twenty years after Ferrari produced the world-famous 250 GTO, a new 2.8-litre twin turbocharged 400 bhp V8 GTO was unveiled in 1984 at the Geneva Motor Show. This car was to be homologated into group 'B' for competition use, but is also being produced as a road-going model.

The 2,855 cc four overhead cam V8 engine is mounted longitudinally at the rear, with the twin turbocharger system mounted to the rear over the transmission, with a single large wastegate between the two units having its own exhaust outlet. The overall layout is similar to the turbocharger system on the Ferrari GP cars. Twin air-to-air intercoolers positioned over each bank of cylinders, cool the charge on its way into the twin inlet manifold. Two separate Weber-Marelli electronic injection and ignition systems are employed, each feeding one bank of the engine.

Performance is quite dramatic for a road vehicle, with the standing start ¼-mile covered in 12.7 seconds with terminal speed of over 190 mph. Likewise, 0-60 mph in 4.9 seconds is equally impressive.

Above and below *Turbocharged Ferrari GTO.*

Lancia Volumex Coupé

After a gap of many years, since a production Lancia appeared with an original equipment supercharger, and possibly the first large volume supercharged as opposed to turbocharged car ever to be offered by a major manufacturer, Lancia launched their Volumex Coupé and HPE models in 1983.

The engine is mounted transversely in this front wheel car. It is a 4-cylinder 1,995 cc unit with cast iron block and dry liners, along with aluminium alloy twin overhead camshaft cylinder head. Compression ratio is 7.5:1.

The supercharger is a 'roots'-type with twin lobed rotors and gear driven from the crankshaft to provide a maximum boost of 0.4 BAR (5.7 psi). Carburation is by single 36 DCA5/250 Weber and no intercooler is fitted. Maximum power output is 135 bhp at 5,500 rpm and maximum torque 152 lb/ft at 3,000 rpm.

Y10 Autobianchi Turbo

Announced in the spring of 1985, this 1,050 cc engined car fitted with an IHI B51 turbocharger with integral wastegate, produces 85 bhp giving an excellent power-to-weight ratio. As might be expected, performance is lively with a 0-60 mph time of 9.5 seconds. A Weber 32 TLF/250 twin choke carburettor and Marelli Digiplex ignition are used.

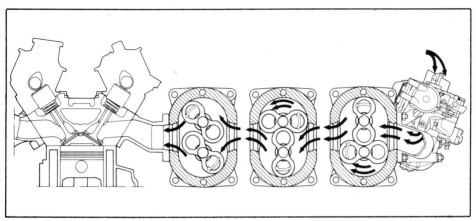

Below left *Supercharged Lancia Volumex Coupé.*

Above Fig 100: *Lancia Volumex Supercharger.*

Below Fig 101: *Lancia Volumex supercharged engine.*

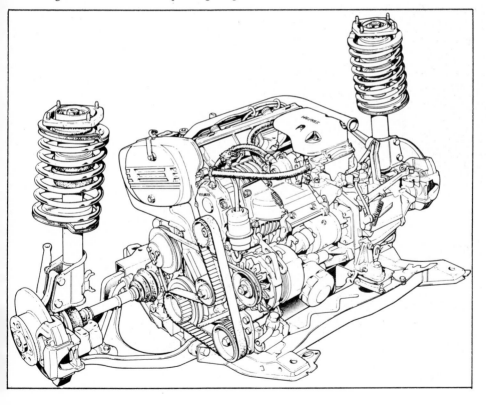

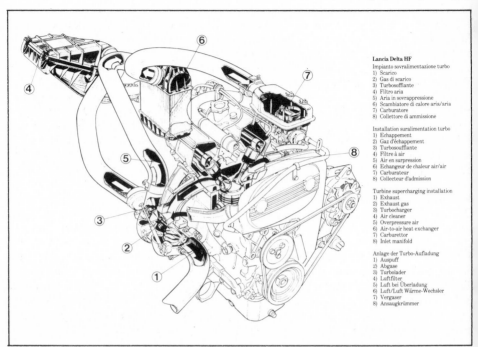

Lancia Delta HF

Impianto sovralimentazione turbo
1) Scarico
2) Gas di scarico
3) Turbosoffiante
4) Filtro aria
5) Aria in sovrappressione
6) Scambiatore di calore aria/aria
7) Carburatore
8) Collettore di ammissione

Installation suralimentation turbo
1) Echappement
2) Gaz d'échappement
3) Turbosoufflante
4) Filtre à air
5) Air en surpression
6) Echangeur de chaleur air/air
7) Carburateur
8) Collecteur d'admission

Turbine supercharging installation
1) Exhaust
2) Exhaust gas
3) Turbocharger
4) Air cleaner
5) Overpressure air
6) Air-to-air heat exchanger
7) Carburettor
8) Inlet manifold

Anlage der Turbo-Aufladung
1) Auspuff
2) Abgase
3) Turbolader
4) Luftfilter
5) Luft bei Überladung
6) Luft/Luft Wärme-Wechsler
7) Vergaser
8) Ansaugkrümmer

Above Fig 102: *Cutaway view of Lancia Delta HF Turbo engine.*

Below *Lancia Delta HF Turbo.*

Lancia Delta HF Turbo

The supercharged Volumex Coupé never quite lived up to its expected image due to a rather conservative power output in relation to the weight of the vehicle. In any case, Lancia were more interested in using this engine as the basis for their world rally championship winner. The latest Lancia 038, 450 bhp Group B rally car, is based on the production Delta HF Turbo, although one would be hard put to find many similarities between the two.

The twin overhead camshaft 1,585 cc power unit produces 130 bhp at 5,600 rpm and maximum torque of 141 lb ft at 3,700 rpm, with the aid of a Garrett T3 turbocharger, maximum boost of 10.0 psi and an air-to-air intercooler. A single pressurised Weber 32DAT twin choke carburettor feeds the engine and other components special to the turbocharged engine include a Microplex electronic ignition system, micro-processor and special cylinder head gasket and sodium cooled exhaust valves.

Maserati Bi-Turbo

One of the most exclusive cars in the world is powered by an engine with a technical specification to match. The engine is a 90° V6 2,491 cc with double overhead camshafts per cylinder head, incorporating four valves and twin plugs per cylinder. Compression ratio is 7.8:1 and power output 195 bhp at 5,500 rpm. The turbocharger system comprises two IHI turbochargers—one per bank of three cylinders, which supply boost to a plenum shrouding a downdraught Weber carburettor. The MABC (Maserati Automatic Boost Control) system is linked to the wastegate on each turbo by microprocessor, solenoid valve and detonation sensor. With this system wastegate opening, and therefore boost pressure, is optimised to match the maximum permissible under the prevailing conditions.

Subaru XT Turbo Coupé

An unusual water-cooled flat four engine design, this 1,781 cc turbocharged version produces 134 bhp at 5,600 rpm and 145 lb/ft of torque at 2,800 rpm, with multi-point electronically controlled fuel injection and ignition.

Chapter 11

Trends and developments

The present trend in the automobile world is towards economy, with smaller, lighter engines which produce less toxic exhaust gases, yet still give a relatively high power output with good bottom end torque. They must be reliable, unfussy to drive and maintain, also smooth and quiet. By turbo-supercharging, excellent results can be achieved in all of these areas, particularly with turbocharged diesels, providing sufficient technical development is carried out with the engine concerned and its related components. But the present production turbocharged engines still have plenty of further potential for development.

The adoption of forced induction could and should have been taken up several years earlier for the smaller automobile diesel engines. If this had been so, the state of the art of supercharging would have been more fully developed. Until such a time as there was a large enough demand for smaller, more efficient turbochargers, no turbocharger manufacturer was particularly interested in developing these units 'on spec', so to speak. However, two principal factors have led in the last few years to a growing interest in forced induction as a means of achieving high power and torque outputs from smaller engines with good specific fuel consumption. Namely, the energy crisis, with a consequent rapid rise in fuel costs, and the need to clean up exhaust emissions.

The energy crisis has led to a considerable reduction in the number of large capacity (over 3.0-litre) engines, yet there is still a demand for good performance. The reduction in fuel octane ratings to reduce the amount of lead additive in the fuel, together with exhaust emission devices to clean up the exhaust gases, led to a reduction in compression ratios, or general 'de-tuning' to meet the ever stricter emission regulations. However, more recently, compression ratios have been rising again in the interests of improved specific performance.

The fact that forced induction can deliver the goods has been proved beyond all doubt.

There is, however, one crucial factor which above all others determines the long-term reliability or otherwise of the pressure-charged engine. This is the average cylinder combustion temperature under full load. The cylinder combustion temperature is primarily governed by the mean compression pressures, inlet charge temperatures, and the engine's heat dissipation ability.

It has been shown that the actual compression pressure peak of a turbocharged petrol engine, using up to 12.0 psi boost with a compression ratio of 7.0:1, is only marginally higher than a normally-aspirated engine running 9.0:1 compression ratio, although the pressure curve is considerably broadened due to the greater weight of charge being burned. Therefore, the second factor to consider is inlet charge temperature. This is a function of the ambient air temperature, the compressor efficiency and induction design, coupled with pressure ratio employed.

Again, it has been shown that a relatively low maximum boost (not more than 10 psi), is all that is required to achieve a substantial power increase provided good boost is available from low rpm. Even so, an intercooler should be incorporated in all production turbo systems as a matter of course. To this day, almost all turbocharging systems, even the extensively developed ones, are additions to a basic normally-aspirated engine, which has been modified to accept the turbocharging system. This is not strictly true, however, as far as some diesel engines are concerned. When the day comes that a manufacturer actually tools up a new engine specifically for supercharging and the normally-aspirated versions are the option packages, that is the time pressurised induction will have come of age.

More recent trends have seen the development of water-cooled bearing housings to extend

Right Fig 103: *The Bendix vane type supercharger. This is a new supercharger designed and developed by the Bendix Company. Although it incorporates some refined design features, in essence it is similar to the Shorrock vane type supercharger in its operating principle, apart from the fact that it has no internal compression. Other features are sealed-for-life bearings, a bypass valve and clutch to disengage the supercharger when it is not required. The Allard Motor Company experimented with a similar arrangement on the Shorrock supercharger back in 1965, but did not have the development facilities to perfect such a system as Bendix have done. This supercharger has the potential for reviving interest in positive displacement supercharging.*

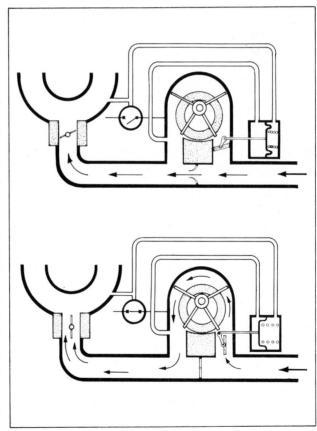

Above *Bendix vane type supercharger installed on VW Scirocco* (Photo courtesy Bendix).

turbocharger bearing life, and ceramic components, principally the turbine wheel assembly which has less weight for a given size of wheel, which improves the rate of acceleration, at the same time allowing higher exhaust gas temperatures before turbine failure.

Other interesting developments include variable vane geometry to improve compressor and turbine efficiency over a wide speed range.

Water-cooled bearing housing

Water-cooled turbocharger bearing housings are now becoming quite commonplace and within a few years all production turbocharged cars will have turbochargers incorporating this feature. For many years one weakness in the design of all turbochargers has been the excessive heat build-up around the turbine shaft and bearing. The most critical period is when the engine is switched off immediately after medium to heavy use. The consequent heat soak is transferred to the remaining lubricating oil residue surrounding the bearings, housing and turbine shaft. The excessive heat soak can be sufficient to burn off the oil film and damage bearings and shaft surfaces, leading to rapid wear of the rotating assembly and bearing housing. By introducing a cooling water flow around the bearing housing, this problem is largely eliminated and the turbocharger core assembly service life can be substantially extended.

I see a move towards better cooling systems, with improved intercoolers and more efficient compressors as essential developments. Smaller, lighter, lower-inertia turbos with built-in wastegates and compressor efficiencies of 80 per cent or higher over a wider operating range, with a 65 per cent overall efficiency, will also come. Higher volumes of production, coupled with improved production techniques and materials, should offset rising costs and help to make the turbocharger more cost-effective.

It should not be assumed, however, that the turbocharger in its present form is the best type of supercharger for all automobile applications. In fact, it is acknowledged that, despite its high peak adiabatic efficiency as compared to current mechanically-driven superchargers, the turbo-supercharger has ideally quite the wrong characteristics for automobile use. There are signs that not all manufacturers have opted for turbochargers to the exclusion of all other supercharging devices. If a pump could be designed which had air delivery characteristics similar to those of a vane-type supercharger, and with overall dimensions similar to current turbo compressors, it might be possible to couple this to an exhaust gas turbine or a device which utilises the exhaust gas heat energy. The Comprex pressure-wave supercharger represents a move in this direction.

The Comprex pressure-wave supercharger

This supercharger was developed by Brown Boveri et Cie in Switzerland, primarily to provide improved low-speed torque and throttle response, as compared to the current turbocharged diesels. The Comprex system employs a method of transferring the exhaust gas energy directly to the inlet charge entering the engine. A rotor with radial vanes is driven from the engine crankshaft in a similar manner to a normal mechanically-driven super-charger at up to twice engine speed. The inlet and outlet ports for the inlet air are at one end of the rotor casing and the exhaust ports at the other end.

Air enters the inlet port and is carried round by the vanes until it is opposite the exhaust gas inlet port. At this point, the high pressure exhaust gases rush into the chamber and compress the inlet charge. During this process the exhaust gases are reflected back out of the exhaust port and the inlet charge directed into the engine. The pressure wave created by the exit of the exhaust gas through the exhaust port, allows a fresh inlet charge to enter the inlet port, and so the cycle continues. Since the exhaust gas does not have to drive any machinery, throttle response should be instantaneous.

On first examination, one would imagine that both heat transfer to the inlet charge and contamination by the hot exhaust gases would be a problem, but due to the very short contact period between inlet charge and exhaust gas this is not a significant drawback. Comparison with a turbocharger system applying a similar maximum boost shows that the Comprex offers much better throttle response and torque at relatively low speeds, but somewhat less maximum power, probably due to the higher back pressure (approx 10-20 per cent higher) reflected back to the engine and power consumed in driving the rotor.

The Comprex is mechanically relatively simple, there being no sophisticated seals or lubrication requirement, but the rotor and housing have to be manufactured from a heat resistant iron-nickel alloy (Inver) with a very low expansion coefficient, so that the vane-to-housing clearances can be kept as close as possible to ensure maximum compression efficiency. Although it has a comparatively flat boost curve, similar in fact to a positive-displacement supercharger, some form of boost limitation is necessary if the torque peak is required at low rpm. Both the rotor size and its drive speed will also, of course, influence the boost versus rpm curve for a given engine displacement.

The Comprex pressure-wave supercharger combines the best features of both a

Below right *The Comprex is a pressure wave supercharger which in essence combines the instant response and high torque back-up at low engine speed characteristic of a positive displacement supercharger, with a mechanical and thermal efficiency approaching that of a turbo supercharger. The Brown Boveri pressure-wave supercharger has a very flat boost curve and a wide operating range. It utilises the energy contained in the exhaust gases to compress the air entering the rotor housing, and the continuous cycle is controlled by the rotor which is driven at approximately 1.5 times engine speed to achieve a charging pressure of up to 3.0:1 pressure ratio (45 psi boost). Two ranges of Comprex units have veen developed, one for commercial vehicles and one for diesel-engined cars in the 50-150 bhp range.*

Below left *Cutaway through the Comprex pressure-wave supercharger* (Brown Boveri).

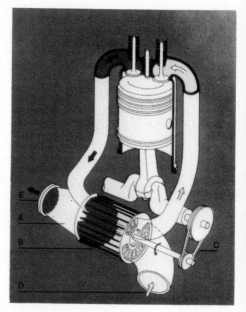

positive-displacement and turbo-supercharger. Thus, by driving the rotor mechanically directly from the engine, almost instant throttle response is an attractive feature of this design, and by using the energy contained in the rapidly expanding exhaust gases to compress the inlet charge, a high degree of mechanical and thermal efficiency is obtained.

Until recently the Comprex supercharger has been applied to the medium and larger diesel engines used in trucks, but tests are being conducted on Comprex supercharged petrol engines with good results, particularly in respect of low speed throttle response. In the competition field, the Ferrari Formula One engine has been Comprex-supercharged and the results so far in terms of power output and throttle response are promising. I have a feeling that others will follow this route and we shall be seeing more Comprex-equipped vehicles.

Although there is likely to be a much wider use of turbocharged petrol engines, when high power output is required from a small cylinder displacement with good fuel economy, and also in the competition field, the large majority of turbocharged automobile engines are likely to be high-speed indirect-injection diesel engines.

Other areas of potential development with pressurised induction include stratified charge and pre-chamber lean burn engines, computer-programmed fuel and ignition systems incorporating detonation sensors, oil-cooled pistons, cylinder heads or gaskets incorporating special high-pressure sealing rings, methanol and other alternative fuels, water and other additive injection, additional air or fuel injection to increase low-speed torque and reduce emissions. Two-stage turbo- and supercharging and turbocharging in series, turbocharged Wankel engines, variable nozzle and blade geometry for turbine and compressor and the Hyperbar system, ceramic turbines, ceramic coatings and Vespel components, are some of the possible and probable development areas. This is just a brief resumé, but may give readers some idea of the considerable area of further development which exists.

Chapter 12

Turbochargers in production

Up until about 1975 there was a relatively small production of turbo units for passenger cars and even total turbocharger production, including all units produced for diesel-engined commercial vehicles, amounted to not much more than one million units per year. However, in the last few years since 1979 there has been a rapid expansion of production, both for passenger car and commercial vehicle use, with production in 1984 for passenger cars amounting to an estimated world production of 1.5 million, which was expected to rise to over two million units in 1985.

The leading manufacturer in number of units produced is the American company Garrett-AiResearch, other major manufacturers being KKK (German), Mitsubishi, IHI, Toyota, Nissan and Hitachi (Japan). Also principally producing units for diesel engine applications are Schwitzer and Cummins (USA) and Holset (UK). Other major manufacturers of turbo units include Rajay and Rotomaster (USA).

Several of these manufacturers are working to produce a production turbocharger using a ceramic turbine wheel, which will allow higher running temperatures with increased speed and therefore higher turbine performance from a very light turbine and compressor wheel assembly.

Rajay

In 1983 Rotomaster took over the manufacturing rights of Rajay turbochargers and now manufacture and market these units. However, the range continues virtually unchanged.

Rajay turbochargers are constructed to the highest technical specifications yet the robust but simple design makes servicing easy, no special tools being necessary to strip and re-assemble the unit. Rajay turbochargers have, unlike most other turbochargers in current production, a diecast aluminium centre body incorporating a dual-feed one piece semi-floating bearing. Such a design allows an extremely short mounting length, only 4.5 in in the case of model 3CC/BB.22.B1, and maximum heat dissipation from around the bearing which is an important factor in maintaining a long service life. The 300 series turbocharger is manufactured with three basic compressor and turbine wheel sizes. In B, F and E trims, each turbine wheel can be used with a range of turbine housings of varying A/R ratio, so that an optimum turbocharger size and match can be selected for each engine. All Rajay turbochargers are fitted with a mechanical face oil seal to allow mounting of a carburettor before the compressor if required. Turbochargers are manufactured suitable for engines ranging in capacity from 750 cc to 7,500 cc.

Rajay turbocharger specifications

Model	*302.B*	*301.F*	*304.E*
Maximum pressure ratio (PR)	3.0	3.2	3.3
Maximum turbine speed (rpm)	110,000	110,000	110,000
Maximum gas temperature (continuous operation) °C	750	750	750
Weight without wastegate (lb)	12	12	14
Air flow range (CFM) at 1.5 (PR)	105-240	125-275	175-500
Engine capacities covered (cc) petrol	750-2,300	1,800-3,800	3,000-6,500
Minimum oil pressure (psi) at idle	10	10	10
under load	25	25	25
Maximum allowable oil drain positioning from vertical	45°	45°	45°
Oil drain pipe ID (in) min	½	½	½

Turbocharger unit range

Model	Approx engine bhp range
302B	45-200
301.F.	55-275
304E	100-400

Rajay turbo, a range of units and housings are available to suit most engines in the 750-7,500 cc range.

To suit certain engine torque and power requirements, it is possible to use alternative matches. For example, an 'F' flow compressor could be used with a 'B' flow turbine wheel, but in general the above specifications will give a good result, with a maximum boost of up to 10.0 psi and maximum engine rpm of 6,000 at up to 3,000 ft.

Rotomaster

Rotomaster has, in relatively few years, become one of the established turbocharger specialists, producing a range of turbochargers and parts similar to and interchangeable with many AiResearch and some Schwitzer, Holset and KKK turbochargers, primarily as replacement units for many commercial vehicles. Rotomaster also manufacture turbocharger units for passenger cars and a range of Turbosonic kits and components. These turbochargers are fitted with mechanical face seals to allow suck-through carburettor arrangement if required. Janspeed Engineering handle the importation and distribution of units for the car market in the UK.

Rotomaster turbocharger specifications

Model T04B	Y.4/N	S.4/0	V.2/P
Maximum pressure ratio (PR)	3.0	3.0	3.2
Maximum turbocharger speed (rpm)	125,000	125,000	125,000
Maximum gas temperature (continuous operation) °C	750	750	750
Weight (lb)	16	16	17
Air flow range (CFM) at 1.5 (PR)	100-300	160-375	180-450
Engine capacities covered (cc) petrol	800-2,800	2,600-4,700	4,300-6,500
Minimum oil pressure (psi) at idle	15.0	15.0	15.0
under load	30.0	30.0	30.0
Maximum allowable oil drain positioning from vertical	35°	35°	35°
Oil drain pipe ID (in) min	½	½	½

A new small turbocharger, the RM-60 with detachable wastegate assembly, was introduced in 1982. This unit is suitable for petrol engines in the range of 30-180 bhp.

Turbocharger unit range

Model	Approx engine bhp range
R-M.60	30-180
T04B.Y.4/N	45-240
T04B.S.4/O	100-275
T04B.V.2/P	130-375

Garrett AiResearch

Garrett are the largest manufacturer of turbochargers worldwide and are able to provide a very wide range of units, backed by some of the best design and research facilities available. A large percentage of the turbocharged cars in production are equipped with AiResearch T3

Right *Rotomaster T04B turbo-charger. Normally available in three trim sizes, each with a range of turbine housings to suit engines ranging in size from 800-6,500 cc.*

Below *Rotomaster RM60 turbo-charger—the smallest model in the range from Rotomaster.*

turbochargers, and the recently introduced T2 as fitted to the Renault 11 which is a very compact lightweight unit yet with a relatively high air flow capacity.

Garrett AiResearch began producing turbochargers suitable for passenger cars back in

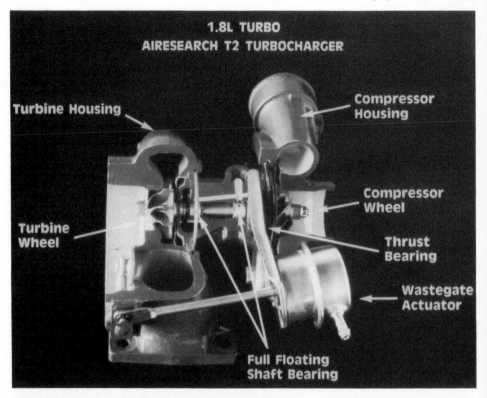

**1.8L TURBO
AIRESEARCH T2 TURBOCHARGER**

Turbine Housing

Compressor Housing

Compressor Wheel

Turbine Wheel

Thrust Bearing

Wastegate Actuator

Full Floating Shaft Bearing

Above *Cutaway view of light-weight 'mini' Garrett AiResearch T2 turbocharger with integral wastegate.*

Left *Cutaway view of a Garrett AiResearch T3 turbocharger with poppet valve wastegate.*

1962; prior to that time all units had been for diesels. The Garrett company foresaw the potential for a greatly expanded market in Europe and in 1970 established the Garrett AiResearch turbocharger division, Skelmersdale, Lancashire, England. Since then establishments have been set up in several European countries, Japan and Argentina, Brazil, Canada and Australia. Some idea of the rapid expansion of the turbocharger market can be realised from these figures. It took 22 years until 1974 to produce the first million units, from 1975-1979 production increased to 3.5 million units with current production at well over 3 million turbochargers per year.

Garrett-AiResearch turbocharger range

Model	Approximate engine bhp range
T2	35-180
T3 (petrol)	50-220
T3 (diesel)	50-160
T31	60-170
T04B	75-375
TV61	220-425
TV71	250-475
TV81	300-575
T18A	420-750

Holset

Apart from the AiResearch and Schwitzer units produced in the UK, Holset are the only other turbocharger manufacturer with manufacturing facilities in the UK. Holset entered the turbocharger business in 1954 when they took out a licence from the inventor of the turbocharger, Dr Alfred Buchi of Switzerland. Then, in 1957, Holset obtained the European manufacturing rights for a smaller and lighter design of turbocharger from the Schwitzer Corporation in Indianapolis, USA. From the early 1960s Holset's turbocharger production became well established, with most of the units going for export. In 1973 Holset was acquired by the Cummins Engine Company Inc, USA. Holset has produced over one million turbocharger units. They manufacture a wide range of small- and medium-sized turbochargers for diesel engine applications. The 3LD model has been widely used in many small diesel engine applications, but the latest turbocharger is the H series, the H1 being the smallest of the range. It has provision for an integral wastegate and is suitable for both diesel and petrol engines in the range of 60-200 hp. Turbochargers are available in the UK through Lucas/Cav Parts Organisation.

Holset turbocharger range

Model	Approximate engine bhp range
H1A	60-180
H1B	90-210
H2A	150-270
H2B	170-300
H3	180-500
H4	300-700

Other models produced: H1 C/D, H2 C/D, 3LD, 3FD, 3FJ, 3LE, 4LE, 4LF, 4LG, 4HD, 4MD, 4MF, 4LEV, 4LEK, 4LFK, 4LFV and 4LGK.

IHI

IHI turbochargers are produced by Ishikawajima-Harima, Heavy Industries Co Ltd in Japan. IHI's involvement with turbochargers began in the 1939-45 period and in 1951 they started production of automotive and small marine turbochargers. By the 1960s the range had expanded to suit larger engines. Later the RH series was developed and between 1977-79 the RB series featuring a backward-curved blade impeller design for improved efficiency and flow range. Current developments include the RU series for pressure ratios of as high as 4.5:1. The RHB51 turbocharger is one of the smallest in the world: with an overall length of 5¾ in and diameter of 4¼ in it weighs only 6.2 lb (2.8 kg) without wastegate. These units are available with integral wastegate and are suitable for petrol engines with draw-through carburettor arrangement. Engines down to 20 bhp can be turbocharged with the RHB51 turbocharger. Also recently developed is an even smaller unit, but this is not currently available in Europe.

Several Japanese car and motor cycle manufacturers use IHI turbochargers. Of the European manufacturers, Maserati use IHI turbos on their bi-turbo and Lancia on their Y10 and Fiat UNO which is water cooled. Production of IHI turbochargers has increased substantially in the last few years with several Japanese manufacturers also using IHI turbochargers.

IHI turbocharger specifications

Model	RHB51	RHB52	RHB6	RHB7
Maximum pressure ratio (PR)	3.0	3.0	3.0	3.0
Maximum turbine speed (rpm)	180,000	180,000	150,000	125,000

Maximum gas temperature				
(continuous operation) °C	750	750	750	750
Weight without wastegate (lb)	6.2	7.0	9.1	14.6
Air flow range (CFM) at 1.5 (PR)	30-300	50-310	67-494	148-664
Engine range covered (bhp)				
petrol	20-200	25-210	35-230	60-305
diesel	15-160	20-170	30-190	60-220
Minimum oil pressure (psi)				
at idle	15	15	15	15
under load	30	30	30	30
Maximum allowable oil drain				
positioning from vertical	15°	15°	15°	15°
Oil drain pipe ID (in) min	7/16	7/16	7/16	½

Turbocharger unit range

Model	Approx engine bhp range (petrol engines)
RHB51	20-200
RHB52	25-210
RHB6	35-230
RHB7	60-305
RHB8	100-435

There is also the RU series for diesel engines up to 1,380 hp with 4.5 pressure ratio.

Above far left *Sectional view of Holset H3 turbocharger with twin tract turbine housing.*

Above left *Holset H1 turbocharger with integral wastegate* (Photos courtesy Holset).

Right *IHI RHB6 turbocharger with integral wastegate.*

Left *KKK turbocharger—sectional view of unit used by Porsche.*

Right *Schwitzer turbocharger. A wide range of units are manufactured for use on diesel engines.*

Far right *Schwitzer turbocharger—one of a wide range produced by this manufacturer for diesel engines.*

Below right *Sectional view of Mitsubishi turbocharger.*

KKK

KKK turbochargers are manufactured in West Germany by Kuhnle, Kopp and Kausch. They came into the turbocharger market in 1962 when they obtained a licence to manufacture with technical information from the Schwitzer Corporation based in Indianapolis, USA. In 1972 KKK took over the manufacturing and marketing of Eberspächer turbochargers and since 1974 have produced their own range of turbocharger units. These units cover engines ranging in power from 80 to over 1,000 bhp. The K24 and 26 turbos, the smallest of the range, have an integral wastegate and the latest range have water-cooled bearing housings.

Porsche have fitted KKK turbochargers almost exclusively since they began using turbochargers both for their production and racing cars. Other manufacturers to use KKK turbochargers include Mercedes and BMW. In Formula One racing, many of the teams incuding BMW, Porsche and Ferrari have used KKK turbochargers.

KKK turbocharger range

Model	Approximate engine bhp range
K2	75-300
K3	100-435
K4	400-620
K5	550-750
K6	700-900

Schwitzer

Schwitzer manufacture turbochargers for a wide range of diesel applications, mainly for the medium to larger engines. Recently however, they have extended their range downwards to cover some of the smaller diesels.

Their S65 and S2 models are now being produced with integral wastegate, so that this model can be used on petrol-engined applications.

Schwitzer have a large manufacturing operation in the UK in Bradford, West Yorks, and in Brazil. Their main factory is in Indianapolis, USA.

Mitsubishi

Another Japanese manufacturer who produces large numbers of turbo units. Some of the smaller range are seen on Mitsubishi cars such as the Starion, Lancer, Galant, Tredia, Cordia and Silvia.

Toyota

Toyota produce their own turbochargers for a range of their turbocharged vehicles, both petrol- and diesel-engined. Although this make of turbocharger is being produced in rapidly increasing numbers, little is seen of it in Europe.

Cummins

An American diesel engine manufacturer which produces units exclusively for its own medium and large diesel engines, although units are occasionally used in other experimental applications.

Alfa Romeo

Alfa Romeo, through their zero engineering operation, currently produce a limited number of units for their own products and this facility may expand when the company produces turbocharged models in larger volume.

Appendix 1

Formulae

To convert CFM to lb/min air flow = CFM × .0765

To convert lb/min to CFM = lb/min × .069

$$\text{Torque} = \frac{\text{BHP} \times 5{,}250}{\text{RPM}}$$

To convert engine cc (cubic centimetres) to CID (cubic inch displacement)
= cc × 0.06102 = CID

To convert engine displacement in litres to CID
= litres × 61.02 = CID

To calculate air flow CFM (cubic feet per minute) for turbocharged engines

$$= \frac{\text{RPM} \times \text{CID} \times \text{volumetric efficiency}}{3{,}456} \times \text{Density ratio}$$

$$\text{HP} = \frac{\text{Torque} \times \text{RPM}}{5{,}250}$$

To calculate compression ratio reduction to maintain standard compression ratio in super-charged engine; where R1 = unsupercharged compression ratio, R2 = compression ratio for supercharged engine, P1 = inlet pressure and P2 = discharge pressure:

$$R2 = R1\left(\frac{P1}{P2}\right) \times 0.5$$

To calculate compressor discharge charge temperature; where T1 = inlet temperature (degrees Rankine), T2 = outlet temperature (degrees Rankine), P1 = inlet pressure and P2 = discharge pressure:

$$T2 = T1\left(\frac{P2}{P1}\right) \times 0.283$$

divided by actual compressor adiabatic efficiency.

To obtain the correct supercharger to engine drive ratio; where R = the required ratio, E = engine capacity, B = required boost (psi) and S = volume of supercharger per revolution:

$$R = E \frac{(1 + B/15)}{2.S}$$

Appendix 2

Useful addresses

AET Engineering Limited, Normanton Industrial Estate, Beckbridge Road, Normanton, Wakefield, WF6 1TE; Tel (0924) 894171. KKK Turbochargers—supply and exchange.

Albert Turbo, Worgl, Austria; Tel 010-05332/2483. Turbo systems.

Allard Turbochargers, Unit 3, Alton Road Industrial Estate, Ross-on-Wye, Herefordshire, HR9 5NB; Tel (0989) 63963. Turbo systems. Turbo overhauls and exchange. Sprintex Superchargers.

Argyll Turbo Cars Limited, Minnow House, Lochgilphead, Argyll, Scotland; Tel (0546) 2418. Turbo systems.

Autopower Services, South March, Long March Industrial Estate, Daventry, Northants; Tel (032872) 76161. Supercharging systems.

A.V.A. Turbo Systems, 16 Beardmore Way, Clydebank Industrial Estate, Clydebank, Glasgow; Tel (041) 952-0807. Turbo systems.

Blower Drive Service, 12140 Washington Blvd, Whittier, CA 90606. Superchargers.

British Brown-Boveri Limited, Glen House, Stag Place, London, SW1E 5AH. Comprex supercharger.

BTN Turbos, Arundel Road, Uxbridge Industrial Estate, Uxbridge, Middlesex; Tel (0895) 56416. Turbo supply, overhaul and exchange.

Camden Superchargers Inc, 2404 Rutland Road, Austin, Texas 78758. Superchargers.

CJ Maintenance, 39 The Ham, Westbury, Wiltshire; Tel (Westbury) 823525. Diesel turbo Systems.

Derek Chinn Esq, Precision Engineering, 34 Howbury Street, Bedford, MK40 3QU; Tel (0234) 214018. Roots-type supercharger manufacturer.

Detroit Diesel Allison, PO Box 6, London Road, Wellingborough, Northants, NN8 2DL. Commercial turbo systems.

Fleming Thermodynamics Limited, 16/17 Fleming Court, Clydebank Business Park, Glasgow, G81 2DR; Tel (041) 952-0933. Manufacturer of Sprintex superchargers.

Gordon-Leeming Motor Engineers, 2-6 Pottery Lane, Newcastle upon Tyne, Tyne and Wear; Tel (Newcastle upon Tyne) 617857. Turbo conversions.

Janspeed Engineering, Castle Road, Salisbury, Wiltshire; Tel (0722) 21833. Turbo systems.

Magnacharger. 1020 N. Fuller Street, Santa Ana, CA 92701. Superchargers.

Malton Autopoint, 2 Scarborough Road, Norton, Malton, North Yorkshire; Tel (0653) 5151. Turbo conversions.

Millers Garage, 51 Kernick Road, Penryn, Cornwall; Tel (0326) 73825. Turbo conversions.

NLR Tuning, Horsley on Tyne, Newcastle, NE15 0NT; Tel (Wylam) 3776. Turbo conversions.

Opico, UK Limited, 47 Westlode Street, Spalding, Lincs; Tel (Spalding) 5691. Tractor turbo conversions.

Pace Products, Bridge House, Stradishall, Suffolk; Tel (044) 082-0687. Turbocharger systems.

PAO Preparations, Lottage Road, Aldbourne, Nr Marlborough, Wiltshire; Tel (0672) 40001/2. Turbo systems.

Rewster Turbos, Unit 7, Silverstone Circuit, Nr Towcester, Northants. Turbo conversions.

Rover Craft, 11 Wastdale Road, Forest Hill, London SE23; Tel (01) 699-8086/9346. Turbo conversions.

Serck Services, Claybrook Drive, Washford Industrial Estate, Redditch, Worcs; Tel (Redditch) 26111. Turbo overhauls. Turbo exchange units.

Southern Supercharger Services, The Race Shop, Railway Sidings, Meopham, Kent; Tel (0474) 812498. Sprintex Supercharger Systems.

T.B. Turbos Limited, Turbo House, Port Royal Avenue, Lancaster, LA1 5QP; Tel (0524) 67157. Diesel turbo systems.

Turbocharger Services, Unit 1, Spenborough Industrial Estate, Union Road, Liversedge, West Yorkshire; Tel (0924) 401066. Turbo supply, overhaul and exchange.

Turbo International, Crofton Drive, Lincoln, LN3 4NR; Tel (Lincoln) 38811. Turbo supply, overhaul and exchange.

Turbo Power, Unit 8, Dock Road, West Bank Dock Estate, Widnes, Cheshire; Tel (051) 424-4204. Exchange turbos.

Turbo Technics Limited, 17 Gallowhill Road, Brackmills, Northampton, NN4 0EE; Tel (Northampton) 64005. Turbo systems. Garrett AiResearch overhauls.

Turbo Tork, Teknol House, Victoria Road, Burgess Hill, Sussex; Tel (04446) 48800. Turbo conversions.

Turbo Torque, 69 Albion Street, Birmingham, B1 3EA; Tel (021) 233-1172. Turbo conversions.

W. Mosselman Turbo Systems BV, Achterdijk 1, 4241 TG Arkel, Netherlands; Tel (01831) 1840. Turbo systems.

Index

Other PSL books for the motoring enthusiast...

Grand Prix Greats
A personal appreciation of 25 famous Formula 1 drivers

Nigel Roebuck — Grand Prix Editor of 'Autosport' and life-long racing enthusiast — presents profiles of the aspect of racing which has always fascinated him — the drivers. His admitted intention is not to concentrate on the most famous or the most successful, but rather to present vivid and highly anecdotal accounts of, in his opinion, the most colourful and charismatic members, both living and dead, of this courageous band of sportsmen. *Highly illustrated with photographs and full-colour specially-commissioned portraits* of such men as: Mario Andretti; Jim Clark; Juan Manuel Fangio; Niki Lauda; Stirling Moss; Nelson Piquet; Alain Prost; Keke Rosberg; Jackie Stewart; Gilles Villeneuve and more. **Destined to become a classic.** *Foreword by Murray Walker.*

Colin Chapman
The Man and His Cars

Gérard ('Jabby') Crombac. *Foreword by Enzo Ferrari.* From small simple beginnings in North London in 1947, Colin Chapman went on to build the world-famous multi-million pound Lotus Car Company. While so doing he also established himself, in Jackie Stewart's words as 'the greatest, most creative, designer of racing cars in the history of motor racing' and left an indelible mark on the sport. This is the definitive, authorized biography of the man and his cars, and of how the two were inseparable for more than forty years. *Includes many previously unpublished photographs from the Chapman family album and other private collections.*